MW00568831

Deer Hunters' 1996 Almanac

FROM THE PUBLISHERS OF DEER & DEER HUNTING MAGAZINE

Published by:

krause
publications

700 E. State Street • Iola, WI 54990-0001
Telephone: 715/445-2214

Please call or write for our free catalog of "outdoor" publications.
Our Toll-free number to place an order or obtain a free catalog is
800-258-0929. Please use our regular business telephone
715-445-2214 for editorial comment or further information.

Library of Congress Catalog Number: 92-74255

ISBN: 0-87341-348-2
Printed in the United States of America

Table of Contents

A Book for Hunters

Something for everyone — that's what you'll find in your 1996 *Deer Hunters' Almanac.*

The editors of *Deer & Deer Hunting* magazine know you are a serious white-tailed deer hunter who spends more than just a couple of days in fall learning about the sport.

History, philosophy, hard facts, and secrets: they're all here.

First, read about the new world record whitetail taken in Biggar, Saskatchewan, in 1993. You get the story first-hand from Milo Hanson, the man who bagged the trophy.

Your amazement won't stop there. Next, look back on some of the most bizarre and intriguing "Deer Browse" stories that have appeared recently on the pages of *Deer & Deer Hunting.* Remember one thing between your gasps and exclamations — all of these stories are true!

We've also included partial listings of the Boone & Crockett and Pope & Young records for both typical- and non-typical bucks. Each entry includes rack score, area where taken, hunter's name, date and rank. The Pope & Young records have been updated and include many new entries.

Looking for some new ways to fix your favorite food? In the middle of this book you will find 13 pages worth of tasty venison recipes.

An extensive how-to section begins on Page 125. Learn how to track wounded deer and what to look for after the shot.

Also, learn how to sight in your rifle, increase arrow velocity, pick the right broadheads and arrows, and determine the ballistics of your muzzleloader.

Find out which scents to use by reading about what works for your fellow hunters.

There's even a section on how to hunt more safely from a tree stand, including sobering information on tree stand accidents.

Other topics include the different whitetail subspecies; the economic impact of shooting sports; and state-by-state hunting regulations and trends.

When it's time to relax, sit back and enjoy a fine selection of short stories, beginning with "Hey Dad. I Got a Buck!" on Page 179. These stories are not only enjoyable, they shed light on the psychological and philosophical aspects of hunting.

Finally, we've included several pages at the end of the book to be used as your own personal reference guide. Find out who to call or write for state-by-state hunting information and log the details of this year's hunts for future reference.

Be it at the hunting camp, the office, or in the comfort of your own home, we hope this book brings you enjoyment throughout the year.

If you have articles, stories or original photos that you would like to have considered for publication in next year's almanac, write to us at: Deer & Deer Hunting, 700 E. State St., Iola, WI 54990.

The Buck of Dreams

Milo Hanson

Milo Hanson shot his record buck on Nov. 23, 1993, in his hometown of Biggar, Saskatchewan. The buck's estimated age was 3.5 to 4.5 years and had a live weight of about 200 pounds. It scored 213-5/8 points on the Boone & Crockett scale.

I was born in 1945 in southwestern Saskatchewan near the town of Eastend. In 1964, I met Olive, and we were married within a year. Four years later, we moved to Olive's family farm near Biggar, where our son, Bradley, was born.

Olive and I operate a grain and cattle farm, where we raise wheat, barley, oats, canola and alfalfa. We farm over five sec-tions, and maintain about 100 cows.

I tell you all this to show I'm not a man who has the time or money to hunt all over the continent. Farming is a full-time job for us.

The area where I shot the world-record whitetail is a mixture of farmlands and aspen bluffs that includes our farm. About 20 percent to 30 percent

> I had heard about this monster buck from neighbors and the bus driver, but none of our hunting party saw the deer before rifle season opened.

of the land has low areas that we didn't clear for crops. These low areas contain a lot of willows and aspens.

When Olive and I moved to the farm in the early 1970s, deer were scarce. The few whitetails that lived there moved out each winter and migrated into nearby hills and pasture land. In recent years, with milder winters and easy access to plentiful crops, the white-tailed deer population has steadily increased. As a result, we now see and shoot large bucks in this area.

Another factor that helped increase deer numbers was the cattle market's decline in the late 1970s. Many local farmers, including us, backed away from cattle and turned more of our efforts and land toward grain production. When cattle herds declined, undergrowth in wooded areas increased. This improved the habitat for wildlife, especially white-tailed deer.

After Olive and I moved to the farm, our friend Walter Meger became our constant hunting partner. Brad also hunts with us regularly, and Olive and I have hunted together since we were married. Each fall the two of us take two to three weeks as a holiday so we can hunt our province for whitetails, mule deer, moose and, occasionally, elk.

In fact, most of our neighbors are avid hunters. During the season, we hunt with all of our friends who farm near us. It seems our farm is always the gathering point for area hunters. It is here that we discuss past hunts and plan future hunts.

Our hunting party — and most hunters in this area — drive around in trucks early in the morning to look for deer and deer sign. We then compare information and form drives, with shooters positioned on the escape routes of our favorite hunting spots. In the evening, just before hunting hours end, we again drive around looking for deer.

On the final day of the 1992 season our school-bus driver saw a monster white-tailed buck feeding in an alfalfa field. The buck's presence soon made the rounds at our coffee shop. Then, in the summer of 1993, a neighbor spotted the big buck near his farm yard. The buck was next seen in a pea field near that neighbor's home. Then, just before rifle season opened Nov. 15, 1993, the buck was seen near a highway several miles north of Biggar. I heard about this monster buck from neighbors and the bus driver, but none of our hunting party saw the deer before rifle season opened.

On opening day we gathered at my farm to plan how we would hunt this buck. We didn't have ideal conditions during the season's first week. The snow was a week old, and deer tracks were everywhere. Two members of our group saw the buck that first week, but had no success getting close to him. On the night of Nov. 22, we had fresh snow so I called the guys to plan our hunt.

The next morning, I met my neighbor John Yaroshko, and we drove out to meet Walter Meger and Rene Igini. When we pulled up I knew something was happening because they were excited. They said they just spotted the monster buck entering a willow grove.

We quickly decided to have Rene walk the track while the rest of us surrounded the willows. I took a position that would keep the buck from running south onto private property. The buck bolted out, giving me my first look at him. Believe me, my heart was pumping! We shot, but missed him.

Rene stayed on his tracks, and eventually lost him in a maze of other deer tracks. Surprisingly, this buck's tracks weren't unusually large.

Just when we were getting frustrated and ready to move

on, the big buck darted out from an aspen bluff and headed toward a willow grove on my land. We posted several hunters around the willows while Rene walked the buck's tracks. The buck again bolted, this time coming within 150 yards broadside from John and myself. I think we both got buck fever this time! We fired several shots, but missed.

Not about to give up, we moved up to the next patch of willows and again jumped the buck. I held steady and shot as he turned straight away from me. He went down to his knees. Just as John hollered, "You got him!," the buck got up and ran into a nearby aspen bluff. I ran up the hill to where he disappeared and could see him below me, standing still.

I aimed through my 4-power scope and fired another shot with my .308 Winchester Model 88 lever-action. Down he went. As I ran down into the bush, I could see his head over a clump of willows. I fired another shot just to make sure he stayed down. It was all over. When I came out of the bluff, the other guys were waiting. They asked, "Did you get him?"

"You bet!" I said, and then I asked for a cigarette. I had not smoked for three years, but I needed one badly!

Shooting this buck gave me a feeling I will probably never experience again, even though I had no idea he was a potential world-record deer. It was the biggest buck I had ever seen, and he left me shaking.

During the next week I realized I had shot the largest deer anyone around Biggar had ever seen. I also knew I would win the trophy at the Big Buck night in a nearby town called Sonningdale. I was also confident of winning the trophy at our local Wildlife Federation branch competition in Biggar.

Still, I had no idea this buck could be the next world record. On Nov. 29, 1993, a neighbor, Adam Evashenko, came over and measured the rack. When he finished entering the numbers on the score sheet, he asked me to go over the numbers because he thought he might have made a mistake. He said if his figures were right, I had the world record. The next day, two other fellows measured it, and they came up with almost identical measurements — between 214 and 215 on the Boone & Crockett scoring system. I suddenly believed I was in the running for the world record!

On Dec. 1, 1993, Norm Parchewsky, an official Boone and Crockett scorer, measured the rack at 214 4/8 for Saskatchewan's Henry Kelsey record book. Soon after, I was interviewed on national television, and then our home was under siege. Phone calls came in by the hundreds; magazine representatives showed up at my door wanting exclusive rights to my story; artists, sculptors, pro-moters, antler collectors, photographers and well-wishers steadily arrived. Life began to change on the farm!

After the 60-day drying period, Norm Parchewsky, Robert Allemand and Allan Holtvogt (all official B&C scorers) measured the buck at 213-1/8 in a scoring ceremony attended by more than 400 people. That was Jan. 22, 1994. My family turned this special day into a family reunion. Olive and I will always remember the happiness everyone felt.

Olive and I have met many nice people, and we have had moments when we wondered about all the hassles. Our lives have changed some, but we treasure our farm life and friendships with our family and neighbors.

After the official scoring ceremony, another important event took place. I offered the taxidermy job to Bub Hill from Briercrest, Saskatchewan, and he immediately started it. Everyone who has seen the mount agrees Bub did a wonderful job.

We have also met Ian McMurchy, a wildlife photographer from our province. Ian does the photography on the Hanson Buck. His photos have shown the buck's beauty to many people, and he shares our pride in this incredible whitetail.

Deer Browse

Be it an unexpected visit to an unfamiliar place, or a fleeting fit of rage, whitetails seem to make the news more often than any other big game animal. The stories, however, go beyond the animals themselves. We've learned that for every curious whitetail there is at least one clever hunter and an occasional villain.

These bits of interesting material are documented regularly in *Deer & Deer Hunting's* "Deer Browse" — one of the more popular sections of the magazine.

The next 34 pages of this book include some of the most bizarre, unbelievable and interesting stories that have occurred over the past few years about white-tailed deer and the people who hunt them.

■ Georgia Hunter Impaled on Antlers

He never had success rattling antlers to attract bucks. And now Woody Rogers cringes at the sight of them.

"I'm not going to carry rattling antlers anymore," the Georgia state patrolman said. "I've never had any luck with them anyway."

Well, Rogers had some luck with the antlers Nov. 23, 1993. But it was bad luck.

Rogers walked out to his stand in Butts County, Ga., which is 40 miles south of Atlanta, with a set of rattling antlers in his fanny pack. He usually carried the antlers around his neck, but decided it would be best to put them in a pack so he wouldn't be mistaken for a deer.

While trying to walk down a steep ditch, Rogers fell backward.

At first, he didn't think much of his fall.

"I just lost my breath," he said.

As he reached around his back, he felt the tip of the antler's main beam had punched through the pack and plunged into his back.

He instantly knew something was seriously wrong. A tine from the other antler was shoved into the ground.

Rogers' training as a police officer might have saved his life. Instead of instinctively reaching for the antler and trying to pull it out, he kept calm.

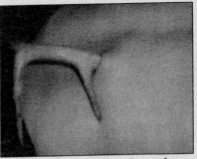

Woody Rogers fell backward onto a set of rattling antlers in Butts County, Ga., Nov. 23, 1993.

"I've heard a lot of stories where some people have pulled out things and bled to death," Rogers said. "I reached back and felt the tine in my back. I then had to get up with the other tine in the ground."

Rogers traveled a quarter-mile to a logging road where his truck was parked.

"I tried not to panic," he said. "I walked slowly out of the woods."

Once in the vehicle, Rogers had to drive a straight-stick transmission while leaning over the steering wheel. His head was touching the windshield to keep the antler off the seat. The one-mile trip to his father's house was no picnic as the truck bounced through a large pothole, sending jolts of pain through his body.

Rogers was taken by ambulance to Henry General Hospital.

"I had to ride on my hands and knees so I wouldn't put pressure on my back," he said.

After he arrived at the hospital, the doctors debated the best procedure. The sight of antlers sticking out of a man's back was foreign to them.

"I told them to do what you have to do," Rogers recalled. "They just snatched it right out. It wasn't all that bad. In fact, it kind of relieved me."

The state patrolman was lucky his injuries weren't more severe. The antler in his back only glanced the liver. After two days in the hospital, he was sent home.

Rogers now has a tough time wearing his bullet-proof vest because of the damage to his ribs, but he has healed and returned to the force.

"After Christmas I went out and killed a couple of more deer," Rogers said.

— *Bart Landsverk*

■ Deer Makes Visit to School

An elementary school in Montevallo, Ala., had a deer attend music class during the 1993 deer hunting season.

The buck ran across campus toward a woods in the city park when it apparently panicked as some fifth-grade boys came out of a door, said Betty Haynie, the school's secretary.

Haynie said the frightened deer ran at the building and leaped through a window.

"Thank goodness no children were in the classroom," she said.

The deer fled from the room immediately, breaking two more windows in the process.

— *Rollin Moseley*

■ Rescue Crew Saves Deer

Two men who work for Georgia's Columbia County rescue squad helped save a 60-pound deer recently near Appling.

John Blankenship found the buck in the well while feeding his horses, said Conservation Ranger Howard Hensley.

Hensley and Danny McGowen climbed down the 12-foot well — which was only 3 feet in diameter — to reach the deer. They roped the deer, tranquilized it, and then volunteers hauled it to safety.

The deer was unhurt, except for a few scrapes.

— *Rollin Moseley*

■ Hunter Bags Last-Minute Trophy

Brian Haralson, Lake Linden, Mich., bagged a trophy buck during the final minutes of the archery season on Jan. 1, 1993, in Houghton County.

"He came right in like I wasn't even there," Haralson said. "My bow creaked when I drew, but he didn't hear it."

The 9-pointer, which was the 23-year-old's first adult buck, was 4.5 years old, and had a dressed weight of 180 pounds. The antlers had a green score of 137, which would have been good enough for entry into state and national records maintained by the Commemorative Bucks of Michigan and the Pope and Young Club.

However, the antlers were knocked off when the animal fell, and can't be entered in national records.

— *Richard P. Smith*

■ Deer Attack Puts Man in Hospital

A Hillsboro, Wis., man considers himself lucky to be alive after being savagely gored by a 9-point buck Sept. 14, 1993.

Cletus Walker, 62, spent a night in the VA Hospital in Madison after being treated for bruises and deep lacerations.

Cletus and his wife, Lois, were at the Burr Ridge home of their son, Kevin, when the attack occurred. Cletus, along with other family members, had stepped onto the deck of the house to enjoy the antics of the 200-pound deer in the front yard.

The buck was well known to people living in Burr Ridge, having been cared for as a fawn by a local resident. The animal was returned to the wild, but had lost its fear of humans.

"Nikki (Cletus and Lois' granddaughter) went out to feed it a cracker," Lois Walker said. "Stella (Kevin's wife) told her to throw it the cracker, though, because she didn't like the way the deer was acting. He was standing on his hind legs, rubbing his antlers in the branches."

The deer accepted the offering, and seemed subdued when Cletus began to pet it.

"I petted it once and it was all right. I petted it a second time, and that was it," Cletus said.

Suddenly the animal lowered its head and drove its antlers into Cletus' shoulder.

"He threw me right up in the air. When I came down, he was on top of me," Cletus said.

The initial attack tore Cletus' jacket and shirt, and bruised his arm and shoulder.

Before Cletus could get to his feet, the deer made another thrust. This time, the injuries were substantial. One prong of the antlers nearly drove through the man's left hand.

"He put two horns into the inside of my right leg. That's what really hurt," Celtus said.

Another tine struck Walker in the wrist.

"It went right through my watch band," he said.

Cletus, who weighs 235 pounds, found his strength was no match for the deer's.

"There was no way I could get up," he said.

Meanwhile, Lois joined in the fray, trying to save her husband.

"I grabbed hold of the deer's antlers," she said. "I was scared. I thought it was killing him. If the buck would have raised his head, its antlers would have got me right in the face."

While her grandmother wrestled with the buck, 10-year-old Nikki dashed into the house in search of a club, and returned with a pair of brooms.

"Stella and I started beating the deer with the brooms," Lois continued. "We broke both broom handles over his head."

Then, however, Cletus was saved by the sound of a loud muffler.

"About the time we broke the broom handles over the deer's head, a car came by," Lois said. "It was real noisy, and the deer just backed off. It whirled around and ran."

In spite of several deep wounds and a severely injured leg, Cletus rose to his feet and stumbled toward the house. He suffered two puncture wounds in the right thigh.

Lois said that because the animal was considered tame, many of the children in Burr Ridge had played with the deer.

"I don't want anybody around Burr Ridge thinking just because this deer comes up to them, they can pet it," Lois said.
— *Steven J. Stanek*

■ Hunter Gets Buck With Antler in its Eye

An Illinois hunter bagged a large, healthy 8-point typical buck during the 1992 bow season.

Everything seemed normal about the 191-pound buck, which Mark West shot at 15 yards in Tazewell County.

That was until West turned the buck over and gazed at what looked like a small stick protruding from the deer's right eye. It wasn't a stick, however. It was a 2.5-inch antler.

"The eyeball was in the back of the socket, but it was dry like a raisin," West said.

Mark West of Illinois shot this 8-point buck during the 1992 bow season. Oddly enough, this buck had a 2.5-inch antler growing out of its right eye.

West said his taxidermist told him the antler was growing on its own pedicel, attached to the bone in the eye socket.
— *Bart Landsverk*

■ Deer Hunting's Success Rates Low

Deer hunting isn't as easy as many non-hunters might believe, according to the National Shooting Sports Foundation.

The organization says deer hunters are unsuccessful 96 percent of the time. NSSF data show that more than 12 million deer hunters in the United States spend an average of 22 days afield for each deer taken.
— *New York Newsday*

■ Old Bucks and Antler Regression

Most white-tailed bucks reach their maximum body size when 5.5 or 6.5 years old, and they normally produce their maximum antler size between ages 6.5 and 8.5 years. Although I've seen some bucks grow their largest antlers late in life, most old bucks in the wild experience antler regression.

Typically, a mature buck grows antlers that are remarkably similar each year. However, at old age, the buck might revert to growing one forked antler or spikes. In a sense, he "goes back" to growing antlers more characteristic of immature bucks, which forecasts his impending demise.

In his book titled *Deer Antlers Regeneration, Function, and Evolution* (Academic Press, 1983) Dr. Richard J. Goss writes: "Whether the stunted antlers of elderly deer are explained in terms of decreased sex hormone secretion, or are attributable to accumulated degenerative effects of old age, is unknown."

Goss emphasizes, however, that antlers carried by "senile" bucks bear no resemblance to those grown by castrated deer. Instead, he suggests that antlers on old bucks are more like the stunted antlers sometimes produced by malnourished deer.

These generalizations do not necessarily apply to captive-raised bucks that receive special care and nutritious food throughout life, as Leonard Lee Rue III points out in "The Deer of North America" (updated and expanded edition, 1989). In reference to an article by Charles J. Alsheimer, published in the November 1985 issue of *Deer and Deer Hunting*, Rue notes that one old pen-raised buck grew its largest set of antlers when 15.5 years old.

Rue, suggests an old buck "may retain a large, spreading rack while the number of points decreases." To substantiate his view, he provides a picture of an old muley buck that has a wide antler spread but only five total points.

Certainly, any white-tailed buck 10 years or older can be considered "very old." Also, quite understandably, few bucks live that long in wild, hunted populations. In the heavily hunted North Woods of lower Michigan, for example, we computed that only one buck in 360,000 ever lived that long. Therefore, few bucks die of old age.

Because of lighter hunting pressure, one buck out of 3,000 might live to age 10 in Michigan's Upper Peninsula, at least when computed in 1987.

Even so, I've personally seen only two old bucks that carried what I would call "degenerate" antlers.

One of those trophies should be in my antler collection, but it is not. My wife, Janice, and son, Keith, on his first deer hunt, missed it in 1987. Minutes later, another hunter took better aim. The antlers, which I did not inspect until a year later, now adorn his hunting cabin wall. The hunter said Michigan DNR biologists aged the deer at 14.5 years old, but I never saw the lower jaw myself.

Still, exactness here isn't important. The fact is, the buck was very old. Its antlers were anything but handsome, consisting of thick 2-inch diameter post-like structures, each 18 to 20 inches long, that grew straight upward and then crossed. Each beam had three or four short tines.

Another old buck was an 11.5-year-old shot by John Rasmussen of Munising, Mich., in November 1993. The animal's age was determined by Michigan DNR biologist Paul Frederick, employing the tooth cementum layering technique. Paul reported good, clear staining results, suggesting the determination was highly accurate.

The old buck's right antler was 19 inches long, the left one 12 inches long. Each beam was about 1.75 inches in diameter, heavily pearled, and with three flattened, blade-like points. The antlers were darkly stained from frequent rubbing. I suspect this buck grew larger antlers earlier in life, and that this set was degenerating because of the buck's old age. (I might add, though, that I've also inspected wild 11.5-year-old bucks with respectable antlers.)

My observations regarding antler configuration among old whitetails differ somewhat from what Rue reported for mule deer. I expect the classic senile whitetail grows short, thick spikes, not wide-spread beams. Regardless, old bucks of both species are rare in the wild, and likely die after casting their final set of degenerating antlers.
— *John J. Ozoga*

■ Lyme Disease Study is Making Progress

Hunters, as well as other citizens, are being threatened by Lyme disease. But if an ongoing experiment is successful, people across the country will be able to breathe easier.

Lyme disease, of course, is caused by a tiny spirochete, a form of bacteria. Its carrier is the deer tick. The disease attacks the muscular, nervous, and skin systems of its victims. Usually, a circular rash is the first of a variety of indicators. Flu-like symptoms, arthritis, and even death can result. Though the disease was identified in Europe decades ago and penicillin was discovered to be a viable treatment, little was done to develop a preventative.

Westchester County, New York, the heavily populated suburb north of New York City, is a center of the Northeast's Lyme disease epidemic.

"One percent to 2 percent of the population in the county's endemic areas are infected each year," said Donna McKenna, nurse practitioner and assistant to Dr. Gary P. Wormser, chief of the Department of Medicine's Division of Infectious Diseases in Westchester County. Therefore, when Connaught Laboratories of Swiftwater, Pa., began developing a vaccine for Lyme disease, Westchester County Medical Center was selected as one of the first of 14 facilities to take part in the experiment.

Preliminary study proved the vaccine was safe and effective for animals, and later demonstrated it was safe for humans. The next step was to see if the immune system of people would manufacture its own antibodies in response to the vaccine.

"We needed 1,000 to 2,000 volunteers," McKenna said. Sportsmen stepped forward, along with other high-risk people such as foresters and landscapers, to participate. The plan was for an early-spring 1994 vaccination of the volunteers. Some of the volunteers received the vaccine, others the placebo. Neither the volunteers nor the people injecting them know which formula is in the syringe, though, of course, the researchers kept accurate records.

Within weeks, people receiving the vaccine should manufacture the antibodies. They will be checked for nine months after the injection to judge the vaccine's effectiveness.

— *Glenn Sapir*

■ Golf Course Poacher Gets 10-Day Term

A Wauwatosa, Wis., man who bragged about killing deer on a golf course and at times videotaped his illegal activities was ordered to serve 10 days in jail and pay more than $4,000 in fines.

In an unusually lengthy oratory before handing down the sentence in July 1993, Milwaukee County Circuit Judge Jeffrey Kremers admonished Robert Schluga for using a high-powered rifle to kill two deer at the Blue Mound Golf and Country Club in Wauwatosa, where he was employed.

He said Schluga's actions were "more than a lapse in judgment and jeopardized the safety of people who jog in the area.

"No one is suggesting that you were spraying bullets all over. Of course, we could have had a real tragedy here. It would not have been intentional on your part in terms of any human being struck.

"You, more than most other people, know how wrong that was because you are — or were — a hunter."

The judge stripped Schluga of his hunting and fishing licenses for three years, sentenced him to 10 days in jail, and ordered him to wear an electronic tether for 25 days so authorities can monitor his whereabouts. He was also told to pay $2,500 in fines and $1,895 to the

Wisconsin Department of Natural Resources.

Kremers could have sentenced Schluga to six months in prison and ordered him to pay $7,000 in fines for the two counts of hunting deer out of season.

Authorities believe Schluga illegally shot at least three deer in 1991 and two deer in 1992. They said there was no information to suggest club officials knew of the poaching.

— *Milwaukee Journal*

■ Unfortunate Event

While bow-hunting in western Wisconsin in 1991, Dave Blaschko of the Arcadia area came across a strange scene in the snow-covered woods.

A white-tailed buck had apparently been trying to drink water from a hollow stump when his antlers became stuck inside the stump. While struggling to free himself, he became wedged even tighter. Sometime later, coyotes showed up, killing and eating him.

— *Tom Indrebo*
Strum, Wis.

This 8-point Wisconsin buck died after his antlers became stuck in this stump.

■ Why You Might Not Find Dead Deer

In winter 1993, I tried to find out how long it takes a dead deer to decompose and "return to nature."

I was curious because I've often heard people say they spend considerable time in the woods but never see a dead deer. Maybe now I can explain why.

On March 15, 1993, I picked up a road-kill. This was a large doe that was carrying three fawns. The doe, labeled No. 1, was placed on the sunny side of a ridge near a trail bordering a swamp's edge.

On March 30, I picked up a second doe on the same highway. This doe was also of good size, but had no fawns. No. 2 was placed on the shady side of the same ridge, about 150 yards from No. 1.

Within days, ravens in the area found both deer. On May 5 I returned to the sites. Only the major bones and hair could be seen. That was only 50 days for doe No. 1, and 36 days for No. 2.

When I again checked the sites June 2, I walked to within five feet before seeing anything. New growth covered all evidence that dead deer had been there. After just 80 days, only a handful of hair remained. No. 1 had returned to nature.

No. 2 was a lot easier to locate in the shade of the large pines and spruce. The hair was spread over an area 6 feet by 15 feet, and the skull was the only bone

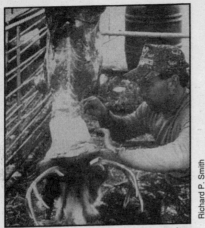

Richard P. Smith

For seamless mounts, no cut is made along the back of the neck. The hide is removed intact. The hide is peeled downward to the skull's base, and the neck severed at the head's base.

Make a vertical cut about 4 inches long in the back of the head. Start between the ears and go downward. From the top of the incision, slice the hide to the base of each antler, forming a Y. The head is then ready for skinning.

in the area. A search located the rib cage and lower leg nearby.

My conclusion is that if you're really not looking for dead deer, you most likely won't find them in the wild. They're quickly broken down by scavengers, the weather and insects.

— Donald L. Seymour
Escanaba, Mich.

■ New Way to Cape Deer Heads

I learned a new way of caping whitetails for mounting while hunting in Texas with guide and outfitter Greg Simons. Although the technique was new to me, Simons and many taxidermists have caped heads this way for seamless mounts

for years.

The standard caping procedure calls for making a cut in the hide on the back of the neck, extending from the top of the shoulders to a point between the ears. The cape and skin covering the head could be removed with the head attached. Taxidermists must sew the hide back together along that incision when completing the mount, creating a seam.

For seamless mounts, make no cuts in the back of the neck. The job is made easier by hanging the buck head down. The hide is simply peeled down to the skull's base. Then the head, with cape attached, is removed from the carcass.

Now, with the head resting on a table and the cape hanging

down hair side out, make a vertical cut of about 4 inches in the back of the head. Start the cut between the ears and go downward. From the top of the incision, slice the hide to the base of each antler, forming a Y. The head is then ready for skinning.

When completing the mount, taxidermists must do far less sewing than with the conventional method.
— *Richard P. Smith*

■ Checking on Deer Health in Tennessee

The Tennessee Wildlife Resources Agency is checking blood samples from 10 deer, five from its Catoosa Wildlife Management Area and five from the Fairfield Glade region.

The blood is tested to check for tick fever (ehrlichiosis). The TWRA is cooperating with Dr. Steven Standaert and others at the Center for Disease Control on the project, which began after ehrlichiosis was diagnosed in some residents of the Fairfield Glade community.

Though it's possible to contract tick fever from a deer, it's highly unlikely. Spokeswoman Charlotte Quist of the Southeastern Cooperative Wildlife Disease Center in Athens, Ga., says: "The only possibility of catching the disease if deer were carrying it would be blood to blood contact." Also, she emphasizes the likelihood of deer being infected is slim.
— *Jim Casada*

Tim Geitner of St. Marys, Pa., shot this 'corkscrew' buck in November 1993 while hunting in Ohio.

■ Corkscrew Buck Bagged in Ohio

Tim Geitner wanted to bag a Pope & Young-class buck when he and his veteran bow-hunting buddies headed to southeastern Ohio in November 1993. That didn't happen.

No, the Saint Marys, Pa., resident struggled to see any big deer the first five days. One reason was temperatures climbed into the 60s and 70s, which was unusually warm for that time of the year.

On the sixth day, however, he shot a unique white-tailed buck.

"As the buck came closer, my eyes were glued to its unusual headgear," Geitner said. "The antlers were symmetrical, but twisted like a laurel branch. I remember thinking, 'He ain't a wall-hanger as far as size goes, but the shape of that rack is so unique, he's a shooter as far as I'm concerned.'"

The three-blade broadhead took the buck through both lungs at 25 yards.

Professor George Bubenik at the University of Guelph, Ontario, one of the continent's top antler experts, studied pictures of the buck.

Bubenik said research has shown corkscrew antlers have a higher mineral content than normal antlers. He believes the photos of Geitner's buck showed well-mineralized antler tips.

How does over-mineralization result in corkscrew antlers?

"Mineralization of the bony tissue depends on the development of the bone matrix," Bubenik said. "The over-mineralization in corkscrew antlers indicates some kind of improper development of the matrix."

— *Larry Holjencin*

■ Delaware Hunter Shoots Cactus Buck

Delaware hunter Jimmie D. Schuman shot this large, multi-tined "cactus" buck Nov. 22, 1991, while hunting near his home in Cantebury, Del.

Jimmie D. Schuman shot this 180-pound 'cactus' buck Nov. 22, 1991. Antlers form like this after a buck is injured or loses his testicles during antler development.

The buck weighed 180 pounds field-dressed. At the time Schuman shot the buck he had never heard of the term "cactus" buck. He almost discarded the head, but decided to keep it.

Antler formations like this sometimes result after a buck injures or loses his testicles during antler development. The antlers remain in velvet indefinitely, and sometimes grow strange formations. The condition is seen more often in mule deer and blacktails than whitetails, and is more common in the South and West.

This might be related to cold weather, which can freeze the velvet-covered masses and cause them to fall off.

— *Jimmie D. Schuman Felton, Del.*

■ Key Deer Herd Improving

Fish and Wildlife scientists in Florida report that at least 61 endangered Key deer fawns were born at their refuge at Big Pine Key in 1992. That is an increase of 11 over the previous year. In addition, there were only 54 known deer losses last year, down from the 60 the year before.

Fewer than 300 of these miniature whitetails survive on a few small islands in the lower Florida Keys, their native range.

Although about half of the

The Big Pine Key white-tailed deer refuge located in the lower Florida Keys had 61 fawns born in 1992. That is an increase of 11 from 1991. The Key deer are an endangered species.

Key deer that die each year are road kills, the most critical threat to their existence is the loss of habitat.

The increased number of births, along with the declining mortality figures, are good news for the only subspecies of white-tails on the endangered species list.

— *Dinny Slaughter*

■ Summer Scouting Pays Off

A summer scouting trip in late August 1992 piqued my curiosity for the upcoming bow-hunting season.

As I watched a doe, two fawns and a 6-point buck enter their feeding grounds from a bordering woodlot, I gazed back toward the woods and saw a velvet-antlered buck appear.

I was happy to have found a good buck to hunt, and I was even more pleased when a second big buck, larger than the first, followed his peer into the field. At first they were too far away to know exactly how big they were, but soon both bucks, accompanied by the doe, fawns and 6-pointer, stood within 40 yards of me.

I could see one of the bucks sported a beautiful 9-point rack with good mass and a wide spread. The second buck was a 10-pointer with a sticker point that hooked toward the inside at the end of the right main beam.

I saw the 9-pointer again in late October. He was following a doe down a lane toward me, but the doe wasn't ready for him and broke away into the woods 50 yards from me. He stopped, gave me a view of his headgear, and took off after the doe.

While hunting in early November, I turned my head

Dave Bennett, Wisconsin, saw these 9- and 10-point bucks in August while scouting. He shot the 10-pointer in November 1992. In February 1993, he found the shed antlers of the 9-pointer and mounted them.

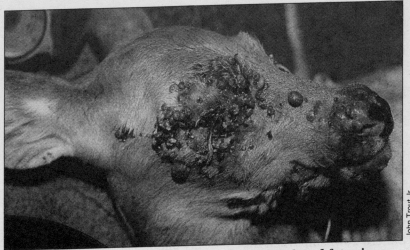

Don Powers of Boonville, Ind., found this tick-infested fawn in early July 1994. Powers contacted conservation wardens and then plucked more than 100 ticks from the fawn's head.

and saw a good buck only 10 yards behind me. As soon as I saw the sticker point at the end of the main beam, I knew this was the 10-pointer. I made the most of my opportunity with a heart shot. When I found him I was disappointed to find that he broke off both of his G-2 tines.

The story didn't end there. In early February 1993 I found both shed antlers from the 9-pointer lying only three feet apart in a bedding area.

— *Dave Bennett*

■ Tick-Infested Fawn Rescued by Hunter

People who go afield in spring and summer should avoid fawns. However, at least one exception to the rule occurred in early July when Don Powers of Boonville, Ind., walked into the woods.

Powers, an avid deer hunter and president of the Tecumseh Conservation Corps Inc. in Warrick County, was tending outdoor duties when three fishermen reported that they heard a fawn bleating excessively in the area. Powers and the group walked up a nearby hill to investigate. What they found was unbelievable.

They spotted three fawns bedded closely together. Two of them ran about 15 yards and stopped to look back. Both looked healthy.

The third, bleating frantically, stood up but could not escape. When the fawn stopped a few feet from Powers, he realized it couldn't see. Ticks covered the fawn's head, particularly near its eyes.

Knowing the fawn needed extensive help, Powers took it to authorities.

After notifying a conservation officer, Powers plucked more than 100 ticks from the deer's head.

— *John Trout Jr.*

■ Woman Killed In Deer-Bicycle Crash

A deer collided with a bicycle on a rural Teleford, Pa., road July 11, killing a Wisconsin woman, Pennsylvania State Police said.

Julia Weiler, 22, of Kenosha, Wis., was riding on a road in Salford Township when the deer bolted from between two trees and ran into her, police said. Weiler died of head injuries after falling head first over her handlebars.

"She was going downhill at a high rate of speed and after the collision she flipped over the handlebars and landed on her head," Trooper Reynold Steptoe said. "It's just a real freak accident."

The deer fled to a wooded area nearby, apparently unhurt. Weiler, who had been wearing a helmet that was found shattered on the ground, was pronounced dead on arrival at Grand View Hospital in Sellersville, a Philadelphia suburb.

■ Lone Coyote Kills Adult Doe

Several winters ago I witnessed a classic predator/prey confrontation that left a lasting impression. I was photographing deer one February afternoon along the frozen Mississippi River in central Minnesota. Because daylight was fading fast, I was preparing to leave my blind.

Suddenly, across the river, a lone doe bounded onto the ice. Behind her was what I at first thought was her fawn. Only when the two animals were in full view did I realize the trailing fawn was not a deer at all. It was a coyote. Following the deer by 10 yards, the coyote loped at the deer's pace. The doe did not appear to panic.

A week earlier, the water level in the river had dropped. The ice sagged with the lower water level, leaving cracks that forced water onto the ice in the center of the river. This water had since frozen, and without

Bill Marchel

Lone coyotes can kill deer under certain circumstances. This doe fell to a coyote on the frozen Mississippi River in central Minnesota.

snow cover, was extremely slick.

For no apparent reason, the doe left the firm footing of the snow-covered ice and ran for the center of the river with the coyote in pursuit. The pair went into a spin as they hit the slick ice.

Although both regained their footing, the coyote now had the advantage. It jumped at the doe's hindquarters, pulling out mouthfuls of hair. The deer fell onto the ice, although the coyote inflicted no perceptible damage. After it was knocked down, the doe seemed to give up.

The coyote circled its prey several times. Though the deer occasionally lashed out with its forelegs as the coyote approached, it made no attempt to regain its footing. Now and then, the doe emitted a pitiful bleat.

I cursed the lack of light needed for photography as the event unfolded. The camera's light meter told me a full 4-second shutter speed would be needed to properly expose the slow-speed film. Peering through the telephoto lens, I watched as the coyote began the grisly task of eating the deer alive.

It pulled mouthfuls of hair and flesh from a hindquarter — all as the doe laid on the ice with its head up. Finally, darkness and cold chased me back to my truck.

I returned to the scene before sunrise the next morning. From a distance, I could see three deer standing near what was left of the fallen doe. A bald eagle and several crows were already cashing in on the free meal.

Closer inspection of the kill site revealed an untouched fetus the doe had been carrying. Other than the doe's head, little else remained of the carcass.

— *Bill Marchel*

■ Four Charged in Deer's Death

A Georgia correctional officer and four inmates of the Macon Youth Development Campus face cruelty-to-animal charges for the beating death of a deer on the grounds of the correctional facility.

The four inmates — three juveniles and a 17-year-old — chased down the doe and beat her to death after the officer challenged them to catch the deer, according to a ranger with the Georgia Department of Natural Resources.

The inmates' supervising officer, Charles Jackson will have to appear in state court in Macon, said Ranger 1st Class Ben H. Weatherly of the Department of Natural Resources. Jackson has also been fired from his position with the correctional department.

Three of the inmates were charged in juvenile court. Seventeen-year-old Keith Wemberly will have to appear in state court with Jackson.

The four youths were given

in-house punishment, according to Ranger Weatherly, who is handling the case. The three juveniles and the 17-year-old will receive two additional months of incarceration at the facility.

All five face one misdemeanor count of cruelty to animals, which carries a possible penalty of a $1,000 fine and up to one year in prison for adults. The juveniles, who range in age from 13 to 16, could be required to perform community service at a wildlife management area, said Weatherly.

Weatherly said the doe wandered onto the correctional campus one morning.

"They ran the deer up against a security fence and commenced to whip it," he said. "The deer was hit with bricks, sticks and kicked in the stomach."

The doe died during the beating and a fawn that was seen with it ran away. The ranger said the inmates were able to catch the deer because it had recently given birth.

The fired Jackson told officers the inmates ran out of his sight.

"He said by the time he caught them, the damage was done," Weatherly said. "We didn't buy it (his story)."

— *Rollin Moseley*

■ Deer Infertility Study Costs $100,000

Concerned that deer in New York need to stop multiplying, New York lawmakers approved $100,000 to come up with birth control for white-tailed deer.

The appropriation was part of a budget bill approved by the New York State Legislature on March 31. It drew some snickers.

"We give them birth control pills," Herman Farrell, chairman of the Assembly's budget-writing Ways and Means Committee, replied when asked to explain the program.

But Assemblyman Richard Brodsky, the suburban lawmaker who got the money put into the budget, isn't joking. With 1 million deer roaming New York, the state needs to control deer populations in areas where hunting is illegal, Brodsky said.

The lawmaker said deer cause problems in populated areas, ranging from nibbled shrubs to Lyme disease, which is transmitted by deer ticks.

The $100,000 state legislators approved will be used to study how to make deer infertile in populous areas where hunting is banned. That might be done with drug-laced darts or treated salt licks, Brodsky said.

Assemblyman Donald Davidsen, a veterinarian, said he wasn't sure the state should spend money on a program that might not work.

"This is almost the kind of thing you'd expect to come out of Washington, where they print their own money," the Steuben County Republican said.

— *Rochester (N.Y.) Democrat*

■ Hunter Shoots Huge Yearling Buck

When Don Haueter of Ripon, Wis., shot a 12-point buck on Nov. 23, 1985, in Waushara County, he figured he had shot one of the herd's senior citizens. After all, the buck's "green" rack grossed 140-6/8 Boone & Crockett points, which is impressive by anyone's standards.

But Haueter was in for a huge surprise. This was not a buck that had grown a huge rack by somehow surviving more than one gun season in this heavily hunted area.

After shooting the buck, Haueter took it to be mounted by Mike Yeska of White River Taxidermy in Neshkoro, Wis. Yeska, who has been at the trade 18 years, ages deer for his customers. He couldn't believe what he saw when he opened the buck's mouth: temporary premolars. Deer usually lose these premolars at 1 year, 7 months of age.

"I never expected that," Yeska said, adding that he thought the deer would be 2.5 to 3.5 years old. "We've had deer with the opposite problem, 3.5-year-olds that only had small forkhorns. This was something special. It just adds something more to the deer and the hunt."

Yeska was fairly certain he had a yearling trophy buck on his hands, but wanted confirmation. He called his friend, Larry Gohlke of Neshkoro, for assistance.

Yeska and Gohlke are knowledgeable about white-tailed deer and aging, so they caped the buck and took numerous pictures of the deer's teeth and antlers. Gohlke sent eight sets of pictures to the University of Wisconsin and the Wisconsin Department of Natural Resources.

Keith McCaffery, Wisconsin's chief deer-research biologist, confirmed Gohlke and Yeska's thoughts. This was definitely a yearling buck.

"I saw the jaw and even submitted a tooth (for analysis)," McCaffery said. "Unfortunately, the tooth was in such poor shape that it didn't produce a good slide. In all respects this appeared to be a 1.5-year-old deer."

McCaffery added that he has seen some deer that didn't replace their temporary premolars. This was not the case with Haueter's buck, however.

"This deer had normally worn premolars with not much more than a year of wear," McCaffery said. "Plus, it had the weight of a 1.5-year-old deer. It appeared to be a normal 1.5-year-old deer. There wasn't any excessive wear (on the teeth). I've looked at thousands of deer jaws. You can spot a yearling with a reasonable amount of accuracy. There wasn't any indication that it was a 2.5-year-old deer that had retained its premolars."

McCaffery took pictures of the teeth and antlers to a Great Lakes Deer Group meeting in

Don Haueter of Berlin, Wis., shot this 12-point yearling buck Nov. 23, 1985 in Waushara County, Wis. An analysis of the teeth, right, shows the buck is only 1.5 years old.

September 1991.

"They were impressed. It's the largest yearling antlers I've ever seen," McCaffery said. "It's not the heaviest yearling buck I've heard of, however. I've shot heavier yearling bucks in Rhinelander, Wis., which has a much harsher environment. The largest was 151 pounds. Bruce Moss at Spooner, Wis., shot a huge yearling in the 180-pound range."

Haueter was hunting near Poy Sippi, Wis., with three of his friends on opening day in 1985. He sat back in his deer stand, listened to shots echo in the distance, and hoped he would get a chance.

As noon approached, Haueter saw a huge buck following a doe 75 yards away between two small woods.

"I missed the first shot, and if he would have kept running away from me, I never would have gotten him," Haueter said.

Instead, the buck turned, giving Haueter a quartering-away shot.

"After I took the second shot, I was pretty sure that I got him," he said.

The buck bolted into a nearby 5-acre woods of oaks and pines. Haueter and two of his partners took stands around the woods while the other hunting partner followed the blood trail. Haueter went to the back side of the woods to make sure the buck didn't sneak out.

The partner who followed the blood trail didn't have to go far.

Few bucks of this class or larger are shot in Waushara County. In fact, the buck won a local big buck contest. Yeska and Gohlke wonder how big this buck would have been at 3.5 or 4.5 years old.

— *Bart Landsverk*

■ Doe Impales Herself on Cemetery Fence

An 80-pound doe jumped over a cemetery fence, browsed on luscious grasses, and then tried to get back to a nearby woods before dawn broke in January 1992.

When it tried to crawl back through the lance-type fence, the doe caught herself on one of the fence's sharp points. Struggling to get off, the young deer literally disemboweled herself on the spear tip of the wrought iron fence.

During the past 25 years, Ohio Conservation Warden Larry Toki has seen deer killed by sharp sticks, wire fences and, of course, motor vehicles.

So when he was called to a cemetery in the township of Deerfield, Toki wasn't caught off guard to see the doe hanging from the fence.

"Mother Nature is unique," he said.

Toki contacted Pat Goebel, who happens to be the local funeral director, to take the animal to be processed.

— *Bart Landsverk*

■ Deer are Problem for Wisconsin Drivers

At least one of every six car crashes in Wisconsin in 1993 in involved a deer, the Wisconsin Department of Transportation

A young doe impaled herself on a Ohio cemetery fence in January 1992.

reported.

Three people were killed in accidents involving deer, 68 people were seriously hurt, and 486 others were less badly injured, the agency reported.

The department counted 22,819 crashes involving deer in 1993. Not included in the total were cases in which drivers struck another object to avoid hitting a deer and, of course, those in which drivers hit a deer but did not report the incident.

Dane County led the state in 1993 in reported car-deer crashes with 1,145, followed by Marathon County with 967, and Columbia County with 845.

In Marquette, Adams and Green Lake Counties, car-deer crashes outnumbered other types of collisions, the department said.

Car-deer crashes typically peak in October and November.

■ Man Arrested for Killing Deer

A Dalton, Ga., man faces charges for killing deer at Chickamauga National Battlefield Park out of season and keeping a fawn at his home.

Lawrence Howell Dorman, 23, was under investigation for having the fawn when Dalton police arrested him on unrelated theft charges, said Detective Ken Brooks. Dorman was charged with illegal possession of wildlife, hunting out of season, and holding game without a permit.

Natural Resources Cpl. Billy Powell said investigators also found out Dorman is awaiting trial in Florida for felony charges of arson, burglary and theft in connection with the destruction of a hunting lodge.

Some of the game law charges stem from two deer killings at Chickamauga battlefield, while others include the killing of a Canada goose in Whitfield County, Ga.

Dorman, who police say used a bow to kill two deer and the goose, was arrested after a three-day investigation. The young fawn was seized at the time of his arrest.

Powell said Dorman admitted he killed two does using a compound bow, and that he also captured the fawn during a spree in the Chickamauga and Chattanooga National Military Park.

Powell said he received information from the Georgia State Patrol that a fawn less than 3 weeks old was being held captive by Dorman. He said someone saw the fawn running loose in Dorman's apartment and called the state patrol, which then notified the Department of Natural Resources' Wildlife Resources Division.

Powell said when he went to serve the warrant and pick up the fawn, Dorman had just been picked up by the Dalton police. He was charged by city officers on a warrant sworn by his former employer for theft.

The wildlife officer said Dorman's girlfriend said the fawn "had been found." But Powell reported the carcass of one deer and a Canada goose were found near Dorman's apartment complex.

Charges placed against Dorman in Whitfield County include holding a game animal without a permit, illegal storage of wildlife parts, and taking a migrant game bird out of season.

Dorman could receive a maximum fine of $3,000 and a prison term of three years. An additional six charges were awaiting Dorman in Catoosa County.

Warrants say Dorman is wanted on two counts of hunting deer out of season, two counts of hunting from a vehicle, and two counts of hunting from a public road. Bond in Catoosa County is set at $15,000.

— *Rollin Moseley*

■ Buck Overcame Injury to Hind Leg

"I wonder what happened to him?"...was the first thought that came to mind as I watched the buck limp through the soybean field Aug. 15, 1993.

The answer to my question was 3.5 months away. I was watching the field to see what bucks were in the area. The Maryland archery season began in one month.

The buck had an injury to his left hind leg near the hoof. True to form, his right antler's growth had been affected by the injury.

When the buck passed within 50 yards of me I could see the baseball-sized knot his hoof had become. Even with binoculars the true nature of his injury was not evident, but his new name was obvious, "Clubby."

Shortly after the archery season began I passed up an opportunity to shoot Clubby. This began a long series of encounters with the buck that my brother, Chris, two hunting partners and I talked about and looked forward to. Check-in-time on the walkie-talkies would always find someone asking the question, "Anyone see Clubby?"

His limp was unmistakable. Several times he was identified by nothing more than his painful-looking gait. Clubby avoided confrontations and competition with other bucks, however, he was often seen following single does. Clubby, although seen limping when feeding or following does, could run at a moment's notice with no indication there was ever a problem.

Chris and I saw him crossing a barren field on the way to our stands the first morning of rifle season, Nov. 30. Under the light of a full moon there was no doubt who the hobbling deer was.

When a shot rang out from the top of a hollow, I dug my walkie-talkie out of my daypack and asked, "Hey Chris, did you get him?"

"Yeah, it's Clubby, but you won't believe what's wrong with his hoof," Chris said.

Hazards to wildlife come in strange forms. Clubby had been the victim of a freak accident. Apparently, when he was a yearling he had stepped on a piece of threaded PVC pipe. The pipe had wedged onto his hoof under the dew claw. As he grew, the pipe caused a severe deformation to his hoof.

Clubby was a 5-point, 120-pound buck, who became the victim of someone's improperly disposed trash.

— *Rusty Metcalf*

■ Doe Dies after Running into Fence

On a warm, partly cloudy afternoon in mid-March, I was photographing waterfowl along a river that had become ice-free only a few days earlier. Much of the snow and ice had also melted from farm fields, and white-tailed deer had been using those fields at night, feeding heavily after a long winter.

I was surprised, however, to see three deer in a field at midday. The animals seemed particularly jumpy for that time of the year, especially considering the area was popular among deer watchers. Deer had become accustomed to the traffic. At times there were 10 vehicles on the road watching the animals.

The three deer became startled and ran toward the protection of a woods about a half-mile away. I pulled my vehicle over to study the deer with binoculars. Between the animals and their destination was another road paralleled by a woven wire fence. The snow in the road ditch had drifted deep during the winter but, because of the sun and warm temperatures, was soft and slushy.

The first two deer sailed over the fence, but the third landed directly in the ditch. Losing its spring because of the deep snow, the deer's momentum carried it straight into the wire. The whitetail rebounded hard off the fence, fell over, and didn't move.

I arrived on the scene within 30 seconds but the deer was already dead, apparently of a broken neck. On numerous occasions I've seen whitetails come away from similar encounters unscathed.

— *Bill Marchel*

Bill Marchel

This doe didn't jump high enough to clear a woven wire fence. She hit the fence, and died from the impact.

■ Disabled Hunter Shoots First Buck

Wisconsin's Jeff Pues killed an 8-point, 101-pound buck with his Remington shotgun Nov. 22, 1994, in Leeman, Wis. It was the first buck the 34-year-old has shot in 10 years since an automobile accident left him quadraplegic.

"I never thought I would hunt again," he said.

Instead of holding the gun with his hands, aiming at the deer, and squeezing the trigger with his index finger, Pues used his mouth to perform the tasks.

He would not have hunted again if it he hadn't attended the Craig Institute in Colorado, a rehabilitation center for the handicapped. Pues read about the W/C SR-77, a shooting rest for the disabled.

The rest allows people who don't have use of their arms to

Jeff Pues used his mouth and the W/C Sr-77 shooting rest to shoot an 8-point buck in Leeman, Wis.

hunt. The triggering mechanism plugs into the wheelchair's battery pack. The hunter moves the tube with his mouth to raise and lower the gun, or to move it left and right. After sighting in on a target, the hunter uses a quick sip on a vacuum tube to activate the trigger.

The device was designed by Jerry Olson of Sidney, Neb., who invented the rest for his disabled friend Bob Bowen of Chadron, Neb. Bowen marketed the shooting rest and worked with Pues to get him back into the woods.

Bowen had some initial difficulties receiving protective liability insurance, said Dave Pues, Jeff's father. So Jeff stayed in telephone contact with Bowen until he was able to purchase the gun rest.

"It took about 1-1/2 years to get this insurance," Dave Pues said. "We have never met the man in person and he's the greatest man we know."

Pues has been using the rest for the past eight years. He has been hunting in a shanty the family built for him the past seven. The ice fishing shanty has a heater and two large windows. Air temperatures below 50 degrees cause problems for Pues.

"The problem I have with hunting is the weather," Pues said. "Once I get cold, it takes four to five hours to get warm with an electric blanket."

Pues is also an artist. Using his mouth for his artwork made the transition to using the gun rest easier.

"You learn how to use your eye and mouth at the same time," he explained. "You have to move your mouth, try to keep an eye on the target, and sight in your gun at the same time."

Pues added that some people thought the motor to move the gun would frighten the deer. He said that wasn't the case.

"It was more of a help than a hindrance. The buck was more curious and it helped slow him down," Pues said. "It gave me more time to move the gun."

— *Bart Landsverk*

■ Pictures Help Solve Hunter's Puzzle

It's not uncommon for me to see 10 to 20 does and fawns, and a couple of different bucks on opening day of the deer gun season on my farm in Wisconsin.

When scouting, I had difficulty determining when sign was made, and which deer made the tracks, droppings and beds. Also, I couldn't tell if more than one buck was responsible for the rubs and scrapes.

To help answer my many questions, I conducted my own research. I bought a few CamTrakker motion-sensing cameras to gather information. The candid shots, with the date and time on each photo, helped me piece together this complex puzzle.

Since starting this study two years ago I have done more scouting than ever throughout the year. This taught me much about the deer on my 120-acre plot. The photos give me the "who was there" and "when they were" pieces to the puzzle.

Ada Klute of Stoughton, Wis., used a CamTrakker motion sensing camera to better identify white-tailed bucks on her property.

Deer movements are easier to figure out when I get a series of photos of the same deer. Unlike hunting, when I could wait for hours or days to see a deer for a few seconds, I now savor the deer's images as often and as long as I like.

I had the chance to watch a few deer get their pictures taken. I was stunned to see their lack of response to the sound or flash from the camera. Some deer just look its way for a bit afterward, but then quickly return to their business.

As I expected, most photos show does with their fawns. It's fun to see the fawns grow. After a few weeks it gets easier to pick out family groups by slight differences in appearance. Even when the fawns are young with spots still on their coats, I can see the gender differences. The buck fawns start forming their pedicles, which cause bumps on their heads. They outnumber the doe fawns I've photographed.

My husband and I stopped killing 1.5-year-old bucks in 1989. That is the reason we get to take pictures of bucks with large racks. Everybody around us talks quality deer management, but they don't follow through.

After carefully studying each photo or series of photos, I have counted 15 different bucks that were at least 2.5 years old.

That number doesn't include the 1.5-year-olds I have on film. This age group makes up the bulk of my buck pictures, but it is harder to distinguish between

them. I can say there are at least as many 1.5-year-olds as there are older bucks.

Even with this setup, the deer are hard to pattern. I have taken more than 3,200 photographs in the past year, but I know I have not photographed all of the deer.

One of those unphotographed deer is a 10-point buck I named "Tricky Dick." It's my goal to get a picture of him this year.

— *Ada Klute*

■ Purdue Researchers Test Contraceptives

Researchers at Purdue University are shooting deer with contraceptive drugs to reduce the herd's reproduction.

Two contraceptive drugs for deer and a new delivery system, a biodegradable bullet, are being tested in northern Indiana and Connecticut.

The three-year research project comes when wildlife management policy is under consideration by the Indiana Department of Natural Resources.

The idea came from public hearings in 1994 on a deer hunt in Brown County State Park.

On Dec. 4, 1993, 463 hunters participated in the controlled hunt. They killed 392 deer, many of which were underweight and malnourished because the park's herd had depleted food sources.

One contraceptive being tested is a synthetic hormone used in cattle. The other contraceptive is being developed by the University of Illinois.

The biodegradable bullet that delivers the contraceptive dissolves in the animal. The other delivery system consists of a dart and needle. Both systems only seem to work well when the animals can be monitored.

In a proposed policy, the DNR said it "strongly encourages the use of hunting as the primary method of population reduction. It is both safe and cost effective."

— *Welton W. Harris III*
The Indianapolis News

■ Buck Can't Keep His Antlers Clean

"Bucky" is a white-tailed deer that tends to stick his nose where it doesn't belong. And in this case, he ends up with several woody knots on his head when logs become wedged between his antlers.

You might recall seeing and reading about this buck in "Tangled: Bucks in a Bind," in the November 1994 issue of *Deer & Deer Hunting*. He is one of several deer living in a pen at the La Crosse County Lakeview Health Center in West Salem, Wis. He leads a normal life most of the year, but lands in trouble in late fall and early winter.

The buck became a celebrity in 1993 when he managed to live for two weeks with an 8-foot log jammed between his antlers. He wound up shaking the log loose, but hasn't been

This buck's antlers became tangled up in logs three times in 13 months. The buck lives in a pen at the La Crosse, Wis., County Lakeview Health Center.

able to avoid similar mishaps.

His woes started when the Wisconsin Department of Agriculture requested the club build a huge brush pile to serve as a windbreak in winter. The brush pile worked fine for the other deer but not for this buck.

Three times in less than 13 months, logs of different sizes have become wedged between his antlers.

None of the members of the West Salem Rod and Gun Club, which owns the deer, could get close enough to dislodge the first log. A few weeks later, he freed himself of the extra luggage and everything returned to normal.

Then, in December 1994, the buck had his second woody encounter. A smaller log, less than 4 feet long, became wedged between his 10-point

34

rack, but only for a week.

He had his third bout with brush this January when a Y-shaped log about 7 to 8 feet long found its way onto his head.

"Why and how he gets tangled up is beyond me," said Harry Meinking, a member of the club. "He apparently can't keep his head from where it doesn't belong."

Now, everything is back to normal. The buck shed one of his antlers and the log in early February. The club has taken steps to keep him out of trouble when he grows new antlers this summer. Two wooden windbreaks will replace the brush pile.

— Bob Lamb

■ In Search of Birds, They Find Dead Buck

Todd Smith, an avid Indiana deer hunter for many years, decided on the morning of Dec. 26, 1994, that he and his father would go bird hunting. However, what he found a short time later was far from a covey of quail.

The two were hunting a wooded area of Spencer County when Smith's father hollered for him. As Smith approached his father he could not believe what he saw. A few feet away lay a respectable 8-point buck with its neck and antlers lodged between a large split tree limb.

"The head of the buck was about three feet off the ground, and his shoulders were just bare-ly above the ground," Smith said.

He said the deer thrashed violently before its death, probably in an attempt to get free. "Several leaves and small limbs were kicked back away from his front and hind hoofs. I could tell that he had really struggled," Smith said.

He speculated that the buck was rutting and became aggressive with the split limb, pushing, shoving, and rubbing the limb until his head became stuck.

— John Trout Jr.

■ Second Deer Hunt Was a Success

My father and I were making plans for our second deer hunt together. We did the usual stuff — shoot rifles, get groceries, set our orange clothes out, etc.

Dad seems to get a kick out of me going hunting with him, and it really doesn't matter if we get anything. I'm still learning the part where you don't see anything for hours in a freezing wind, rain, sleet or sometimes nice weather, and still call it a successful hunt.

Seeing snow geese, turkeys, muskrats and deer is interesting. I always take a book to read to pass the slow times away. I get cold easily. If I can stay warm and dry, it's fun.

It wasn't very windy, which is good because we sit 25 feet high in a box stand. We practiced climbing in the daylight so I'd know what I was doing in the dark.

At 6:30 a.m., I snuggled in

Thirteen-year-old Sabrina Balzer of Pardeeville, Wis., shot this 9-point buck with her father, Jim, on the first day of the 1994 Wisconsin deer gun season.

for a nap, but no sooner had I gotten comfortable when deer started snorting across the marsh. We heard ice crash, and several deer were visible in the bright moonlight.

After another crash, two deer, one of which was a buck, walked right underneath our stand.

I saw a big doe 30 yards away at 9:15 a.m., but I still wanted to wait for a buck. I started having second thoughts. I asked Dad if I should take her, and he said to wait because she was looking back into the brush. A buck was probably following her.

Sure enough, Dad said he saw a huge buck, and I should concentrate holding the cross-hairs on his shoulder. What ever you do, don't look at the antlers, he said. I waited until a clear shot presented itself, and I shot.

My heart was pounding so hard I'm not sure how I held so steady. We watched as the magnificent whitetail ran only a short ways and dropped. We waited for 20 minutes, and climbed down.

The reality of what I had accomplished began to set in as I caught that "buck-of-a-lifetime" look from Dad. He hugged me and said I had just taken a bigger buck than he had ever seen in the wild his entire life. I had tears of excitement and Dad did, too.

The 9-point buck weighed 175 pounds field dressed, had a 20.25-inch inside spread, and a 22.5-inch outside spread.

Maybe there is more to hunting than I thought. Dad said I can have the head mounted and that my great grandchildren will tell stories about this one.

— *Sabrina Balzer, age 13*
Pardeeville, Wis.

■ Deer Declined During Late '80s

Amid growing evidence, the Institute for White-tailed Deer Management and Research at Stephen F. Austin State University now is convinced there indeed was a deer die-off over much of the eastern half of Texas in the late 1980s. Dr. James C. Kroll, director of the institute reports: "Our data and increasing numbers of reports by landowners and hunters as far west as Bosque County, north to northeast Texas, support the idea we lost several hundred thousand deer in a very short time!"

Reports continue to accumulate of landowners and hunters finding large numbers of deer carcasses and skeletons near water — a sure sign these deer probably died from a disease known as "Blue tongue." The disease is carried by biting gnats or midges which emerge in late summer and early fall: a significant stress time for whitetails. "They don't die a pretty death," asserts Kroll. "The virus causes high fever and totally destroys the stomach and mouth lining." High fever forces deer to water to cool their bodies. That's why so many are found dead around water.

In addition to reports of dead deer, the institute's comprehensive study, funded primarily by Temple-Inland Inc., an east Texas forest products company, revealed post-mortem indicators of a die-off. 'We are seeing a herd that without doubt is building back from a significant crash," warns Kroll. "The average age of deer on hunting clubs and leases in 14 east Texas counties has steadily increased for the last three years."

Kroll points out that, after a herd crash there are many young deer. As the herd builds back up, average age climbs until the herd reaches saturation. "At this point," he adds, "the herd has two basic choices; it can stagnate with low fawn survival or crash when conditions are right."

Are conditions right? "We really don't know at this time," he notes. "It all depends on weather conditions this winter and next summer." Most biologists report low acorn crops in general - important for energy sources during cold weather. However, most deer deaths in east Texas occurs during the late summer stress period.

Kroll reports many calls in 1995 about dead or sick deer. He suggests landowners and hunters look for signs of unhealthy deer. "Deer management is site specific," he adds. "That's why you cannot make broad statements about the herd in general."

He suggests you look for any sign of over-population problems. Unusual numbers of deer carcasses, especially around water; or deer harvested that have hoofs that appear to have sloughed off, or spongy antlers are indicators of Blue tongue.

Fawn survival is extremely low on most hunting clubs, the Institute has discovered. On average, less than 35percent of fawns survive to the fall hunting season. During the last three years, the conception rate of does (fetuses per doe) also has slipped; indicating a significant nutritional problem.

"When a herd has declined," Kroll adds, "important deer foods also decline and even become extinct. We are seeing this trend in many southeastern counties."

Kroll believes primary deer foods such as greenbrier and honeysuckle rarely recover after a decline, lowering the overall carrying capacity. "For years, biologists have used the estimated carrying capacity of east Texas in general of 40 deer per thousand acres," he said. "Now it looks like this number has declined to about 25 per thousand."

Hunters and landowners are encouraged to use their doe permits and doe days whenever possible. Also, planting of summer or winter food plots will help alleviate some of the nutritional problems.

■ He Makes Bucks, Gobblers Tremble

The Virginia deer and turkey seasons sometimes overlap. On these occasions Charles Corder, an active hunter of both species loads his 12-gauge pump with one double aught buck shell in the chamber and a pair of No. 6s in it's tubular magazine.

If he unexpectedly flushes a turkey while deer hunting he can quickly shuck the first round to get to the birdshot. One November morning while still-hunting through dense honeysuckle, Charles jumped a deer, got a glimpse of white antler, and fired off a point and shot as the animal disappeared into the thicket.

When Charles recovered the dead whitetail, he was astonished to find an animal that would later be judged the biggest buck killed in Virginia that season. With it's heavy beams, 12 points and spread of 23 inches, the rack scored 213 points.

After the buck's hide was removed it was discovered that the 3.5-year-old animal had previously received multiple gunshot wounds. Charles has taken 71 deer: all bucks, six points or better.

Incredibly, eight of those had 20-inch spreads. One old trophy buck possessed an antler spread of 27-3/8 inches, and no teeth at the ripe age of 10-plus years.

During the same period he also killed 51 gobblers. And here is the kicker for other hunters to contemplate. This top gun has never used an elevated deer stand. Every single whitetail was taken while still-hunting within five miles of his home.

— *Dinny Slaughter*

■ Hunters Helped Hungry in '94

Missourians who had difficulty making ends meet received a helping hand from deer hunters in 1994, according to Protection Programs Supervisor Dave Beffa with the Missouri Department of Conservation (MDC).

Despite difficulties complying with regulations enforced by state and federal health and wildlife management agencies, Missouri hunters persevered in efforts to share meat with the needy. In 1992, members of the Columbia Area Archers went door to door delivering venison to families identified by food pantries and other social service organizations.

Support from MDC and the Conservation Federation of Missouri helped gain legislative approval for changes in the law to make it easier to donate deer. This made it possible for deer hunters to funnel donations through food pantries. Beffa hopes the program will grow this year.

"Hunters are becoming more aware that they have the option of donating meat in some areas," said Beffa.

Hunters who want to donate meat for distribution by charitable organizations take their deer to participating meat processing operations and specify how much ground deer meat they want to give.

To encourage such efforts, the Columbia Area Archers have published a booklet of guidelines about setting up deer-meat donations programs. Copies are available from: Dennis Ballard, 17200 North Route V, Sturgeon, MO 65284.

■ Deer Contraception Program Dropped

Citing cost and time constraints, officials of the East Bay Regional Park District in Fremont, Calif., have abandoned an annual $60,000 deer contraception program.

In 1993, 15 does at Coyote Hills Park were injected with birth control drugs and have since received annual booster shots. Despite the attempt to curb the deer numbers, the population has outgrown the park's carrying capacity by 20 percent in just two years.

Park officials said they will shoot abundant deer and donate the venison to food pantries.
— Wildlife Legislative Fund of America

■ Cusino Releases its Final Bucks

A square mile enclosure that played a prominent role in Michigan deer research for many years no longer holds any deer. The last whitetails at the Cusino Wildlife Research Station in Shingleton were trapped and released into the wild this winter.

An effort was made to capture and release all deer inside the enclosure during early 1994 before researcher John Ozoga retired because there were no plans to conduct further deer research.

The trio of remaining bucks was captured during early 1995 and released. Cusino employee Jeff Lukowski said the oldest buck was 11.5 years old and weighed 216 pounds at the time of release. Its last set of antlers were between 10 and 14 points.

The next oldest was a 6.5-year-old 12-pointer that weighed 221 pounds. The other buck was 4.5 years old, had 10 points and weighed 175 pounds.

Lukowski added that six of the 16 bucks released from the enclosure during 1994 — identifiable through ear tags — were killed last fall. He said the biggest buck was hit by a vehicle one night during the first days of gun season. Gary Virta of Shingleton tagged a 10-pointer while hunting that day, and was driving home on H-58 in Alger County when he struck and killed a 17-pointer weighing more than 250 pounds.

An unidentified hunter shot a 7.5-year-old, 15-pointer.

A trio of 2.5-year-olds, two of which were shot by bow-hunters, field-dressed between 175 and 210 pounds.
— *Richard P. Smith*

■ Huge Albino Buck Captured on Video

Video footage of an albino whitetail documents what is believed to be the largest white buck on record.

"The Albino Monarch," shown here in a still-shot taken from video footage, lived in western Wisconsin for 10 years. The buck weighed nearly 300 pounds and sported a 15-point rack.

The buck, known as "The Albino Monarch," lived for 10 years in western Wisconsin and reached a live weight of nearly 300 pounds. Its impressive 15-point rack — 10 main tines and five non-typical points — was estimated to have an inside spread of 27 inches.

It was previously thought that the largest albino on record was a 7.5-year-old 8-pointer shot illegally in 1992 near Florence, Wis. (see "Albinos in the Deer Herd," *Deer & Deer Hunting*, March 1995).

Jane Symiczek, an avid bow-hunter, went afield more than 500 times to film "The Albino Monarch," first seeing him when he was a fawn in 1983. She said the buck's senses grew just as quickly as his body and antlers.

It's a common belief that albino bucks are smaller, sterile, and lack the acute senses of "normal" whitetails. That was not the case with this albino.

"He could see as good and smell as good as a brown one," Symiczek recalled, adding that she witnessed the buck tending scrape lines on several occasions.

While most of her video-taping encounters were brief, Symiczek said she once climbed into a tree stand and filmed the buck for 30 minutes.

The buck died in 1993 after its hips degenerated to the point where it was left crippled. A farmer found the buck while it was still alive and called a warden to shoot it. A full body mount of the animal is displayed at the high school in Arcadia, Wis.

Though research indicates albinism is a recessive characteristic that diminishes through reproduction, Symiczek reports to have seen the numbers of albinos increase near her home since the big buck was around. "When I first filmed him, he was the only one. ... There seems to be more and more every year," she said, adding that she recently saw four albinos at one time.

— *Dan Schmidt*

Though already mortally wounded with buckshot, this North Carolina whitetail's escape from hunters was cut short when it became wedged between two trees.

■ Trees Stop Wounded Buck in His Tracks

Furman Ivey has hunted deer in eastern North Carolina for nearly 26 years, and has experienced literally hundreds of unusual occurrences.

What he witnessed during a hunt in 1989, however, ranks as his all-time strangest.

During an afternoon hunt, Ivey and his hunting party pursued a lung-shot spike buck. The deer was shot as it crossed an open field, and fled into an adjacent swamp.

Its escape attempt was short.

No more than 100 yards into the swamp, the buck tried to pass between two trees and became stuck. It had died from the gun-shot wound by the time Ivey and his party found it.

Ivey said the deer was so tightly wedged between the trees that the men had to elevate it to head level to free it.

That made for a humorous end to a successful hunt, Ivey said.

"We laughed so hard we couldn't even stand up," he said. "The guy who shot it said this was one solution to (stopping a deer)."
— *Dan Schmidt*

■ Hunter Shrugs Off Rain For Trophy

After hunting in the rain for a week near Mount Forest, Ontario, in November 1994,

A downpour didn't stop Ritchie Castonguay of Capreol, Ontario, from hunting on Nov. 3, 1994. His perseverance paid off when he arrowed this buck. The rack had a rough score of 160-1/8.

things were not looking good. My partner and I both knew there were some big deer in the area from the tracks and deer sign.

The last morning of the hunt looked grim, but we decided to go out anyway. Of course, as soon as I was settled in my tree stand, it started to pour! I sat tight, however, and about an hour later, I heard a deer jump a steel fence behind me. It was still too dark to see so I decided to try to keep the deer around by using my grunt call.

When there was shooting light, I could see a doe feeding 30 yards away. I soon had eight does right under my stand. Suddenly, there he was — a bruiser buck — trotting down one of the deer runs with his nose to the ground.

I now have a super 10-point buck that rough-scored 160-1/8.

Rain or shine, you never know when the big one might walk under your tree stand.

— *Ritchie Castonguay*

■ Rare Albino Buck Shot in Wisconsin

A Minnesota man was charged for shooting a rare albino deer south of Minong, Wis., in Washburn County in 1994.

Department of Natural Resources Warden Supervisor Dale Corbin said the 64-year-old man, of Owatonna, Minn., went to officials and said he had found the dead albino deer in the woods.

A subsequent investigation, however, revealed the man had killed the animal. Corbin said.

In Wisconsin, it is against the law to shoot albino deer. Fines of up to $4,000 can be imposed for breaking the law.

"It's an adult deer that people have seen in the area for four or five years at least," Corbin said. "It has a really nice eight-point rack, a nice heavy rack. It's a magnificent looking animal. It's not typical in that its an albino, and we don't have many albino. It has the pink eyes and the pink hooves."

The "nice heavy rack" will be mounted and placed in a DNR office, he said.

In another hunting incident, DNR spokesman Jim Bishop said a buck has been spotted near Spooner sporting a hunter's tag on its antlers.

The hunter apparently shot the deer and, thinking it was dead, tagged it.

The deer apparently was only wounded and took off after being tagged, Bishop said.

WHITE-TAILED DEER HARVEST RECORDS

The following harvest figures were obtained from Department of Wildlife officials.

Though the numbers were updated as much as possible before press time, harvest totals for the 1994 season were not available for some states.

Also note that some states in the West combine mule deer and whitetails in their harvest statistics. In many of these cases we used the best estimates of deer biologists to determine what percentage of the kill were whitetails.

In addition, be aware that all states do not use the same procedures to arrive at a total deer harvest for the year. Some are more precise than others. Still, the figures will show harvest trends in each state.

ALABAMA

Year	Firearm	Bow	Total
1963-64			31,123
1964-65			59,230
1965-66			37,819
1966-67			47,842
1967-68			68,406
1968-69			63,674
1969-70			74,239
1970-71			63,502
1971-72			80,184
1972-73			82,555
1973-74			121,953
1974-75			120,727
1975-76			125,625
1976-77			144,155
1977-78			147,113
1978-79			152,733
1979-80			140,685
1980-81			130,532
1981-82			202,449
1982-83			141,281
1983-84			192,231
1984-85			237,378
1985-86			280,436
1986-87	288,487	17,653	306,140
1987-88	309,517	15,683	325,200
1988-89	257,734	18,854	276,588
1990-91	263,100	31,300	294,400
1991-92	269,500	25,500	295,000

Ala. (cont.)

Year	Firearm	Bow	Total
1992-93	261,500	31,600	293,100
1993-94	305,300	45,200	350,500

ARIZONA

Year	Firearm	Bow	Total
1958	5,096		5,096
1959	5,421		5,421
1960	4,982		4,982
1961	4,734		4,734
1962	4,194		4,194
1963	4,343		4,343
1964	4,339		4,339
1965	3,612		3,612
1966	2,993		2,993
1967	2,662		2,662
1968	2,927		2,927
1969	2,202		2,202
1970	2,232		2,232
1971	1,535		1,535
1972	1,673		1,673

	Ariz. (cont.)				Ark. (cont.)		
Year	Firearm	Bow	Total	Year	Firearm	Bow	Total
1973	2,097		2,097	1953	6,245		6,245
1974	3,248		3,248	1954	7,343		7,343
1975	2,870		2,870	1955	6,856		6,856
1976	2,662		2,662	1956	8,249		8,249
1977	2,319		2,319	1957	9,438		9,438
1978	2,287		2,287	1958	9,993		9,993
1979	3,264		3,264	1959	12,280		12,280
1980	3,523		3,523	1960	15,000		15,000
1981	3,504		3,504	1961	19,359		19,359
1982	4,002	60	4,062	1962	27,772		27,772
1983	4,221	71	4,292	1963	25,148		25,148
1984	7,116	65	7,181	1964	16,637		16,637
1985	6,902	138	7,040	1965	17,138		17,138
1986	5,934	94	6,028	1966	20,028		20,028
1987	4,895	115	5,010	1967	21,751		21,751
1988	4,600	108	4,708	1968	20,063		20,063
1989	4,387	189	4,576	1969	24,018	1,678	25,696
1990	4,449	100	4,549	1970	24,784	1,233	26,017
1991	5,375	129	5,504	1971	23,375	1,345	24,720
1992	5,737	95	5,832	1972	31,415	672	32,087
1993	5,556	152	5,772	1973	32,292	1,502	33,794
1994	5,363		5,363	1974	32,168	1,595	33,763
				1975	32,210	1,112	33,322
				1976	27,249	540	27,789
				1977	27,862	1,247	29,109
				1978	41,018	2,434	43,452
				1979	32,841	3,233	36,074
				1980	41,693	3,509	45,202
				1981	41,567	3,024	44,591
				1982	35,051	7,822	42,873
				1983	42,709	17,539	60,248
				1984	53,679	12,360	66,039
				1985	48,027	12,049	60,076
				1986	67,941	11,939	79,880
				1987	89,422	16,970	106,392
				1988	94,193	16,014	110,207
				1989	97,031	16,048	113,079
				1990	70,498	20,412	90,910
				1991			110,896
				1992			110,401

ARKANSAS

Year	Firearm	Bow	Total
1938	203		203
1939	540		540
1940	408		408
1941	433		433
1942	1,000		1,000
1943	1,723		1,723
1944	1,606		1,606
1945	1,687		1,687
1946	1,661		1,661
1947	2,016		2,016
1948	2,779		2,779
1949	3,075		3,075
1950	4,122		4,122
1951	4,600		4,600
1952	6,090		6,090

COLORADO

NOTE: Colorado does not distinguish between white-tailed deer and mule deer in its harvest statistics. Biologists there estimate that approximately 1,000 white-tails have been taken during each of the past five years. Most of these animals come from the river bottoms of the eastern plains of Colorado.

CONNECTICUT

Year	Firearm	Bow	Total
1975	475	75	550
1976	530	100	630
1977	780	125	905
1978	805	125	930
1979	870	140	1,010
1980	2,189	376	2,565
1981	2,463	393	2,856
1982	2,233	391	2,624
1983	3,152	639	3,791
1984	3,742	596	4,338
1985	3,817	722	4,539
1986	4,575	819	5,394
1987	5,618	854	6,472
1988	6,843	799	7,642
1989	7,837	926	8,763
1990			9,896
1991			11,311
1992			12,486
1993			10,360
1994			10,438

DELAWARE

Year	Firearm	Bow	Total
1976-77	1,475	19	1,494
1977-78	1,630	22	1,652
1978-79	1,679	20	1,699
1979-80	1,783	20	1,803
1980-81	1,737	17	1,754
1981-82	2,080	31	2,111
1982-83	2,046	48	2,094
1983-84	2,210	21	2,231
1984-85	2,473	41	2,514
1985-86	2,383	58	2,439
1986-87	2,772	78	2,850
1987-88	3,420	121	3,541
1988-89	3,844	154	3,998
1989-90	4,292	212	4,504
1990-91	4,814	252	5,066
1991-92	4,970	362	5,332
1992-93	6,721	524	7,245
1993-94	6,917	548	7,465

FLORIDA

Year	Firearm	Bow	Total
1971			48,900
1972			58,500
1973			57,122
1974			54,102
1975			54,380
1976			60,805
1977			85,744
1978			NA
1979			54,765
1980			72,039
1981			66,489
1982			64,557
1983			77,146
1984			73,895
1985			80,947
1986			89,212
1987			105,917
1988			107,240
1989			85,753
1990			79,170
1991			81,255
1992			81,942
1993			104,178

GEORGIA

Year	Firearm	Bow	Total
1980-81			135,500
1981-82			134,000
1982-83			144,000
1983-84			164,000
1984-85			177,000
1985-86			189,600
1986-87			226,000
1987-88			280,536
1988-89			300,624
1989-90			293,167
1990-91			351,652
1991-92	265,352	15,708	281,060
1992-93	284,412	21,841	306,253

IDAHO

Year	Firearm	Bow	Total
1980			45,988
1981			50,580
1982			48,670
1983			50,600
1984			42,600
1985			48,950
1986			59,800

Idaho (cont.)

Year	Firearm	Bow	Total
1987			66,400
1988			82,200
1989			95,200
1990			72,100
1991			NA
1992			44,590
1993			NA

NOTE — These harvest figures include white-tailed deer and mule deer because Idaho has not traditionally distinguished between the two in its harvest totals. However, whitetails made up 53 percent of the 1992 harvest, meaning 23,633 whitetails were taken.

ILLINOIS

Year	Firearm	Bow	Total
1957	1,709		1,709
1958	2,493		2,493
1959	2,604		2,604
1960	2,438		2,438
1961	4,313		4,313
1962	6,289		6,289
1963	6,785		6,785
1964	9,975		9,975
1965	7,651		7,651
1966	7,357		7,357
1967	6,588		6,588
1968	8,202		8,202
1969	8,345		8,345
1970	8,889	590	9,479
1971	10,359	566	10,925
1972	10,100	552	10,652
1973	12,902	960	13,862
1974	12,853	1,425	14,278
1975	15,614	1,608	17,222
1976	15,308	1,600	16,908
1977	16,231	2,810	19,041
1979	20,058	1,074	21,132
1980	20,825	1,463	22,288
1981	20,800	1,766	22,566

Ill. (cont.)

Year	Firearm	Bow	Total
1982	22,657	2,205	24,862
1983	26,112	2,554	28,666
1984	29,212	3,023	32,235
1985	31,769	3,746	35,515
1986	36,056	4,357	40,413
1987	42,932	6,646	49,578
1988	47,786	7,820	55,606
1989	56,143	10,000	66,143
1990			81,000
1991	83,191	18,099	101,290
1992	84,537	19,564	104,101
1993	92,276	23,215	115,491
1994	99,319	25,571	124,890

INDIANA

Year	Firearm	Bow	Total
1951			1,590
1952			1,112
1953			83
1954			68
1955			149
1956			198
1957			NA
1958			592
1959			800
1960			1,523
1961			2,293
1962			3,212
1963			4,634
1964			6,001
1965			4,155
1966			5,775
1967			6,560
1968			6,659
1969			7,323
1970			5,175
1971			5,099
1972			NA
1973			8,244
1974			9,461
1975			8,758
1976			11,344
1977			12,476
1978			9,896
1979			13,718
1980			19,780
1981	12,600	5,527	18,127
1982	16,267	4,651	20,918
1983	21,244	3,988	25,232

Ind. (cont.)

Year	Firearm	Bow	Total
1984	21,944	5,640	27,584
1985	25,768	6,371	32,139
1986	33,837	9,621	43,458
1987	38,937	12,841	51,778
1988	46567	13,667	60,234
1989	62,901	16,417	79,318
1990	70,928	17,775	88,703
1991	77,102	21,581	98,683
1992	73,396	21,918	95,314
1993	77,226	23,988	101,214
1994	89,037	23,379	112,416

IOWA

Year	Firearm	Bow	Total
1953	4,007	1	4,008
1954	2,413	10	2,423
1955	3,006	58	3,064
1956	2,561	117	2,678
1957	2,667	138	2,805
1958	2,729	162	2,891
1959	2,476	255	2,731
1960	3,992	277	4,269
1961	4,997	367	5,364
1962	5,299	404	5,703
1963	6,612	538	7,151
1964	9,024	670	9,694
1965	7,910	710	8,620
1966	10,742	579	11,321
1967	10,392	791	11,183
1968	12,941	830	13,771
1969	10,731	851	11,582
1970	12,743	1,037	13,780
1971	10,459	1,232	11,691
1972	10,485	1,328	11,813
1973	12,208	1,822	14,030
1974	15,817	2,173	17,990
1975	18,948	2,219	21,167
1976	14,257	2,350	16,607
1977	12,788	2,400	15,188
1978	15,168	2,957	18,125

Iowa (cont.)

Year	Firearm	Bow	Total
1979	16,149	3,305	19,454
1980	18,857	3,803	22,660
1981	21,578	4,368	25,946
1982	21,741	4,720	26,461
1983	30,375	5,244	35,619
1984	33,756	5,599	39,355
1985	38,414	5,805	44,219
1986	52,807	9,895	62,702
1987	66,036	9,722	75,758
1988	83,184	9,897	93,756
1989	87,300	11,857	99,712
1990	87,856	10,146	98,002
1991	74,828	8,807	83,635
1992	68,227	8,814	77,684
1993	67,139	9,291	76,430

KANSAS

Year	Firearm	Bow	Total
1965	1,340	164	1,504
1966	2,139	376	2,515
1967	1,542	434	1,976
1968	1,648	614	2,262
1969	1,668	583	2,251
1970	2,418	793	3,211
1971	2,569	578	3,147
1972	2,318	664	2,982
1973	3,220	892	4,112
1974	4,347	1,130	5,477
1975	4,352	1,136	5,488
1976	3,955	1,114	5,069
1977	3,766	1,174	4,940
1978	4,942	1,738	6,680
1979	5,810	2,259	8,069
1980	7,296	3,007	10,303
1981	9,413	2,939	12,352
1982	11,446	3,441	14,887
1983	13,640	3,918	17,558
1984	19,446	4,167	23,613
1985	21,296	4,230	25,526
1986	24,123	4,358	28,481
1987	31,664	4,329	35,993
1988	35,236	5,118	40,354
1989	34,000	5,550	39,550
1990	40,800	5,000	45,800
1991	34,770	4,500	39,270
1992	26,400	4,500	30,900

KENTUCKY

Year	Firearm	Bow	Total
1976	3,476		3,476
1977	5,682		5,682
1978	6,012	421	6,433
1979	7,442	620	8,062
1980	7,988	1,714	9,702
1981	13,134	1,849	14,983
1982	15,804	2,165	17,969
1983	16,027	2,705	18,732
1984	20,344	2,668	23,012
1985	26,024	4,051	30,075
1986	34,657	4,863	39,520
1987	54,372	6,000	60,372
1988	57,553	6,707	64,260
1989	62,667	7,482	70,149
1990	66,151	7,767	73,918
1991	84,918	8,016	92,934
1992	73,664	8,274	81,938
1993	64,598	8,680	73,278

NOTE: These harvest totals don't include open counties. It is estimated that 30 percent of hunters in open counties fail to check in otherwise legally harvested deer.

LOUISIANA

Year	Firearm	Bow	Total
1960-61	16,500		16,500
1961-62	NA		NA
1962-63	NA		NA
1963-64	24,000		24,000
1964-65	23,000		23,000
1965-66	26,000		26,000
1966-67	32,500		32,500
1967-68	36,000		36,000
1968-69	50,000		50,000
1969-70	53,000		53,000
1970-71	53,500		53,500
1971-72	61,000		61,000
1972-73	65,000		65,000
1973-74	74,500		74,500
1974-75	82,000		82,000
1975-76	77,000		77,000
1976-77	84,500		84,500
1977-78	82,500		82,500
1978-79	85,000		85,000
1979-80	90,000	5,000	95,000
1980-81	105,500	5,000	110,500
1981-82	115,000	5,500	120,500

La. (cont.)

Year	Firearm	Bow	Total
1982-83	132,000	5,500	137,500
1983-84	131,000	6,000	137,000
1984-85	128,000	6,500	134,500
1985-86	139,000	7,500	146,500
1986-87	149,000	8,750	157,750
1987-88	164,000	9,500	173,500
1988-89	161,000	10,500	171,500
1989-90	162,000	11,000	173,000
1990-91	176,200	18,200	194,300
1991-92	186,400	17,700	204,100
1992-93	192,300	22,600	214,900
1993-94	193,000	20,100	213,100

MAINE

Year	Firearm	Bow	Total
1919	5,784		5,784
1920	5,829		5,829
1921	8,861		8,861
1922	7,628		7,628
1925	8,379		8,379
1927	8,112		8,112
1928	9,051		9,051
1929	11,708		11,708
1930	13,098		13,098
1931	14,694		14,694
1932	15,465		15,465
1933	18,935		18,935
1934	13,284		13,284
1935	19,726		19,726
1936	19,134		19,134
1937	19,197		19,197
1938	19,363		19,363
1939	19,187		19,187
1940	22,201		22,201
1941	19,881		19,881
1942	22,591		22,591
1943	24,408		24,408
1944	21,708		21,708
1945	24,904		24,904
1946	31,728		31,728

	Maine (cont.)				MARYLAND		
Year	Firearm	Bow	Total	Year	Firearm	Bow	Total
1947	30,349		30,349	1983	16,239	2,181	18,420
1948	35,364		35,364	1984	17,324	2,501	19,825
1949	35,051		35,051	1985	17,241	2,549	19,790
1950	39,216		39,216	1986	22,411	3,404	25,815
1951	41,730		41,730	1987	24,846	4,216	29,062
1952	35,171		35,171	1988	27,625	5,983	33,608
1953	38,609		38,609	1989	38,305	7,988	46,293
1954	37,379		37,379	1990	37,712	8,605	46,317
1955	35,591		35,591	1991	36,169	10,454	46,623
1956	40,290		40,290	1992	39,858	11,240	51,098
1957	40,125	17	40,142	1993	39,429	11,251	51,234
1958	39,375	18	39,393				
1959	41,720	15	41,735				
1960	37,752	22	37,774				
1961	32,740	7	32,747				
1962	38,795	12	38,807				
1963	29,816	23	29,839				
1964	35,286	19	35,305				
1965	37,266	16	37,282				
1966	32,142	18	32,160				
1967	34,693	14	34,707		MASSACHUSETTS		
1968	41,064	16	41,080	Year	Firearm	Bow	Total
1969	30,388	21	30,409	1989	5,818	890	6,708
1970	31,738	12	31,750	1990	5,829	1,061	6,890
1971	18,873	30	18,903	1991	8,085	1,378	9,463
1972	28,664	34	28,698	1992	8,470	1,570	10,040
1973	24,681	39	24,720	1993	6,514	1,387	8,345
1974	34,602	65	34,667	1994	7,545	1,587	9,132
1975	34,625	50	34,675				
1976	29,918	47	29,965		MICHIGAN		
1977	31,354	76	31,430	Year	Firearm	Bow	Total
1978	28,905	97	29,002	1878			21,000
1979	26,720	101	26,821	1879			80,000
1980	37,148	107	37,255	1880			70,000
1981	32,027	140	32,167	1881			80,000
1982	28,709	125	28,834	1899			12,000
1983	23,699	100	23,799	1900			12,000
1984	19,225	133	19,358	1911			12,000
1985	21,242	182	21,424	1916			8,000
1986	19,290	302	19,592	1919			20,000
1987	23,435	294	23,729	1920			25,000
1988	27,754	302	28,056	1921			11,520
1989	29,844	416	30,260	1922			11,700
1990	25,658	319	25,977	1923			13,270
1991	26,236	500	26,736	1924			15,190
1992	28,126	694	28,820	1925			18,120
1993	26,608	682	27,402	1926			20,200
1994	23,967	716	24,683	1927			22,810
				1928			24,810

Mich. (cont.)

Year	Firearm	Bow	Total
1929			28,710
1930			32,150
1931			23,500
1932			20,500
1933			25,500
1934			27,000
1935			30,000
1936			42,000
1937	39,760	4	39,764
1938	44,390	8	44,398
1939	44,770	6	44,776
1940	51,380	10	51,390
1941	73,430	24	73,454
1942	62,190	22	62,212
1943	51,610	37	51,647
1944	51,730	37	51,767
1945	85,080	68	85,148
1946	90,510	170	90,680
1947	82,360	390	82,750
1948	64,540	580	65,120
1949	77,750	780	78,530
1950	84,410	1,340	85,750
1951	82,240	1,320	83,560
1952	162,630	1,840	164,470
1953	97,650	1,820	99,470
1954	67,740	1,820	69,560
1955	74,160	2,310	76,470
1956	74,050	2,430	76,480
1957	77,300	1,760	79,060
1958	100,010	2,570	102,580
1959	115,400	1,840	117,240
1960	75,490	1,230	76,720
1961	58,090	1,980	60,070
1962	95,917	1,643	97,560
1963	124,217	2,143	126,360
1964	141,466	2,814	144,280
1965	112,347	2,173	114,520
1966	94,327	1,933	96,260
1967	104,170	2,650	106,820
1968	101,669	2,681	104,350
1969	106,698	2,582	109,280
1970	68,843	3,187	72,030
1971	62,076	3,354	65,430
1972	55,796	3,694	59,490
1973	66,359	4,631	70,990
1974	92,111	7,969	100,080
1975	106,800	8,790	115,590
1976	107,625	10,365	117,990
1977	137,110	21,250	158,360

Mich. (cont.)

Year	Firearm	Bow	Total
1978	145,710	25,140	170,850
1979	119,790	25,640	145,430
1980	137,380	28,110	165,490
1981	175,090	33,320	208,410
1982	163,520	38,420	201,940
1983	127,770	30,640	158,410
1984	131,280	32,630	163,910
1985	197,370	42,050	239,420
1986	219,260	57,960	277,220
1987	265,860	72,820	338,680
1988	311,770	72,020	383,790
1989	355,410	97,080	452,490
1990	338,890	93,800	432,690
1991	318,460	115,880	434,340
1992	274,650	99,990	374,640
1993	232,820	98,160	330,980

NOTE: Firearm harvest totals prior to 1975 did not include muzzleloader harvest. Also, harvest totals since 1978 do not include deer taken with camp deer permits. In addition, prior to 1961, camp deer harvests were not separated by firearm and bow.

MINNESOTA

Year	Firearm	Bow	Total
1918	9,000		9,000
1919	18,300		18,300
1920	18,600		18,600
1921	13,600		13,600
1922	11,200		11,200
1923	closed		
1924	15,600		15,600
1925	closed		
1926	28,000		28,000
1927	closed		
1928	27,300		27,300
1929	closed		
1930	27,800		27,800
1931	closed		
1932	42,300		42,300

	Minn. (cont.)				Minn. (cont.)		
Year	Firearm	Bow	Total	Year	Firearm	Bow	Total
1933	26,200		26,200	1982	107,000	5,566	112,566
1934	39,100		39,100	1983	NA	5,977	NA
1935	closed			1984	132,000	6,390	138,390
1936	50,100		50,100	1985	138,000	7,575	145,575
1937	33,600		33,600	1986	129,800	7,610	137,410
1938	44,500		44,500	1987	135,000	7,535	142,535
1939	closed			1988	138,900	8,262	147,162
1940	56,000		56,000	1989	129,600	9,307	138,907
1941	closed			1990	166,600	11,106	177,706
1942	77,000		77,000	1991	206,300	12,964	219,264
1943	67,700		67,700	1992	230,064	13,004	243,068
1944	62,800		62,800	1993	188,109	13,722	202,928
1945	67,100		67,100	1994	180,008	13,818	193,826
1946	93,400		93,400				
1947	74,400		74,400				
1948	61,600		61,600				
1949	49,900		49,900				
1950	closed						
1951	72,700	43	72,743				
1952	57,300	34	57,334				
1953	61,000	66	61,066				
1954	56,000	182	56,182				
1955	79,000	214	79,214		MISSISSIPPI		
1956	69,000	325	69,325	Year	Firearm	Bow	Total
1957	67,000	392	67,392	1971-72	580	39	619
1958	75,000	403	75,403	1972-73	816	53	869
1959	104,000	390	104,390	1973-74	919	57	976
1960	95,000	445	95,445	1974-75	NA	NA	NA
1961	107,000	490	107,490	1975-76	NA	NA	NA
1962	96,000	519	96,519	1976-77	2,529	975	3,504
1963	113,000	713	113,713	1977-78	NA	NA	NA
1964	122,000	780	122,780	1978-79	NA	NA	NA
1965	127,000	871	127,871	1979-80	NA	NA	NA
1966	115,000	604	115,604	1980-81	184,163	17,437	201,600
1967	107,000	598	107,598	1981-82	196,856	14,860	211,716
1968	103,000	819	103,819	1982-83	227,432	16,222	243,654
1969	68,000	776	68,776	1983-84	176,400	19,747	196,147
1970	50,000	453	50,453	1984-85	209,574	17,815	227,389
1971	closed	1,279	1,279	1985-86	216,959	18,120	235,079
1972	73,400	1,601	75,001	1986-87	237,075	19,209	256,284
1973	67,100	1,935	69,035	1987-88	240,337	24,662	264,999
1974	65,000	2,176	67,176	1988-89	236,012	28,744	264,756
1975	63,600	2,265	65,865	1989-90	236,012	28,744	262,386
1976	36,200	1,167	37,367	1990-91	218,347	29,982	249,572
1977	58,100	2,609	60,709	1991-92	243,175	33,940	277,714
1978	57,800	2,608	60,408	1992-93	260,093	40,886	300,980
1979	55,400	2,578	57,978	1993-94	229,425	32,971	262,409
1980	77,100	3,641	80,741				
1981	108,100	5,535	113,635				

	MISSOURI				Mo. (cont.)		
Year	Firearm	Bow	Total	Year	Firearm	Bow	Total
1944	583		583	1993	156,704	14,696	172,120
1945	882		882				
1946	743		743				
1947	1,387		1,387				
1948	1,432		1,432				
1949	1,353		1,353				
1950	1,623	1	1,624				
1951	5,519		5,519				
1952	7,466	2	7,468				
1953	7,864	5	7,869		MONTANA		
1954	7,648	22	7,670	Year	Firearm	Bow	Total
1955	7,988	37	8,025	1984			56,760
1956	7,864	33	7,897	1985			43,019
1957	9,986	58	10,044	1986			44,733
1958	13,610	71	13,681	1987			40,675
1959	16,306	90	16,396	1988			43,971
1960	17,418	263	17,681	1989			44,261
1961	15,967	116	16,083	1990			49,419
1962	16,516	231	16,747	1991			56,789
1963	17,304	268	17,572	1992	58,565	2,067	60,632
1964	20,619	316	20,935	1993	60,369	2,038	62,407
1965	18,785	371	19,156				
1966	27,965	458	28,423		NEBRASKA		
1967	22,802	380	23,182	Year	Firearm	Bow	Total
1968	22,090	559	22,649	1945	2		2
1969	23,265	619	23,884	1949	0		0
1970	28,400	828	29,228	1950	7		7
1971	31,722	962	32,684	1951	2		2
1972	30,084	1,130	31,214	1952	7		7
1973	33,438	1,285	34,723	1953	353		353
1974	29,262	1,437	30,699	1954	219		219
1975	51,823	1,850	53,673	1955	189		189
1976	40,683	1,973	42,656	1956	344	8	352
1977	36,562	2,199	38,761	1957	258	21	279
1978	40,261	2,781	43,042	1958	340	103	443
1979	53,164	3,327	56,491	1959	975	111	1,086
1980	49,426	3,661	53,087	1960	1,355	108	1,463
1981	50,183	3,495	53,678	1961	1,443	198	1,641
1982	55,852	4,191	60,043	1962	3,280	194	3,474
1983	57,801	4,626	62,427	1963	3,710	246	3,956
1984	71,569	5,134	76,703	1964	5,138	326	5,464
1985	80,792	5,621	86,413	1965	6,853	338	7,191
1986	102,879	5,832	108,711	1966	6,920	375	7,295
1987	132,500	8,077	140,577	1967	4,773	546	5,319
1988	139,726	10,183	149,909	1968	5,067	399	5,466
1989	157,506	10,970	168,476	1969	5,440	524	5,964
1990	161,857	11,118	172,975	1970	6,460	654	7,114
1991	149,112	14,096	164,384	1971	6,343	662	7,005
1992	150,873	15,029	166,929	1972	5,635	624	6,259

Neb. (cont.)

Year	Firearm	Bow	Total
1973	7,090	865	7,955
1974	7,894	1,032	8,926
1975	8,404	1,155	9,559
1976	7,595	831	8,426
1977	5,921	769	6,690
1978	6,164	958	7,122
1979	7,899	1,151	9,050
1980	9,939	1,639	11,578
1981	11,364	2,025	13,389
1982	12,957	2,049	15,006
1983	15,980	2,781	18,761
1984	19,679	2,471	22,150
1985	20,930	2,593	23,523
1986	22,859	2,291	25,150
1987	24,266	2,812	27,078
1988	24,938	2,951	27,889
1989	24,359	2,847	27,206
1990	21,973	2,716	24,689
1991	20,820	2,931	23,751
1992	20,125	3,141	23,266
1993	23,377	3,282	26,683
1994	26,050	3,830	29,880

NEW HAMPSHIRE

Year	Firearm	Bow	Total
1922	1,896		1,896
1923	1,402		1,402
1924	1,537		1,537
1925	1,493		1,493
1926	1,665		1,665
1927	1,481		1,481
1928	1,474		1,474
1929	1,598		1,598
1930	1,735		1,735
1931	1,498		1,498
1932	1,687		1,687
1933	2,064		2,064
1934	1,526		1,526
1935	1,845		1,845
1936	2,751		2,751
1937	3,216		3,216

N.H. (cont.)

Year	Firearm	Bow	Total
1938	3,363		3,363
1939	3,820		3,820
1940	5,699		5,699
1941	3,897		3,897
1942	4,844		4,844
1943	5,029		5,029
1944	5,029		5,029
1945	6,449		6,449
1946	6,356		6,356
1947	10,172		10,172
1948	6,767		6,767
1949	9,852		9,852
1950	10,051		10,051
1951	11,462		11,462
1952	6,932		6,932
1953	9,517		9,517
1954	9,328		9,328
1955	10,275		10,275
1956	10,917		10,917
1957	9,901		9,901
1958	10,221		10,221
1959	8,435		8,435
1960	7,560	9	7,569
1961	7,763	12	7,775
1962	7,917	5	7,922
1963	8,626	2	8,628
1964	7,559	9	7,568
1965	9,676	3	9,679
1966	9,105	16	9,121
1967	14,153	33	14,186
1968	12,712	36	12,748
1969	8,778	13	8,791
1970	7,214	17	7,231
1971	7,263	12	7,275
1972	6,923	20	6,943
1973	5,440	22	5,462
1974	6,875	20	6,895
1975	8,308	24	8,332
1976	9,076	14	9,090
1977	6,877	62	6,939
1978	5,545	57	5,602
1979	4,939	42	4,981
1980	5,353	31	5,384
1981	6,028	125	6,153
1982	4,577	97	4,674
1983	3,156	124	3,280
1984	4,169	120	4,289
1985	5,523	148	5,671
1986	6,557	263	6,820

	N.H. (cont.)				N.J. (cont.)		
Year	Firearm	Bow	Total	Year	Firearm	Bow	Total
1987	5,864	257	6,121	1939	2,336		2,336
1988	5,900	225	6,125	1940	2,622		2,622
1989	6,749	489	7,238	1941	2,182		2,182
1990	6,466	482	7,872	1942	2,532		2,532
1991	8,060	732	8,792	1943	2,458		2,458
1992	9,013	1,202	10,215	1944	2,633		2,633
1993	9,012	877	9,889	1945	2,704		2,704
1994	7,478	901	8,379	1946	3,043		3,043
				1947	3,938		3,938
				1948	3,249		3,249
				1949	3,618	9	3,627
				1950	3,796	12	3,808
				1951	5,005	14	5,019
				1952	4,514	141	4,655
				1953	4,824	287	5,111
				1954	4,767	319	5,086
				1955	6,114	368	6,482

	NEW JERSEY						
Year	Firearm	Bow	Total	Year	Firearm	Bow	Total
				1956	6,070	690	6,760
1909	86		86	1957	6,643	1,104	7,747
1910	127		127	1958	6,115	1,252	7,367
1911	141		141	1959	9,612	1,230	10,842
1912	109		109	1960	6,072	1,298	7,370
1913	149		149	1961	11,325	1,081	12,406
1914	149		149	1962	7,219	978	8,197
1915	180		180	1963	7,868	952	8,820
1916	481		481	1964	6,933	1,116	8,049
1917	255		255	1965	5,136	1,109	6,245
1918	327		327	1966	8,517	1,329	9,846
1919	353		353	1967	8,467	1,456	9,923
1920	522		522	1968	7,100	1,501	8,601
1921	834		834	1969	7,121	1,356	8,477
1922	771		771	1970	6,866	1,387	8,253
1923	890		890	1971	6,111	1,434	7,545
1924	1,216		1,216	1972	9,557	1,464	11,021
1925	1,063		1,063	1973	9,629	1,689	11,318
1926	1,249		1,249	1974	11,429	1,717	13,146
1927	1,790		1,790	1975	10,675	2,013	12,688
1928	1,415		1,415	1976	10,908	2,110	13,018
1929	1,331		1,331	1977	11,828	2,591	14,419
1930	1,484		1,484	1978	13,177	2,641	15,818
1931	1,702		1,702	1979	13,843	2,263	16,106
1932	1,575		1,575	1980	16,030	5,161	21,191
1933	1,875		1,875	1981	16,291	5,846	22,137
1934	2,466		2,466	1982	16,817	6,928	23,745
1935	2,387		2,387	1983	16,403	6,902	23,305
1936	2,034		2,034	1984	17,920	7,699	25,619
1937	2,173		2,173	1985	21,480	7,971	29,451
1938	2,339		2,339	1986	23,590	10,187	33,777
				1987	27,415	11,813	39,228

N.J. (cont.)

Year	Firearm	Bow	Total
1988	33,140	12,760	45,900
1989	34,812	13,714	48,526
1990	34,372	13,850	48,222
1991	29,936	15,480	45,416
1992	31,257	16,418	47,675
1993	32,936	17,006	49,942
1994	32,602	18,840	51,442

NEW YORK

Year	Firearm	Bow	Total
1941	18,566		18,566
1942	19,217		19,217
1943	31,510		31,510
1944	38,808		38,808
1945	15,136		15,136
1946	22,296		22,296
1947	24,194		24,194
1948	54,896	8	54,906
1949	27,584	13	27,597
1950	38,924	47	38,971
1951	31,049	75	31,124
1952	59,986	341	60,327
1953	29,273	529	29,802
1954	37,879	670	38,549
1955	58,593	939	59,532
1956	71,208	1,107	72,315
1957	71,478	1,199	72,677
1958	65,439	1,030	66,469
1959	41,345	961	42,306
1960	44,913	842	45,755
1961	57,723	731	58,454
1962	62,042	739	62,781
1963	63,244	623	63,867
1964	60,174	582	60,756
1965	66,577	843	67,420
1966	73,092	1,065	74,157
1967	77,834	821	78,655
1968	90,758	1,407	92,165
1969	86,888	1,241	88,129
1970	63,865	1,148	65,013
1971	47,039	1,243	48,282

N.Y. (cont.)

Year	Firearm	Bow	Total
1972	54,041	1,596	55,637
1973	73,191	2,002	75,193
1974	100,097	3,206	103,303
1975	99,835	3,288	103,123
1976	86,421	3,794	90,215
1977	79,035	4,169	83,204
1978	81,749	3,810	85,559
1979	90,691	3,368	94,059
1980	131,606	4,649	136,255
1981	161,593	3,792	165,385
1982	178,825	6,175	185,000
1983	161,640	5,466	167,106
1984	124,244	5,400	129,644
1985	142,802	9,705	152,507
1986	168,366	9,705	178,071
1987	192,867	11,325	204,192
1988	181,186	11,644	192,830
1989	167,558	12,770	180,328
1990	175,544	14,664	190,208
1991	192,812	19,008	211,820
1992	212,988	18,947	231,935
1993			220,288

*NORTH CAROLINA

Year	Firearm	Bow	Total
1949			14,616
1951			17,739
1952			15,572
1953			18,598
1954			20,084
1955			20,114
1962			28,808
1964			39,793
1967			38,688
1970			38,405
1972			47,469
1974			53,079
1976			45,077
1982			90,242
1983			96,236
1986			133,160
1989			148,208
1992			217,743
1993	107,669	8,727	118,638

* — harvest figures are from mail survey estimates.

NORTH DAKOTA

Year	Firearm	Bow	Total
1941			2,665
1943			2,765
1950			13,933
1952			27,024
1954			22,705
1955			17,123
1956			21,790
1957			19,714
1958			9,828
1959			23,812
1960			25,262
1961			26,324
1962			23,429
1963			9,929
1964			24,311
1965			25,837
1966			26,469
1967			26,524
1968			10,761
1969			18,367
1970			22,882
1971			28,673
1972			25,424
1973			27,780
1974			23,445
1975			20,666
1976			19,969
1977			17,201
1978			17,120
1979			18,118
1980			24,179
1981			27,006
1982			31,210
1983			35,709
1984			41,582
1985			43,074
1986			60,122
1987			47,157
1988			41,190
1989			46,739
1990			41,372
1991			46,632

N.D. (cont.)

Year	Firearm	Bow	Total
1992			51,903
1993			62,252
1994			59,592

OHIO

Year	Firearm	Bow	Total
1952			450
1953			4,000
1954			closed
1955			4,200
1956			3,911
1957			4,784
1958			4,415
1959			2,960
1960			2,584
1961			closed
1962			2,114
1963			2,074
1964			1,326
1965			406
1966			1,073
1967			1,437
1968			1,396
1969			2,105
1970			2,387
1971			3,831
1972			5,074
1973			7,594
1974			10,747
1975			14,972
1976			23,431
1977			22,319
1978			22,967
1979			34,874
1980			40,499
1981			47,634
1982			52,885
1983			59,812
1984			66,860
1985			64,263
1986			67,626
1987			79,355
1988			100,674
1989			91,236
1990	80,109	12,087	92,196
1991	94,342	17,109	111,451
1992	97,676	19,577	117,253
1993	104.540	23,160	138,752

NOTE: Harvest totals for Ohio do not include deer taken during the primitive weapons hunt.

OKLAHOMA

Year	Firearm	Bow	Total
1964	3,368	140	3,508
1965	4,090	213	4,303
1966	4,925	275	5,200
1967	4,976	259	5,235
1968	5,490	260	5,750
1969	6,069	304	6,373
1970	6,895	331	7,226
1971	6,587	465	7,052
1972	7,714	508	8,222
1973	7,140	427	7,567
1974	7,821	489	8,310
1975	9,028	649	9,677
1976	10,544	1,004	11,548
1977	10,192	680	10,872
1978	13,080	1,028	14,108
1979	13,023	1,185	14,208
1980	12,800	1,497	14,297
1981	11,446	1,964	13,410
1982	17,006	2,249	19,255
1983	19,222	2,698	21,920
1984	20,041	2,568	23,609
1985	16,664	3,523	20,187
1986	25,096	3,320	28,416
1987	29,239	4,115	33,354
1988	34,436	4,414	38,850
1989	33,752	4,589	38,341
1990	38,545	5,525	44,070
1991	40,197	7,079	47,286
1992	42,620	7,792	50,412
1993	49,978	7,853	57,831
1994	51,145	9,054	60,199

OREGON

Year	Firearm	Bow	Total
1992	422	NA	422
1993			
1994	707	NA	707

NOTE: The 1992 season was the first time Oregon Department of Wildlife officials distinguished between mule deer and white-tailed deer in its harvest totals.

PENNSYLVANIA

Year	Firearm	Bow	Total
1949	130,723		130,723
1950	54,817		54,817
1951	72,534		72,534
1952	64,969	24	64,993
1953	53,552	84	53,636
1954	40,870	55	40,925
1955	86,036	119	86,155
1956	41,697	224	41,921
1957	103,758	1,358	105,116
1958	110,567	1,358	111,925
1959	88,845	1,327	90,172
1960	67,489	1,174	68,663
1961	54,515	1,517	56,032
1962	71,603	1,310	72,913
1963	83,028	1,388	84,416
1964	89,534	1,600	91,134
1965	97,669	2,119	99,788
1966	116,416	2,337	118,753
1967	141,164	3,251	144,415
1968	139,127	2,747	141,874
1969	113,515	3,169	116,684
1970	96,688	2,998	99,686
1971	101,458	2,769	104,227
1972	104,270	2,945	107,215
1973	123,239	3,652	126,891
1974	121,743	3,909	125,652
1975	133,134	5,061	138,195
1976	118,385	3,648	122,033
1977	141,400	4,678	146,078
1978	116,188	5,053	121,241
1979	110,562	4,232	114,794
1980	129,703	5,774	135,477
1981	142,592	5,938	148,530
1982	130,958	7,264	138,222
1983	130,071	6,222	136,293
1984	133,606	6,574	140,180
1985	154,060	7,368	161,428
1986	148,562	8,570	157,132
1987	164,055	8,901	172,956
1988	185,565	9,834	195,399
1989	184,856	10,951	195,807
1990	396,529	19,032	415,561
1991	365,267	22,748	388,015
1992	335,439	25,785	361,224
1993	359,224	49,409	408,557

RHODE ISLAND

Year	Firearm	Bow	Total
1972	93	57	150

R.I. (cont.)

Year	Firearm	Bow	Total
1973	46	56	102
1974	62	48	110
1975	57	54	111
1976	61	50	111
1977	95	62	157
1978	91	78	169
1979	103	93	196
1980	145	72	217
1981	155	88	243
1982	112	104	216
1983	123	99	222
1984	139	109	248
1985	144	112	256
1986	299	126	425
1987	252	179	431
1988	323	125	448
1989	466	169	635
1990	701	238	939
1991	850	291	1,141
1992	1,045	417	1,462
1993	938	378	1,316

SOUTH CAROLINA

Year	Firearm	Bow	Total
1972			18,894
1973			23,703
1974			26,727
1975			29,133
1976			33,749
1977			36,363
1978			39,721
1979			43,569
1980			44,698
1981			56,410
1982			54,321
1983			57,927
1984			60,182
1985			62,699
1986			69,289
1987			86,208
1988			98,182

S.C. (cont.)

Year	Firearm	Bow	Total
1989			107,081
1990			125,171
1991			130,848
1992			126,839
1993			142,795

SOUTH DAKOTA

Year	Firearm	Bow	Total
1985	43,989	2,738	46,727
1986	40,798	1,953	42,751
1987	32,018	2,456	34,474
1988	33,265	2,327	35,592
1989	42,947	3,081	46,028
1990	38,902	2,986	41,888
1991	39,915	2,686	42,601
1992	41,959	2,964	44,923
1993	45,431	2,963	48,394
1994	47,142	2,325	49,467

TENNESSEE

Year	Firearm	Bow	Total
1970	8,258	372	8,630
1971	6,202	365	6,567
1972	7,354	499	7,853
1973	10,937	474	11,411
1974	12,624	685	13,309
1975	13,897	993	14,890
1976	16,374	1,739	18,113
1977	19,527	1,770	21,297
1978	22,819	2,465	25,284
1979	25,970	2,570	28,540
1980	27,196	3,457	30,653
1981	28,885	3,407	32,292
1982	35,726	4,644	40,370
1983	42,528	6,347	48,875
1984	49,493	5,883	55,376
1985	53,118	7,278	60,396
1986	69,044	8,578	77,622
1987	86,777	12,040	98,817
1988	81,469	10,796	92,265
1989	95,475	13,287	108,762
1990	97,172	16,061	113,233
1991	105,832	15,764	121,596
1992	106,168	19,728	125,896
1993	118,946	19,596	138,542

TEXAS

Year	Firearm	Bow	Total
1980	253,993	6,390	260,383
1981	292,525	7,527	300,052

	Texas (cont.)				Vt. (cont.)		
Year	Firearm	Bow	Total	Year	Firearm	Bow	Total
1982	328,678	8,943	337,621	1931	1,758		1,758
1983	309,409	8,935	318,344	1932	1,992		1,992
1984	361,811	11,451	373,262	1933	2,397		2,397
1985	370,732	12,767	383,499	1934	1,633		1,633
1986	431,002	14,117	445,119	1935	2,039		2,039
1987	489,368	15,585	504,953	1936	1,997		1,997
1988	458,576	16,392	474,968	1937	2,446		2,446
1989	460,896	16,595	477,491	1938	2,433		2,433
1990	413,910	15,622	429,532	1939	2,589		2,589
1991	459,083	14,964	474,047	1940	3,400		3,400
1992	453,361	15,532	468,893	1941	3,111		3,111
1993			452,509	1942	3,280		3,280
				1943	2,871		2,871
	VERMONT			1944	3,657		3,657
Year	Firearm	Bow	Total	1945	3,510		3,510
1897	103		103	1946	4,523		4,523
1898	134		134	1947	5,635		5,635
1899	90		90	1948	4,298		4,298
1900	123		123	1949	5,983		5,983
1901	211		211	1950	6,106		6,106
1902	403		403	1951	6,940		6,940
1903	753		753	1952	6,554		6,554
1904	541		541	1953	7,475	7	7,482
1905	497		497	1954	8,402	8	84,10
1906	634		634	1955	9,936	42	9,978
1907	991		991	1956	9,645	62	9,707
1908	2,208		2,208	1957	11,293	142	11,435
1909	4,597		4,597	1958	10,510	150	10,660
1910	3,609		3,609	1959	11,268	232	11,500
1911	2,644		2,644	1960	11,164	261	11,425
1912	1,692		1,692	1961	15,526	297	15,823
1913	1,802		1,802	1962	15,898	277	16,175
1914	2,041		2,041	1963	10,024	176	10,200
1915	6,042		6,042	1964	14,502	352	14,854
1916	1,630		1,630	1965	16,029	544	16,573
1917	992		992	1966	20,616	704	21,320
1918	825		825	1967	21,942	934	22,876
1919	4,092		4,092	1968	12,934	1,432	14,366
1920	4,477		4,477	1969	20,753	1,547	22,300
1921	1,507		1,507	1970	17,592	1,197	18,789
1922	787		787	1971	7,760	604	8,364
1923	686		686	1972	8,980	1,073	10,053
1924	1,537		1,537	1973	8,560	1,040	9,600
1925	952		952	1974	11,254	1,580	12,834
1926	882		882	1975	9,939	1,606	11,545
1927	869		869	1976	10,278	1,200	11,478
1928	1,063		1,063	1977	10,029	2,094	12,123
1929	1,438		1,438	1978	7,087	1,688	8,775
1930	1,481		1,481	1979	14,936	1,587	16,523

	Vt. (cont.)				Va. (cont.)		
Year	Firearm	Bow	Total	Year	Firearm	Bow	Total
1980	24,675	1,257	25,932	1966			25,920
1981	19,077	1,169	20,246	1967			24,934
1982	9,148	798	9,946	1968			28,041
1983	6,092	538	6,630	1969			34,150
1984	12,418	630	13,048	1970			38,138
1985	13,150	727	13,877	1971			42,369
1986	11,943	810	12,753	1972			48,775
1987	8,046	958	9,004	1973			60,789
1988	6,451	627	7,078	1974			61,989
1989	8,030	1,202	9,232	1975			63,443
1990	7,930	1,053	8,983	1976			63,671
1991	9,993	1,591	11,584	1977			67,059
1992	11,215	3,245	14,460	1978			72,545
1993	10,043	2,999	13,333	1979			69,940
1994	9,177	3,276	12,903	1980			75,208
				1981			78,388
	VIRGINIA			1982			88,540
Year	Firearm	Bow	Total	1983			85,739
1935			1,158	1984			84,432
1936			1,475	1985			101,425
1937			1,526	1986			121,801
1938			1,391	1987			119,309
1939			1,365	1988			114,562
1940			1,691	1989			135,094
1941			1,901	1990			160,411
1942			1,448	1991			179,344
1943			2,282	1992			200,446
1944			3,433	1993	185,222	15,900	201,122
1945			4,545				
1946			6,543		**WASHINGTON**		
1947			4,019	Year	Firearm	Bow	Total
1948			5,162	1992	10,593	1,007	11,600
1949			6,910	1993	7,430	882	8,312
1950			5,699	1994	9,709	1,153	10,860

NOTE: Washington does not differentiate between black-tailed deer, mule deer and white-tailed deer in its harvest totals. The total deer kill in 1994 was 46,618 and it is estimated that 23 percent of those animals were white-tailed deer.

Year			Total
1951			7,230
1952			10,874
1953			11,797
1954			14,079
1955			14,227
1956			20,855
1957			22,473
1958			26,841
1959			28,969

	WEST VIRGINIA		
Year	Firearm	Bow	Total
1933	379		379
1934	309		309
1936	242		242
1937	456		456
1938	896		896
1939	897		897

Year			Total
1960			36,145
1961			32,875
1962			38,838
1963			38,391
1964			31,179
1965			27,983

	W. Va. (cont.)				W. Va. (cont.)		
Year	Firearm	Bow	Total	Year	Firearm	Bow	Total
1940	1,116		1,116	1992	177,265	28,659	205,924
1941	1,064		1,064	1993	142,589	26,425	169,014
1942	1,575		1,575	1994	120,954	24,448	145,402
1943	1,827		1,827				
1947	5,473	2	5,475				
1948	4,958	5	4,963				
1949	6,466	6	6,472				
1950	6,549	10	6,559				
1951	21,851	22	21,873				
1952	17,140	16	17,156				
1953	19,844	13	19,857				
1954	16,703	29	16,732				
1955	13,081	67	13,148		**WISCONSIN**		
1956	18,158	87	18,245	Year	Firearm	Bow	Total
1957	6,187	19	6,206	1897	2,500		2,500
1958	18,436	117	18,553	1898	2,750		2,750
1959	19,588	90	19,678	1899	3,000		3,000
1960	15,850	80	15,930	1900	3,500		3,500
1961	4,930	113	5,043	1901	4,000		4,000
1962	5,627	152	5,779	1902	4,000		4,000
1963	7,609	119	7,728	1903	4,250		4,250
1964	8,474	183	8,657	1904	4,500		4,500
1965	19,686	226	19,912	1905	4,250		4,250
1966	21,249	199	21,448	1906	4,500		4,500
1967	18,318	163	18,481	1907	4,750		4,750
1968	10,364	187	10,551	1908	5,000		5,000
1969	13,620	470	14,090	1909	5,550		5,550
1970	13,399	589	13,988	1910	5,750		5,750
1971	15,905	714	16,619	1911	9,750		9,750
1972	20,960	1,443	22,403	1912	8,500		8,500
1973	24,179	1,684	25,863	1913	9,750		9,750
1974	27,821	2,119	29,940	1914	9,850		9,850
1975	32,368	2,968	35,336	1915	5,000		5,000
1976	38,712	2,323	41,035	1916	7,000		7,000
1977	37,987	2,531	40,518	1917	18,000		18,000
1978	40,096	4,350	44,446	1918	17,000		17,000
1979	49,625	5,461	55,086	1919	25,152		25,152
1980	47,022	7,144	54,166	1920	20,025		20,025
1981	65,505	9,003	74,508	1921	14,845		14,845
1982	74,642	13,454	88,096	1922	9,255		9,255
1983	78,605	11,235	89,840	1923	9,000		9,000
1984	94,132	12,578	106,710	1924	7,000		7,000
1985	71,183	13,416	84,599	1926	12,000		12,000
1986	101,404	17,207	118,611	1928	17,000		17,000
1987	109,367	19,742	129,109	1930	23,000		23,000
1988	112,155	16,537	128,692	1932	36,000		36,000
1989	129,350	16,217	145,567	1934	21,251	1	21,252
1990	148,233	21,715	169,948	1936	29,676	1	26,677
1991	149,536	27,448	176,984	1937	14,835	0	14,835

Wis. (cont.)

Year	Firearm	Bow	Total
1938	32,855	1	32,856
1939	25,730	6	25,736
1940	33,138	5	33,142
1941	40,403	18	40,421
1942	45,188	15	45,203
1943	128,296	76	128,372
1944	28,537	78	28,615
1945	37,527	160	37,687
1946	55,276	256	55,532
1947	53,520	368	53,888
1948	41,954	279	42,233
1949	159,112	551	159,663
1950	167,911	383	168,294
1951	129,475	188	129,663
1952	27,504	126	27,630
1953	19,823	355	20,178
1954	24,698	743	25,441
1955	35,060	na	na
1956	35,562	na	na
1957	68,138	na	na
1958	95,234	na	na
1959	105,596	na	na
1960	61,005	na	na
1961	38,772	na	na
1962	45,835	na	na
1963	65,020	na	na
1964	93,445	3,164	96,609
1965	98,774	4,995	103,769
1966	110,062	5,986	116,048
1967	128,527	7,592	136,119
1968	119,986	6,934	126,920
1969	98,008	5,987	103,995
1970	72,844	6,520	79,364
1971	70,835	6,522	77,357
1972	74,827	7,087	81,914
1973	82,105	8,456	90,561
1974	100,405	12,514	112,919
1975	117,378	13,588	130,966
1976	122,509	13,636	136,145
1977	131,910	16,790	148,700
1978	150,845	18,113	168,958
1979	125,570	16,018	141,588
1980	139,624	20,954	160,578
1981	166,673	29,083	195,756
1982	182,715	30,850	213,565
1983	197,600	32,876	230,476
1984	255,240	38,891	294,131
1985	274,302	40,744	315,046
1986	259,240	40,490	299,730

Wis. (cont.)

Year	Firearm	Bow	Total
1987	250,530	42,651	293,181
1988	263,424	42,393	305,817
1989	310,192	46,394	356,586
1990	350,040	49,291	399,331
1991	352,328	67,005	419,333
1992	288,906	60,479	349,385
1993	217,584	53,008	270,592
1994	307,629	66,254	373,883

WYOMING

Year	Firearm	Bow	Total
1968	13,891		13,891
1969	12,863		12,863
1970	9,878		9,878
1971	7,806		7,806
1972	4,306		4,306
1973	9,174		9,174
1974	12,832		12,832
1975	14,001		14,001
1976	11,298		11,298
1977	11,049		11,049
1978	7,796		7,796
1979	7,452		7,452
1980	7,014		7,014
1981	7,286		7,286
1982	7,608		7,608
1983	8,498		8,498
1984	9,888		9,888
1985	9,267		9,267
1986	7,983	254	8,237
1987	5,628	192	5,820
1988	7,005	174	7,179
1989	8,903	197	9,100
1990	9,535	147	9,632
1991	10,240	139	10,379
1992	14,533	216	14,749
1993	12,623	1,322	13,945

Boone and Crockett Records

The information reproduced in this chapter is taken from the Boone and Crockett Club's *Records of North American Whitetail Deer*, second edition, 1991, with the express written permission of the Boone and Crockett Club. The information that follows is only a partial listing of the top whitetails. For information on the complete record book, write: Boone and Crockett Club, 250 Station Drive, Missoula, MT 59801.

ALABAMA
TYPICAL WHITE-TAILED DEER

Score	Locality Killed / By Whom Killed	Date Killed
186-3/8	Lee County / Picked Up	1986
182-7/8	Hale County / James C. Bailey	1974
172-1/8	Pickens County / Walter Jaynes	1968
170-2/8	Lee County / George P. Mann	1980
168-2/8	Marengo County / William L, Wright	1979
162-7/8	Perry County / Rodney A. Pilot	1987
161-6/8	Greene County / William H. Fincher	1982
161-4/8	Barbour / Craig Thompson	1979

NON-TYPICAL WHITE-TAILED DEER

2245/8	Perry County / Robert E. Royster	1976
223-1/8	Sumter County / James 1, Spidle, Sr,	1942
217-2/8	Dallas County / Robert Tate	1988
199-2/8	Winston County / James W. Huckbay	1973
187	Greene County / William H. Fincher	1976

ARKANSAS
TYPICAL WHITE-TAILED DEER

189	Crawford County / Tom Sparks, Jr.	1975
186-7/8	Arkansas County / Walter Spears	1952
184-6/8	Desha County / Lee Perry	1961
183	Desha County / R.J. Diekoff	1954
180	Desha County / Turner Neal	1962
179-2/8	Prairie County / Charles Newsom	1962
177-7/8	Chicot County / George Matthews	1923
173-3/8	Arkansas County / Jimmy Hanson	1948
173-2/8	Chicot County / Yan Sturdivant	1951
172	Bearden / Buddy Wise	1962

NON-TYPICAL WHITE-TAILED DEER

208-5/8	St. Francis County / George W. Hobson	1987
206-1/8	Boydel / Picked Up	1959

ARKANSAS (continued)

Score	Locality Killed / By Whom Killed	Date Killed
201-1/8	Arkansas County / Daniel B. Bullock	1953
196-4/8	Desha County / Turner Neal	1955

COLORADO
TYPICAL WHITE-TAILED DEER

182-5/8	Yuma County / Ivan W. Rhodes	1978
175-7/8	Logan County / Picked Up	1971
171-2/8	Yuma County / John O. Cletcher	1985

NON-TYPICAL WHITE-TAILED DEER

204-2/8	Yuma County / Jeff L. Mekelburg	1986

CONNECTICUT
TYPICAL WHITE-TAILED DEER

177-2/8	Litchfield County / Picked Up	1984
176-2/8	Litchfield County / Frederick H. Clymer	1987

NON-TYPICAL WHITE-TAILED DEER

195	Windham County / Harold Tanner	1970

FLORIDA
NON-TYPICAL WHITE-TAILED DEER

186-1/8	Jackson County / Henry Brinson	1959

GEORGIA
TYPICAL WHITE-TAILED DEER

184-3/8	Paulding County / Floyd Benson	1962
184	Newton County / Gene Almand	1966
184	Hart County / Kenton L. Adams	1986
180-7/8	Jones County / James H.C. Kitchens	1957
180-2/8	Newton County / David Moon	1972
179-2/8	Lamar County Gary Littlejohn	1968
179-1/8	Twiggs County Cy Smith	1970
179	Jasper County Hubert R. Moody	1957
179	Dooley County Shannon Akin	1981
177-5/8	Macon County James W. Athon	1976

NON-TYPICAL WHITE-TAILED DEER

240-3/8	Monroe County John L. Hatton, Jr.	1973
215-7/8	Putnam County Thomas H. Cooper	1974
208-3/8	Decatur County James L. Darley	1964

GEORGIA (continued)

Score	Locality Killed / By Whom Killed	Date Killed
199-6/8	Harris County / Kenneth H. Brown	1974
198-4/8	Wheeler County / David Frost	1983
197-4/8	Dooly County / Wayne Griffin	1984
197-3/8	Newton County / R.H. Bumbalough	1969
195-4/8	Worth County / Shane Calhoun	1985
195-3/8	Colquitt County / Olen P. Ross	1976
193-5/8	Henry County / Jason J. Patrick	1986

IDAHO
TYPICAL WHITE-TAILED DEER

181-7/8	Clearwater County / Richard E. Carver	1985
177-5/8	Idaho County / Donna M. Knight	1986
176-6/8	Idaho County / Edward D. Moore	1986
176-6/8	Idaho County / Frank J. Loughran	1987
175-5/8	Benewah County / Carl Groth	1982
174-2/8	Clearwater County / Douglas B. Crockett	1983
173-6/8	Bonner County / Robert L. Campbell	1967
172	Joseph Plains / Jim Felton	1965
171-4/8	Latah County / Darwin L. Baker	1986
170	Latah County / Lewis L. Turcott	1974

NON-TYPICAL WHITE-TAILED DEER

267-4/8	Idaho/Jack Brittingham	1923
248-1/8	Nez Perce County / John D. Powers, JR.	1983
226-3/8	Nez Perce County / Mrs. Ralph Bond	1964
213-5/8	Bonner County / Rodney Thurlow	1968
203-1/8	Kootenay County / William M. Ziegler	1965
201-3/8	Bonner County / Leroy Coleman	1960
200-3/8	Nez Perce County / Tim C. Baldwin	1987
198-1/8	Kootenai County / Frank J. Cheney	1967
197	Kootenai County / D.L. Whatcott & R.C. Carlson	1980

ILLINOIS
TYPICAL WHITE-TAILED DEER

204-4/8	Peoria County M.J. Johnson	1965
182-7/8	Rock Island County / Clifton C. Webster	1986
182-2/8	Champaign County / Tom Babb	1985
181-5/8	Wabash County / Mike Drone	1987
181-4/8	Canton / Arnold C. Hegele	1968
181-3/8	Pope County / Jack A. Higgs	1963
180	Pulaski County / Picked Up	1988
179	Perry County / Roy A. Smith	1987
178-4/8	St. Clair County / Emil W. Kromat	1981
178-3/8	Clinton County / Richard V. Spihlmann	1961

Score	Locality Killed / By Whom Killed	Date Killed
178-3/8	Jo Daviess County / Gary J. Flynn	1986

NON-TYPICAL WHITE-TAILED DEER

267-3/8	Peoria County / Richard A Pauli	1983
238-1/8	Madison County / Joe Bardill	1985
236-5/8	Pike County / Floyd Pursley	1987
231-4/8	Perry County / Unknown	1968
223-6/8	Greene County / Terry L. Walters	1982
221	Pike County / Frank C. Skelton	1987
220-4/8	Mercer County / Roger D. Hultgren	1970
217-6/8	Macoupin County / Albert Grichnik	1966
215-7/8	Schuyler County / Donald E. Ziegenbein	1981
213-4/8	Pike County / Donald L. Roseberry	1984

INDIANA
TYPICAL WHITE-TAILED DEER

195-1/8	Parke County / B. Dodd Porter	1985
194-2/8	Vigo County / D. Bates & S. Winkler	1983
185-1/8	Franklin County / Gayle Fritsch	1972
185	Putnam County Earl G. McCammack	1985
183-6/8	Clinton County / Stuart C. Snodgrass	1977
177	Cass County / Herbert R. Frushour	1974
177	Jasper County / Dan Haskins	1975
175-2/8	Fulton County / Larry A. Croxton	1984
172-7/8	Jefferson County / Chet A. Nolan	1987
171	Pike County / Phil Lemond	1986

NON-TYPICAL WHITE-TAILED DEER

226-3/8	Clark County / Robert L. Bromm, Sr.	1985
215-4/8	Wayne County / Clyde L. Day	1986
205-7/8	Switzerland County / Paul Graf	1981
198-7/8	Ripley County / William L. Wagner	1982
191-2/8	Delaware County / Robert D. McFarland	1986

IOWA
TYPICAL WHITE-TAILED DEER

194-4/8	Monroe County / Lloyd Goad	1962
186-6/8	Johnson County / Gregg R. Redlin	1983
187-5/8	Cherokee County / Dennis R. Vaudt	1975
187-2/8	Warren County / Dwight E. Green	1964
185-1/8	Warren County / Joyce McCormick	1968
185-1/8	Harrison County / Marvin E. Tippery	1971
184-7/8	Delaware County / R.E. Stewart	1953
184-2/8	Hardin County / Robert D. Imsland	1985

IOWA (continued)

Score	Locality Killed / By Whom Killed	Date Killed
183-7/8	Taylor County / Wayne Swartz	1947
182-5/8	Jefferson County / William J. Waugh	

NON-TYPICAL WHITE-TAILED DEER

282	Clay County / Larry Raveling	1973
256-2/8	Monona County / Carroll E. Johnson	1968
229-6/8	Decatur County / Edgar Shields	1986
229-3/8	Wapello County / Robert D. Harding	1985
222-4/8	Davis County / James L. Fine	1987
222-1/8	Hancock County / Jerry M. Monson	1977
221-7/8	Tama County / Charles Upah	1959
221-4/8	Humboldt County / Donald Crossley	1971
220-2/8	Union County / George Foster	1968
220	Wayne County / Dallas Patterson	1975

KANSAS
TYPICAL WHITE-TAILED DEER

198-2/8	Nemaha County / Dennis P. Finger	1974
194-7/8	Leavenworth County / William R. Mikijanis	1985
191-4/8	Chautauqua County / Michael A. Young	1973
186-3/8	Morris County / Garold D. Miller	1969
185	Seward County / Michael D. Gatlin	1987
184-4/8	Chase County / Thomas D. Mosher	1984
184	Saline County / James R. Bell	1985
182-3/8	Waubausee County / Norman Anderson	1966
181-6/8	Lyon County / Kenneth C. Haynes	1969
180	Edwards County / David R. Cross	1985

NON-TYPICAL WHITE-TAILED DEER

258-6/8	Republic County / John O. Band	1965
251-1/8	Mitchell County / Theron E. Wilson	1974
248-7/8	Greenwood County / Clifford G. Pickell	1968
239	Lyon County / Don E. Roberts	1987
229-2/8	Linn County / Merle C. Beckman	1984
227	Miami County / Gary A. Smith	1970
216-6/8	Barber County / Robert L. Rose	1972
209-6/8	Edwards County / Tim C. Schaller	1984
206/5-8	Chase County / Jay A. Talkington	1983
205-6/8	Cloud County / Gary G. Pingel	1982

KENTUCKY
TYPICAL WHITE-TAILED DEER

187-1/8	Pulaski County / Scott Abbott	1982
186	Warren County / Arnold M. Bush	1986

KENTUCKY (continued)

Score	Locality Killed / By Whom Killed	Date Killed
185-2/8	Todd County / C.W. Shelton	1964
184	Grayson County / Floyd Stone	1987
181-2/8	Hardin County / Thomas L. House	1963
181	Gallatin County / Kenneth D. Hoffman	1979
178-2/8	Ohio County / Earl R. Trogden	1986
178	Union County / Cary L. Gibson	1983
177-4/8	Grayson County / David W. Mercer	1986
175-3/8	Todd County / Gary W. Crafton	1981

NON-TYPICAL WHITE-TAILED DEER

Score	Locality Killed / By Whom Killed	Date Killed
236-3/8	Union County / Wilbur E. Buchanan	1970
226-5/8	Pulaski County / H.C. Sumpter	1984
221-7/8	Trigg County / Bill McWhirter	1982
218-4/8	Logan County / Robert L. Schrader, Jr.	1987
215	Hardin County / Michael F. Meredith	1980
210-3/8	Lyon County / Roy D. Lee	1975
209-5/8	Butler County / Dean A. Hannold	1979
208-6/8	Daniel Boone Natl. For. / Richard G. Lohre	1968
204	Webster County / Jeff Robinson	1982
202	Powell County / Hershel Ingram	1980

LOUISIANA
TYPICAL WHITE-TAILED DEER

Score	Locality Killed / By Whom Killed	Date Killed
189-5/8	St. Landry Parish / Leonce Mallet	1965
184-6/8	Madison Parish / John Lee	1943
184-4/8	Bossier County / Earnest O. McCoy	1961
184-2/8	Franklin Parish / H.B. Womble	1914
180-5/8	St. Landry Parish / Shawn P. Ortego	1975
180-4/8	Madison Parish / Buford Perry	1961
180-3/8	Union Parish / Picked Up	1963
177-3/8	Claiborne Parish / Steven L. Morton	1986
176-5/8	Tensas Parish / Sam Barber	1974
176-2/8	Richland Parish / Willard Roberson	1968

NON-TYPICAL WHITE-TAILED DEER

Score	Locality Killed / By Whom Killed	Date Killed
218-4/8	St. Martin Parish / Drew Ware	1941
206-7/8	Claiborne Parish / J.H. Thurmon	1970
206-6/8	Grant Parish / Richard D. Ellison, Jr.	1969
201-3/8	Concordia Parish / G.O. McGuffee	1963
198-5/8	Concordia Parish / Raymond Cowan	1961
190-2/8	Concordia Parish / John T. Lincecurn	1986

MAINE
TYPICAL WHITE-TAILED DEER

Score	Locality Killed / By Whom Killed	Date Killed
192-7/8	York County / Alphonse Chase	1920
186-2/8	Hancock County / Gerald C. Murray	1984
184-5/8	Washhington County / Unknown	1944
184-1/8	Waldo County / Christopher Ramsey	1983
18158	Oxford County / Dean W. Peaco	1953
181-1/8	Waldo County / Clarendon Pomeroy	1946
180-6/8	Hancock County / Cyrus IL Whitaker	1912
179-7/8	Hancock County / Butler B. Dunn	1930
179-6/8	Penobscot County / Dale Rustin	1984
178-6/8	Aroostook County / John R. Hardy	1983

NON-TYPICAL WHITE-TAILED DEER

248-1/8	Penobscot County / Unknown	1945
228-7/8	Cherryfield / Flora Campbell	1953
228-1/8	Maine / Henry A. Caesar	1911
224	Hancock County / Picked Up	1975
223-3/8	Maine / Frank Maxwell	1900
219-2/8	Aroostook County / Harold C. Kitchin	1973
218-7/8	Waldo County / Roy C. Guse	1957
28-7/8	Washington County / Robert E. Cooke	1972
208-1/8	Hancock County / Hollis Staples	1922
207-6/8	Aroostook County / Alfred Wardwell	1945

MARYLAND
TYPICAL WHITE-TAILED DEER

183-3/8	Dorchester County / John R. Seifert, Jr.	1973
181-6/8	Montgomery County / Gary F. Menso	1985
172-1/8	Queen Annes County / James R. Spies, Jr.	1976
172	Caroline County / Garey N. Brown	1986
170-6/8	Carroll County / Wes McKenzie	1971
170-5/8	St. Marys County / Brian M. Boteler	1980
170-1/8	Harford County / Edward C. Garrison	1987

NON-TYPICAL WHITE-TAILED DEER

228-4/8	Montgomery County / John W. Poole	1987
217-2/8	Talbot County / Vincent L. Jordan, Sr.	1974
210	Calvert County / Robert E. Barnett	1984
208-7/8	Charles County / Robert A. Boarman	1984
201-3/8	Queen Annes County / Franklin E. Jewell	1978
196-2/8	Dorchester County / Kevin R. Coulboume	1979
185-7/8	Charles County / Robert Sparks	1980

MICHIGAN
TYPICAL WHITE-TAILED DEER

Score	Locality Killed / By Whom Killed	Date Killed
193-2/8	Jackson County / Craig Calderone	1986
186-3/8	Ontonagon County / Unknown	1980
184-7/8	Baraga County / Louis J. Roy	1987
181-5/8	Ionia County / Lester Bowen	1947
180-4/8	Iron County / John Schmidt	1927
180-3/8	Huron County / Picked Up	1985
178	Hillsdale County / Dudley N. Spade	1972
177-7/8	Iron County / Felix Brzoznowski	1939
176-6/8	Clinton County / Ray Sadler	1963
1760/8	Baraga County / Paul Korhonen	1945

NON-TYPICAL WHITE-TAILED DEER

Score	Locality Killed / By Whom Killed	Date Killed
238-2/8	Bay County / Paul M. Mickey	1976
218-3/8	Keweenaw County / Bernard J. Mum	1980
215-5/8	Iron County / C. & R. Lester	1970
212	Iron County / Ben Komblevicz	1942
209-1/8	Keweenaw County / Nathan E. Ruonavaara	1946
201-5/8	Charlevoix County / Robert V. Doerr 1973	
201-5/8	Baraga County / Dennis D. Bess	1981
201	Delta County / Ernest B. Fosterling	1953
198-5/8	Iron County / Eino Macki	1930
197-5/8	Luce County / Sid Jones	1917

MINNESOTA
TYPICAL WHITE-TAILED DEER

Score	Locality Killed / By Whom Killed	Date Killed
202	Beltrami County / John A. Breen	1918
195-5/8	Marshall County / Robe& Sands	1960
193-2/8	Itasca County / Picked Up	1935
192	Pine County / Frank Worlickey	1952
192	(lay County / Mark L. Peterson	1984
191-5/8	Goodhue County / David C. Klatt	1985
189-3/8	Fillmore County / Tom Norby	1975
187-6/8	Houston County / Donald M. Grant	1978
187-5/8	Winona County / Ken W. Koenig	1976
187-4/8	Winona County / Dan Groebner	1974

NON-TYPICAL WHITE-TAILED DEER

Score	Locality Killed / By Whom Killed	Date Killed
268-5/8	Norman County / Mitchell A. Vakoch	1974
258-2/8	Becker County / J.J. Matter	1973
249-2/8	Fillmore County / Dallas R. Henn	1961
245-5/8	Itasca County / Peter Rutkowski	1942
245-3/8	Itasca County / Mike Hammer	1956
240-6/8	St. Louis County / John Cesarek	1964

Score	Locality Killed / By Whom Killed	Date Killed
236	Winona County / Francis A. Pries	1964
232-5/8	Wabasha County / Robert F. Friese	1948
231-5/8	Winona County / Robert E. Bains	1973
230-1/8	Pope County / Harvey J. Erickson	1974

MISSISSIPPI
TYPICAL WHITE-TAILED DEER

182-7/8	Noxubee County / Glen D. Jourdon	1986
182-7/8	Claiborne County / R.L. Bobo	1955
181-5/8	Wilkinson County / Ronnie P. Whitaker	1981
180-4/8	Leflore County / W.F. Smith	1968
178-5/8	Bolivar County / Grady Robertson	1951
176-5/8	Bolivar County / Sidney D. Sessions	1952
175-2/8	Wilkinson County / Johnnie J. Leake, Jr.	1978
174-7/8	Coahoma County / O.P. Gilbert	1960
173-5/8	Lowndes County / Geraline Holliman 1982	
172-5/8	Adams County / Adrian L. Stallone	1983

NON-TYPICAL WHITE-TAILED DEER

217-5/8	Carroll County / Mark T. Hathcock	1978
209-6/8	Franklin County / Ronnie Strickland	1981
205-6/8	Lowndes County / Joe W. Shurden	1976
202-5/8	Carroll County / George Galey	1960
202-1/8	Oktibbeha County / Oliver H. Lindig	1983
201-6/8	Wilkinson County / Jimmy Ashley	1985
196-5/8	Wilkinson County / Robert D. Sullivan	1982
195-7/8	Monroe County / Kenneth A. Dye	1986
195-5/8	Adams County / Kathleen McGehee	1981

MISSOURI
TYPICAL WHITE-TAILED DEER

205	Randolph County / Larry W. Gibson	1971
199-4/8	Clark County / Jeffrey A. Brunk	1969
187-2/8	Scotland County / Robin Berhorst	1971
187-2/8	Atchison County / Unknown	1984
187.1	Cooper County / Joe Ditto	1974
187.1	Mercer County / Picked Up	1986
186-7/8	Atchison County / Mike Moody	1968
186-2/8	Laclede County / Larry Ogle	1972
185-5/8	Dallas County / James E. Headings	1986
183-4/8	Sumner / Marvin F. Lentz	1968

NON-TYPICAL WHITE-TAILED DEER.

333-7/8	St. Louis County / Picked Up	1981
259-5/8	Chariton County / Duane R. Linscott	1985

MISSOURI (continued)

Score	Locality Killed / By Whom Killed	Date Killed
225-1/8	Nodaway County / Ken Barcus	1982
219-5/8	Warren County / James It. Williams	1959
218-5/8	Chariton County / Stanley McSparren	1979
217-7/8	Maries County / Gerald R. Dake	1974
215-5/8	Worth County / B.M. & R. Nonneman	1974
214	Atchison County / Warren E. Davis	1983
208-7/8	Atchison County / Kenneth W. Lee	1964
207-3/8	Lincoln County / Melvin Zumwalt	1955

MONTANA
TYPICAL WHITE-TAILED DEER

199-3/8	Missoula County / Thomas H. Dellwo	1974
191-5/8	Flathead County / Earl T. McMaster	1963
189-1/8	Blaine County / Kenneth Morehouse	1959
187-5/8	Montana / Unknown	1984
186-3/8	Flathead County / Unknown	1973
186	Flathead County / Douglas G. Mefford	1966
184-7/8	Yellowstone County / Picked Up	1984
184-7/8	Missoula County / Jack Greenwood	1985
183-3/8	Flathead County / Unknown	1957
182-7/8	Montana / Unknown	1983

NON-TYPICAL WHITE-TAILED DEER

252-1/8	Hill County / Frank A. Pleskac	1968
248-5/8	Snowy Mts. / Unknown	1980
241-7/8	Flathead County / George Woldstad	1960
234-1/8	Glacier County / Unknown	1968
224	Lincoln County / Ray Baenen	1935
223-4/8	Richland County / Verner King	1960
219-1/8	Flathead County / R.C. Garrett	1962
216-2/8	Richland County / Joseph P. Culbertson	1972
215	Fergus County / Robert D. Fleherty	1958
214-3/8	Missoula County / Lyle Pettit	1962

NEBRASKA
TYPICAL WHITE-TAILED DEER

194-1/8	Dakota County / E. Keith Fahrenholz	1966
189-V8	Nuckolls County / Van Shotzman	1968
185-5/8	Nenzel / Richard Kehr	1965
184-5/8	Polk County / Keith Houdersheldt	1985
182-1/8	Frontier County / Robert . Bortner	1985
180-7/8	Keya Paha County / Steve R. Pecsenye	1966
179-4/8	Pawnee County / Kenneth C. Mort	1975
178-5/8	Harlan County / Don Tripe	1961
178-2/8	Pawnee County / Picked Up	1960
178-1/8	Dismal River / Gift Of G.B. Grinnell	1909

NEBRASKA (continued)
NON-TYPICAL WHITE-TAILED DEER

Score	Locality Killed / By Whom Killed	Date Killed
277-3/8	Hall County / Del Austin	1962
242-5/8	Nance County / Robert E. Snyder	1961
238	Keya Paha County / Donald B. Phipps	1969
233-6/8	Custer County / Lonnie E. Poland	1986
215-7/8	Long Pine / Picked Up	1964
214-6/8	Hitchcock county / David W. Oates	1985
212-3/8	Hershey / Ray Liles	1959
211-5/8	Aida / Donald Knuth	1964
208-4/8	Dixon County / Dan Greeny	1969
208-1/8	Antelope County / Leon McCoy	1965
208-V8	Atkinson Highway / Russell Angus	1966

NEW YORK
TYPICAL WHITE-TAILED DEER

198-3/8	Allegany County / Roosevelt Luckey	1939
181-3/8	Orange County / Roy Vail	1960
180-3/6	Livingstone County / Edward Beare	1943
179-3/8	Essex County / Herbert Jaquish	1953
176-2/8	Erie County / Wesly H. Iulg	1944
176-2/8	Warren County / Frank Dagles	1961
175-7/8	Lewis County / Andrew Lustyik	1942
175-5/8	Allegany County/ William L. Damon	1981
174-2/8	Livingston County / Kenneth Bowen	1941
174-1/8	Essex County / Denny Mitchell	1933

NON-TYPICAL WHITE-TAILED DEER

244-2/8	Allegany County / Homer Boylan	1939
224	New York / Unknown	1983
219-7/8	Genesee County / Robert Wood	1944
207-7/8	Suffolk County / George Hackal	1950
207-4/8	Portageville / Howard W. Smith	1959
206-2/8	Cortland County / Hank Hayes	1947
205-7/8	Steuben County / Fred J. Kelley	1938
199-1/8	Clinton County / Unknown	1971
196-1/8	Wyoming County / Eric D. Ban	1985

NORTH CAROLINA
TYPICAL WHITE-TAILED DEER

181-7/8	Guilford County / Terry E. Daffron	1987
178	Caswel I County / Picked Up	1988
172-1/8	Granville County / Dudley Barnes	1985

NORTH DAKOTA
TYPICAL WHITE-TAILED DEER

Score	Locality Killed / By Whom Killed	Date Killed
189-3/8	McKenzie County / Gene Veeder	1972
187-5/8	Emmons County / Joseph F. Bosch	1959
187-2/8	McLean County / Frank 0. Bauman	1986
182	Zap / Wally Duckwitz	1962
178-1/8	Concrete / Lawrence E. Vandal	1947
177-7/8	Cass County / Joe It Chesley	1987
177-2/8	Golden Valley County / Allen Goltz	1964
175-6/8	Burleigh County / Earl Haakenson	1963
175	New Salem / John T. Cartwright	1957
174-4/8	McKenzie County / Ben Dekker	1976

NON-TYPICAL WHITE-TAILED DEER

Score	Locality Killed / By Whom Killed	Date Killed
254-6/8	Stanley / Roger Ritchie	1968
232-1/8	McLean County / Olaf P. Anderson	1886
220-7/8	Pembina County / Gary F. Bourbanis	1985
216-6/8	Kathryn / Gerald R. Elsner	1963
210-5/8	Rinville County / Glen Southam	1978
206-1/8	Dunn County / Kenneth E. DeLap	1982
203-5/8	Grand Forks County / Thomas G. Bernotas	1975
203-2/8	McHenry County / Garry L. Heizelman	1987
202-6/8	Garrison / Clarence Hummel	1961
201-1/8	Slope County / Arthur Hegge	1961

OHIO
TYPICAL WHITE-TAILED DEER

Score	Locality Killed / By Whom Killed	Date Killed
184-6/8	Muskingum County / Dale Hartberger	1981
184-1/8	Vinton County / Dan F. Allison	1965
183	Piedmont Lake / J. Rumbaugh & J. Ruyan	1958
182-7/8	Wayne County Gary E. Landry	1975
181-4/8	Licking County / Arle McCullough	1962
181-3/8	Portage County / Robert M. Smith	1953
179	Logan County / Gregory K. Snyder	1982
178-7/8	Monroe County / Roger E. Schumacher	1958
178-2/8	Tuscarawas County / Ray D. Gerber, Jr.	1983
177-5/8	Harrison County / Mark Dulkoski	1984

NON-TYPICAL WHITE-TAILED DEER

Score	Locality Killed / By Whom Killed	Date Killed
328-2/8	Portage County / Picked Up	1940
256-5/8	Holmes County / Picked Up	1975
250-6/8	Richland County / David D. Dull	1987
235-4/8	Ashtabula County / James L. Clark	1957
231-3/8	Licking County / Norman L. Myers	1964
226-4/8	Muskingum County / Rex A. Thompson	1981
226-1/8	Trumbull County / Paul E. Lehman	1948

Score	Locality Killed / By Whom Killed	Date Killed
211-5/8	Adams County / William J. DeCamp	1987
210-2/8	Columbiana County / Harold L. Hawkins	1981
207	Stark County / Tad E. Crawford	1987

OKLAHOMA
TYPICAL WHITE-TAILED DEER

177-6/8	Atoka County / Skip Rowell	1972
173-5/8	Woods County / Jack Clover	1983
170-3/8	Haskell County / Loyd Long	1985
160	Le Flore County / Carl E. Hale	1978

NON-TYPICAL WHITE-TAILED DEER

247-2/8	Johnston County / Bill M. Foster	1970
234-2/8	Alfalfa County / Loren Tarrant	1984
299-4/8	Dewey County / Ricky C. Watt	1987
216-3/8	Comanche County / Dwight O. Allen	1962
209	Hughes County / Lane Grimes	1987
206-1/8	Osage County / Wesley D. Coldren	1986
204-4/8	Love County / William B. Heller	1970
203-6/8	McCurtain County / Gary L. Birge	1981
201-3/8	Pushmataha County / Maurice Jackson	1975
197-4/8	Garfield County / Derald D. Crissup	1980

OREGON
TYPICAL WHITE-TAILED DEER

178-2/8	Wallowa County / Sterling K. Shaver	1982

PENNSYLVANIA
TYPICAL WHITE-TAILED DEER

184-6/8	Greene County / Ivan Parry	1974
182-2/8	Sullivan County / Floyd Reibson	1930
177-4/8	Bedford County / Raymond Miller	1957
176-5/8	Mifflin County / John Zerba	1936
176	Bradford County / Clyde H. Rinehuls	1944
175-4/8	McKean County / Arthur Young	1830
174-2/8	Butler County / Ralph Stoltenberg, Jr.	1986
173-3/8	Clarion County / Mead Kiefer	1947
173-3/8	Clarion County / Picked Up	1954
172-6/8	Somerset County / Edward B. Stutzman	1945

NON-TYPICAL WHITE-TAILED DEER

207-7/8	Port Royal / C. Ralph Landis	1951
207	Lycoming County / Al Prouty	1949

PENNSYLVANIA (continued)

Score	Locality Killed / By Whom Killed	Date Killed
201-1/8	Westmoreland County / Richard K. Mellon	1966
196-6/8	Perry County / Kenneth Reisinger	1949
	Westmoreland County / Edward G. Ligus	1956

SOUTH CAROLINA
NON-TYPICAL WHITE-TAILED DEER

208-5/8	Beaufort County / John M. Wood	1971

SOUTH DAKOTA
TYPICAL WHITE-TAILED DEER

193	South Dakota / Unknown	1964
192	Lyman County / Bob Weidner	1957
189-5/8	Tabor / Duane Graber	1954
184-3/8	Kingsbury County / Rudy F. Weigel	1960
181-3/8	Harding County / Gregg Else	1985
180-4/8	Clay County / James E. Olson	1975
180-3/8	Hand County / Vernon Winter	1965
177-1/8	Gregory County / Harold Deering	1969
176-7/8	Day County / William B. Davis	1959
176-5/8	Roberts County / Fred Kuehl	1964

NON-TYPICAL WHITE-TAILED]DEER

256-1/8	Marshall County / Francis Fink	1948
250-6/8	South Dakota / Howard Eaton	1870
249-1/8	Lily / Jerry Roitsch	1965
216-7/8	Brown County / Francis Shattuck	1960
210	Gregory County / Richard C. Berte	1982
208-4/8	Day County / Unknown	1950
207-7/8	Perkins County / W.E. Brown	1957
207-3/8	Roberts County / Delbert Lackey	1975
206-4/8	Yankton County / William Sees	1973
203-4/8	Lawrence County / Ernest C. Larive	1957

TENNESSEE
TYPICAL WHITE-TAILED DEER

186-1/8	Roane County / W.A. Foster	1959
184-4/8	Fayette County / Benny M. Johnson	1979
178-5/8	Scott County / Charles H. Smith	1978
173-4/8	Shelby County / John J. Heirigs	1962
173-2/8	Decatur County / Glen D. Odle	1972
173-1/8	White County / Same H. Langford	1980
173	Sullivan County / C. Alan Altizer	1984
172-3/8	Decatur County / Danny Pope	1982
172-2/8	Stewart County / Joe K. Sanders	1984

TENNESSEE (continued)
NON-TYPICAL WHITE-TAILED DEER

Score	Locality Killed / By Whom Killed	Date Killed
223-4/8	Hawkins County / Luther E. Fuller	1984
209-7/8	Hawkins County / Johnny W. Byington	1982
198-3/8	Montgomery County / Clarence McElhaney	1978
196-6/8	Unicoi County / Elmer Payne	1972

TEXAS
TYPICAL WHITE-TAILED DEER

196-4/8	Maverick County / Tom McCulloch	1963
196-1/8	McMullen County / Milton P. George	1906
192-2/8	Frio County / Basil Dailey	1903
190	Dimmitt County / C.P. Howard	1950
187-7/8	Zavala County / Donald Rutledge	1946
187-5/8	Starr County / Picked Up	1945
187-4/8	Frio County / Kenneth Campbell	1987
186-2/8	La Salle County / Herman C. Schliesing	1967
186-2/8	Kenedy County / Jack Van Cleve III	1972
186-1/8	Zavala County / Picked Up	1965

NON-TYPICAL WHITE-TAILED DEER

286	Brady / Jeff Benson	1892
272	Junction / Picked Up	1925
247-7/8	Frio County / Raul Rodriguez II	1966
240	Kerr County / Walter F. Schreiner	1905
235-1/8	Frio County / C.J. Stolle	1919
226-7/8	Dimmit County / Lake Webb	1937
226-4/8	La Salle County / A.L. Lipscomb, Sr.	1909
220-2/8	Zavala County / J.D. Jarratt	1930
219-3/8	Webb County / Richard O. Rivera	1972
215-2/8	Parker County /'Pleasant Mitchell	1982

VERMONT
TYPICAL WHITE-TAILED DEER

170-1/8	Essex County / Kevin A. Brockney	1986

VIRGINIA
TYPICAL WHITE-TAILED DEER

188-6/8	Shenandoah County / Gene Wilson	1985
178-3/8	Goochland County / Edward W. Fielder	1981
177-2/8	Augusta County / Donald W. Houser	1963
176-7/8	Prince George County / Fred W. Collins	1949
176-2/8	Rappahannock County / George W. Beahm	1959
174-4/8	Charlotte County / Jerry C. Claybrook	1977
17158	Augusta County / David H. Wolfe	1967

Score	Locality Killed / By Whom Killed	Date Killed
172-6/8	Surry County / Edward B. Jones	1984
172-5/8	Surry County / Picked Up	1987
170-7/8	Bath County / Maurice Smith	1953

NON-TYPICAL WHITE-TAILED DEER

232-4/8	Buckingham County / James R. Shumaker	1986
221-3/8	Louisa County / Picked Up	1981
217	Isle Of Wight County / Peter F. Crocker, Jr.	1963
216-4/8	Surry County / Stanley M. Hall	1986
216-3/8	Powhatan County / William E. Schaefer	1970
215-5/8	Wise County / Edison Holcomb	1987
211-7/8	Rockingham County / Dorsey O. Breeden	1966

WASHINGTON
TYPICAL WHITE-TAILED DEER

181-7/8	Whitman County / George A. Cook III	1985
180-4/8	Okanogan County / Joe Peone	1983
179-4/8	Spokane County / Bert E. Smith	1972
178-4/8	Addy / Irving Naff	1957
176-5/8	Washington / Unknown	1953
173-3/8	Pend Oreille County / Tom R. Lentz	1987
172-6/8	Spokane County / Maurice Robinette	1968
171-3/8	Metaline Falls County / Scott Hicks	1970
170-2/8	Spokane County / Edward A. Floch Jr.	1970
170	Stevens County / Clair Kelso	1966

NON-TYPICAL WHITE-TAILED DEER

234-4/8	Stevens County / Larry G., Gardner	1953
233-6/8	Thompson Creek / George Sly, Jr.	1964
231	Stevens County / Joe Bussano	1946
227-4/8	Pullman / Glenn C. Paulson	1965
210-7/8	Stevens County / Charles Tucker	1966
209	Chesaw / Charles Eder	1967
207-2/8	Oroville / Victor E. Moss	1967
206-1/8	Loon Lake / Bill Quirt	1955
204-3/8	Newport / David R. Buchite	1960
203-3/8	Okanogan County / Michael A. Anderson	1962

WEST VIRGINIA
TYPICAL WHITE-TAILED DEER

182-3/8	Braxton County / William D. Given	1976
180-5/8	Cheat Mt. / Joseph V. Volitis	1969
175-1/8	Wetzel County / Matthew Scheibelhood	1984
171	Hampshire County / Conda L. Shanholz	1958

WEST VIRGINIA (continued)
NON-TYPICAL WHITE-TAILED DEER

Score	Locality Killed / By Whom Killed	Date Killed
205-6/8	Ritchie County / Charles E. Bailey, Jr.	1979
204-6/8	Gilmer County / Brooks Reed	1960
203-1/8	Wetzel County / Tom Kirkhart	1981

WISCONSIN
TYPICAL WHITE-TAILED DEER

206-1/8	Burnett County / James Jordan	1914
197-5/8	Wood County / Joe Haske	1945
191-3/8	Vilas County / Robert Hunter	1910
189-7/8	Trempealeau County / Emil Stelmach	1959
186-1/8	Waupaca County / Fred Penny	1963
185	Vernon County / Harold Christianson	1968
184	Menominee County / Keith Miller	1969
183-7/8	Forest County / James M. Thayer	1980
183-6/8	Pepin County / LaVerne Anibas	1965
183-5/8	Buffalo County / Lee F. Spittler	1953

NON-TYPICAL WHITE-TAILED DEER

245	Buffalo County / Elmer F. Gotz	1973
241-3/8	Wisconsin / Unknown	1940
233-7/8	Loraine / Honaer Pearson	1937
233	Burnett County / Victor Rammer	1949
232	Waukesha County / John Herr, Sr.	1955
231-5/8	Dane County / Dennis D. Shanks	1979
231-2/8	Forest County / Robert Jacobson	1958
228-2/8	Cable / Charles Berg	1910
227-4/8	Bayfield County / Earl Holt	1934
226-6/8	Rusk County / Joe Michalets	1911

WYOMING
TYPICAL WHITE-TAILED DEER

191-5/8	Albany County / Robert D. Ross	
177-1/8	Newcastle / H.W. Julien	
174-3/8	Goshen County / Casey L. Hunter	
170-3/8	Niobrara County / Joseph A. Perry III	

NON-TYPICAL WHITE-TAILED DEER

238-7/8	Crook County / Picked Up	1962
224-1/8	Crook County / John S. Mahoney	1947
214-2/8	Crook County / Clinton Berry	1953
211-7/8	Crook County / Curtis U. Nelson	1971
204-2/8	Crook County / David Sipe	1956
202-3/8	Crook County / Marshall Miller	1968

Score	Locality Killed / By Whom Killed	Date Killed
200-3/8	Crook County / Paul L. Wolz	1967
198-7/8	Weston County / G. Huls & B.L. Arfmann	1973
198-4/8	Cow Creek / Thelma Martens	1951

ALBERTA
TYPICAL WHITE-TAILED DEER

204-2/8	Beaverdam Creek / Stephen Jansen	1967
190-5/8	Buffalo Lake / Eugene L. Boll	1969
188-4/8	Metiskow / Norman T. Salminen	1977
184-7/8	Vermilion / C. Letawsky & B. Myshak	1986
183	Red Deer River / Picked Up	1966
181-7/8	Hotchkiss / Andy G. Petkus	1984
181-7/8	Lesser Slave Lake / Picked Up	1985
181-4/8	Pine Lake / Robert Crosby	1977
181	Stettler / Archie Smith	1962
180-7/8	Castor / Norman D. Stienwand	1981

NON-TYPICAL DEER

277-5/8	Hardisty / Doug Klinger	1976
267-7/8	Shoal Lake / Jerry Froma	1984
255-4/8	Pigeon Lake / Leo Eklund	1973
241-1/8	Bighill Creek / Donald D. Dwernychuk	1984
233-2/8	Acadia Valley / James J. Niwa	1973
232-5/8	Winfield / Harry 0. Hueppelshevser	1986
233-2/8	Thursby / Robert G. MacRae	1987
231-6/8	Peace River / Terry Doll	1978
230-6/8	Red Deer / Delmer E. Johnson	1973
222-5/8	Edgerton / Nick Leskow	1964

BRITISH COLUMIBA
TYPICAL WHITE-TAILED DEER

177-7/8	Ymir / Frank Gowing	1961
175-7/8	Pouce Coupe River / Dale Callahan	1986
174-5/8	Baldonnel / D. Ian Williams	1978
174-4/8	Fort Steele /John Lum	1958
174-1/8	Anarchist Mt. / George Urban	1980
173-6/8	Hartr Creek / Greg Lamontange	1984
171-6/8	Gray Creek / Ross Oliver	1982
171-3/8	Whatshan lake / Ernest Roberts	1957
171	Okanagan Range / Picked Up	1984

NON-TYPICAL WHITE-TAILED DEER

245-7/8	Elk River / James I. Brewster	1905
218	West Kootenay / Karl H. Kast	1940

Score	Locality Killed / By Whom Killed	Date Killed
205-5/8	Midway / Gordon Kamigochi	1980
202-2/8	East Klooteney / Andrew W. Rosicky	1956
198-1/8	Nelway / Edward John	1935

MANITOBA
TYPICAL WHITE-TAILED DEER

197-7/8	Assiniboine River / Larry H. MacDonald	1980
189	Red Deer Lake / Will Bigelow	1986
188-4/8	Souris River / Wes Todoruk	1986
188-3/8	Sanford / Picked Up	1982
187-6/8	Mantagao Lake / Picked Up	1988
183	Lorne / Alain G. Comte	1987
182-5/8	Virden Darryl Gray	1957
179-7/8	Hamiota / Alan J. Sheridan	1984
179-4/8	Whitemud River / L. Greg Fehr	1985
179-3/8	Oberon / Arnold W. Poole	1968

NON-TYPICAL WHITE-TAILED DEER

257-3/8	Elkhorn / Harvey Olsen	1973
241-6/8	Manitoba / Unknown	1984
238-3/8	Assiniboine River / Doug Hawkins	1981
237-3/8	Whiteshell / Angus McVicar	1925
231-3/8	Holland / W. Ireland	1968
214-7/8	Aweme / Criddle Bros.	1954
212-1/8	Minnedosa / Albert Pfau	1966
208-1/8	Griswold / J.V. Parker	1946
207-7/8	Assiniboine River / Terry L. Simcox	1987
206-7/8	Whitemouth River/ Tom Clark, Jr.	1987

NEW BRUNSWICK
TYPICAL WHITE-TAILED DEER

180-6/8	New Brunswick Unknown	1937
178-3/8	Queens County Bert Bourque	1970
176-4/8	Charlotte County / Albert E. Dewar	1960
175-6/8	Nine Mile Brook / Leopold Leblanc	1973
175-4/8	Canaan / Marcel Poirier	1985
171-V8	Kings County / Wayne F. Anderson	1987
173-1/8	St. George / Gilbert Leavitt	1962
172-3/8	Snider Mt. / Jack W. Brown	1975
172	Westmoreland County / Edgar Cormier	1983
171-5/8	Bonnell Brook / Steve R. McCutcheon	1984

NON-TYPICAL WHITE-TAILED DEER

249-7/8	Kings County / Ronald Martin	1946

NEW BRUNSWICK (continued)

Score	Locality Killed / By Whom Killed	Date Killed
243-7/8	Wirral / H. Glenn Johnston	1962
242-2/8	Auburnville / John L. MacKenzie	1958
224-2/8	Salmon River / Ford Fulton	1966
214-7/8	St. John County / T. Emery	1968
204-118	Charlotte County / Gary L. Lister	1984
204-6/8	George Lake / Henry Kirk	1903
199-7/8	Queens Lake / George Lacey	1915
198-3/8	Clark's Brook / Bernard V. Sharp	1985
196-4/8	Charlotte County / Clayton Tatton	1959

NOVA SCOTIA
TYPICAL WHITE-TAILED DEER

170-6/8	Guysborough County / Roy B. Simpson	1968

NON-TYPICAL WHITE-TAILED DEER

264-5/8	West Afton River / Alexander C. MacDonald	1960
253	Goldenville / Neil MacDonald	1945
233-1/8	Condon Lakes / Don McDonnell	1987
222-4/8	Ostrea Lake / Verden Baker	1949
218-7/8	Bay of Fundy / Basil St. Lewis	1983
200-1/8	Parrsboro / Allison Smith	1960
196	Annapolis Valley / David Cabral	1984

ONTARIO
TYPICAL WHITE-TAILED DEER

174-1/8	Amherstview / Tony H. Stranak	1987

SASKATCHEWAN
TYPICAL WHITE-TAILED DEER

200-2/8	Whitkow / Peter J. Swistun	1983
195-4/8	Porcupine Plain / Philip Philipowich	1985
193-6/8	Christopher Lake / Jerry Thorson	1959
191-6/8	Hudson Bay / George Chalus	1973
188-4/8	Burstall / W.P. Rolick	1957
185-3/8	Canwood / Clark Heimbechner	1984
184-6/8	Dore Lake / Garvis C. Coker	1971
184-5/8	Hudson Bay / Picked Up	1986
182-4/8	Carrot River / Lori Lonson	1960
182-1/8	Round Lake / Jesse Bates	1984

NON-TYPICAL WHITE-TAILED DEER

265-3/8	White Fox / Elburn Kohler	1957
248-4/8	Moose Mtn. Park / Walter Barkto	1964

Score	Locality Killed / By Whom Killed	Date Killed
245-4/8	Carrot River / Picked Up	1962
243-5/8	Govan / A.W. Davis	1951
238- 1/8	Whitewood /Jack Davidge	1967
236-4/8	Reserve / Harry Nightingale	1959
235-4/8	Pipestone Valley / E.J. Marshall	1958
233-7/8	Tompkins / Don Stueck	1961
233	Punnichy / Steve Kapay	1968
231-7/8	Harris / Herman Cox	1954

MEXICO
TYPICAL WHITE-TAILED DEER

181-7/8	Coahuila / German Lopez Flores	1986
181-6/8	Nuevo Leon / J.P. Davis	1985
180-5/8	Nuevo Leon / Charles H. Priess	1985
174-2/8	Cerralvo / Unknown	1900
173-4/8	Tarnaulipas / John F. Sontage, Jr.	1987
172	Coahuila / Picked Up	1986
170-1/8	Coahuila / Rodolfo F. Barrera	1988
160-2/8	Coahuila / Jesus H.G. Villarreal	1988

NON-TYPICAL WHITE-TAILED DEER

233-6/8	Nuevo Leon / Ron Kolpin	1983
210-6/8	Coahuila / Picked -Up	1981
208-1/8	Mexico / Unknown	1959

ARIZONA
TYPICAL COUES' WHITE-TAILED DEER

143	Pima County / Ed Stockwell	1953
131-7/8	Cochise County / George W. Kouts	1935
130-4/8	Pima County / Kim J. Poulin	1981
126-5/8	Cochise County / Mike Kasun	1959
126-5/8	Pima County / DeWayne M. Hanna	1977
126-1/8	Pima County / Robert G. McDonald	1986
125-4/8	Arivaca / Gerald Harris	1953
125	Ft. Apache Res. / Picked Up	1969
124-5/8	Rincon Mts. / James Pfersdorf	1936
123-7/8	Gila County / Stephen P. Hayes	1965

NON-TYPICAL COUES' WHITE-TAILED DEER

158-4/8	Santa Cruz County / Picked Up By Walter H. Pollock	1988
151-4/8	Cochise County / Charles C. Mabry	1929
150-5/8	Sasabe / Robert Rabb	1954
149-7/8	Chiricaua Range / Marvin R. Hardin	1950

Records of the Pope & Young Club

Your 1996 *Deer Hunters' Almanac* includes the most up-to-date listings of the Pope and Young Club. The records listed here are taken from the club's *Bowhunting Big Game Records of North America*, fourth edition 1993, with the permission of the Pope and Young Club. The records appearing here are only a partial listing of the top whitetails. For information on the complete record book, write Pope and Young Club Inc., Box 548, Chatfield, MN 55923.

WHITE-TAILED DEER (Typical Antlers)
Minimum Score: 125

Score	Area	State	Hunter's Name	Date	Rank
204 4/8	Peoria County	IL	M.J. Johnson	1965	1
197 6/8	Monroe County	IA	Lloyd Goad	1962	2
197 6/8	Wright County	MN	Curt Van Lith	1966	2
197 1/8	Edmonton	ALB	Don McGarvey	1961	4
194 2/8	Jones County	IA	Robert L. Miller	1977	5
194 0/8	Logan County	CO	Stuart Clodfielder	1981	6
193 2/8	Jackson County	MI	Craig Calderone	1986	7
190 5/8	Warren County	IA	Richard Swim	1981	8
190 4/8	Parke County	IN	B. Dodd Porter	1985	9
189 1/8	Kearney County	NE	Robert Vrbsky	1978	10
188 1/8	Des Moines County	IA	Kevin Peterson	1989	11
186 1/8	Sumner County	KS	Greg Hill	1988	12
186 1/8	Morris County	KS	Craig Johnson	1991	12
185 1/8	Jackson County	IL	Mark Guetersloh	1990	14
183 2/8	Shawnee County	KS	Mark W. Young	1990	15
182 2/8	Jefferson County	KS	John Welborn	1982	16
182 0/8	Jefferson County	KS	Michael J. Rose	1982	17
181 7/8	Greenwood County	KS	Boyd Schneider	1984	18
181 7/8	Dakota County	MN	Eugene Lengsfeld	1985	18
181 7/8	Logan County	IL	Terry Lee Rich	1986	18
181 7/8	Jefferson County	OH	Brad L. Eibel	1988	18
181 6/8	Wabasha County	MN	Lee G. Partington	1971	22
181 6/8	Sussex County	DE	Donald Betts	1989	22
181 4/8	Keya Paha County	NE	Steve R. Pecsenye	1966	24
181 4/8	Fulton County	IL	Arnold Hegele	1968	24
181 4/8	North Norfolk	MAN	Lloyd Lintott	1986	24
180 5/8	Jefferson County	KS	Ron Artzer	1987	27
180 4/8	Henry County	IA	Jeff L. Weigert	1991	28
180 4/8	Ross County	OH	Gerald F. Hamm	1991	28
180 1/8	Winona County	MN	Kenneth W. Schreiber	1980	30
180 1/8	Mahoning County	OH	Robert A. Haney	1987	30

Pope & Young White-Tailed Deer Records, Typical Antlers

Score	Area	State	Hunter's Name	Date	Rank
179 5/8	Lac qui Parle County	MN	Mary A. Barvels	1978	32
179 4/8	Clark County	IA	Rodney D. Hommer	1990	33
179 3/8	Marshall County	SD	Phyllis Roehr	1976	34
179 1/8	Osage County	KS	Ralph Batchelor, Jr.	1985	35
179 0/8	Scotland County	MO	David Smith	1985	36
179 0/8	Wapello County	IA	Robert L. McDowell	1985	36
179 0/8	Edgar County	IL	Edward A. Inman	1985	36
179 0/8	Des Moines County	IA	Glen M. Thompson	1987	36
178 7/8	Washington County	IA	Ronald A. Murphy	1990	40
178 7/8	Whiteside County	IL	Bernard Higley, Jr.	1990	40
178 4/8	Meade County	KS	Tim Ross	1985	42
178 4/8	Fulton County	IL	Locie L. Murphy	1985	42
178 4/8	Firdale	MAN	Randy Bean	1988	42
178 3/8	McPherson County	KS	Larry Daniels	1967	45
178 0/8	Carroll County	IL	Art Heinze	1988	46
177 3/8	Greene County	IA	Roger V. Carlson	1973	47
177 3/8	Wayne County	OH	Gary E. Landry	1975	47
177 3/8	Jones County	IA	Ken Dausener	1984	47
177 3/8	Miami County	KS	Keith L. Groshong	1991	47
177 1/8	Washington County	IA	Ernie Aronson	1985	51
177 1/8	St. Croix County	WI	Phillip R. Hovde	1990	51
177 0/8	Baltimore County	MD	Richard B. Traband	1990	53
176 7/8	Will County	IL	David Davis	1990	54
176 6/8	Marshall County	KS	Ray A. Mosher	1966	55
176 6/8	Muscatine County	IA	Don McCullough	1980	55
176 6/8	McHenry County	IL	Gene Melby	1988	55
176 6/8	Kane County	IL	Mark DuLong	1991	55
176 4/8	Davis County	IA	Jeffrey A. Getz	1991	59
176 2/8	Houston County	MN	John Zahrte	1981	60
176 2/8	Kingman County	KS	Gerald Stroot	1981	60
176 1/8	Lewis County	KY	Alfred Simms	1985	62
176 1/8	Clay County	KS	Larry L. Thompson	1988	62
176 1/8	Johnson County	MO	James Stephens	1990	62
176 0/8	Clay County	KS	Rayford W. Willingham	1985	65
175 7/8	Kandiyohi County	MN	Eldon Hauser	1969	66
175 5/8	Burnett County	WI	Myles Keller	1977	67
175 5/8	Pratt County	KS	Gary Brehm	1984	67
175 5/8	Dickinson County	KS	Gary Stroda	1985	67
175 5/8	Woodbury County	IA	Paul Feddersen	1988	67
175 5/8	Lucas County	IA	Dean Chandler	1991	67
175 4/8	Murray County	MN	Steven Wynia	1973	72
175 4/8	Jo Daviess County	IL	Richard McCartin	1991	72
175 3/8	Ottawa County	KS	Gary Gans	1985	74
175 2/8	Sangamon County	IL	Wm. Richard Olsen	1978	75
175 2/8	St. Mary Parish	LA	Shannon Presley	1981	75
175 1/8	Marion County	IA	Gordon Hayes	1973	77
175 1/8	Dodge County	MN	Bill Chase	1976	77
175 0/8	Lee County	IA	Stephen D. McKeehan	1989	79
174 6/8	Randolph County	IL	Jack D. Carter	1988	80
174 5/8	Pickaway County	OH	Hunter R. Certain	1985	81
174 5/8	Livingston County	MI	Nicholas Scott Converse	1987	81
174 4/8	Toole County	MT	Dale Fames	1979	83

Pope & Young White-tailed Deer Records, Typical Antlers

Score	Area	State	Hunter's Name	Date	Rank
174 4/8	Chariton County	MO	Roger D. Guilford	1988	83
174 3/8	Taylor County	KY	Barry Eastridge	1987	85
174 2/8	Ashland County	WI	Kelly McClaire	1986	86
174 2/8	Mower County	MN	Jason Blom	1987	86
174 2/8	Wabaunsee County	KS	Henry C. Boss II	1991	86
174 0/8	Harrison County	IA	Ricky G. Seydel	1989	89
173 7/8	Noble County	OK	Danny McCants	1968	90
173 6/8	Mercer County	IL	Floyd A. Clark	1961	91
173 6/8	Winneshiek County	IA	Herbert Amundson	1985	91
173 6/8	Crawford County	IA	Ed Willroth	1991	91
173 5/8	Muskingum County	OH	David R. Hatfield	1980	94
173 4/8	Lac qui Parle County	MN	Dale W. Shackelford	1981	95
173 4/8	McHenry County	IL	Gordon Sunderlage	1987	95
173 3/8	Warren County	IL	Larry C. Harding	1974	97
173 2/8	Miami County	KS	Dan R. Moore	1982	98
173 2/8	Monroe County	IN	Jake Wineinger	1990	98
173 1/8	Dunn County	WI	Jack K. Dodge	1987	100
173 0/8	White County	IN	Eric L. Mohler	1978	101
173 0/8	Russell County	KS	Michael J. Pasek	1990	101
172 7/8	Vermillion County	IL	Ed Gudgel	1988	103
172 7/8	Walworth County	WI	Robert Peterson	1988	103
172 6/8	Ripley County	IN	Steve A. Allen	1982	105
172 6/8	Sullivan County	TN	C. Alan Altizer	1984	105
172 6/8	Saline County	KS	Bruce Brown	1986	105
172 6/8	Fairfield County	OH	James Carmichael	1988	105
172 6/8	Pike County	IL	Jimmy Howard	1989	105
172 6/8	Moultrie County	IL	Joe Nelson	1991	105
172 5/8	Rosebud County	MT	Michael E. Gayheart	1989	111
172 4/8	Lucas County	IA	Jim Barlow	1985	112
172 4/8	Scotland County	MO	Charlie L. Smith	1985	112
172 4/8	Shelby County	IL	Gene E. Thoele	1991	112
172 3/8	Clinton County	IL	James D. Rueter	1984	115
172 3/8	Marshall County	IA	Dale E. Smith	1988	115
172 3/8	Johnson County	KS	David Reed	1990	115
172 2/8	Iowa County	IA	Ardith Lockridge	1965	118
172 2/8	Clinton County	IA	Robert S. Stankee	1985	118
172 2/8	Butler County	PA	Ralph W. Stoltenberg, Jr.	1986	118
172 2/8	Saunders County	NE	John L. Kunert	1986	118
172 2/8	Clay County	KS	Scott Otto	1989	118
172 1/8	Rice County	MN	Mike Sannan	1989	123
172 1/8	Russell County	KS	James H. Skucius	1990	123
172 1/8	Lake County	IL	Mark J. Kramer	1990	123
172 0/8	Whiteside County	IL	Noel Feather	1977	126
172 0/8	Greene County	IN	Jason Anderson	1991	126
172 0/8	Nicolet County	MN	Bruce Kramer	1991	126
172 0/8	McMullen County	TX	Steve Best	1991	126
171 7/8	Scotland County	MO	David Smith	1984	130
171 7/8	Linn County	IA	Charles Bemer	1985	130
171 7/8	Lucas County	IA	Tim M. Whitlatch	1989	130
171 6/8	Richland County	ND	Todd Funfar	1982	133
171 6/8	Carroll County	OH	Randy S. Mulheim	1983	133
171 6/8	Dunn County	WI	James W. Belmore	1991	133
171 6/8	Edmonton	ALB	Warren Witherspoon	1991	133

Pope & Young White-tailed Deer Records, Typical Antlers

Score	Area	State	Hunter's Name	Date	Rank
171 5/8	Calgary	ALB	Scott Simi	1979	1937
171 5/8	Cowley County	KS	Michael L. Snyder	1985	137
171 5/8	Logan County	KY	Alan Scott	1987	137
171 4/8	Ellsworth County	KS	Jim Willems	1985	140
171 3/8	Cass County	ND	Warren Buss	1966	141
171 3/8	Harrison County	IA	R.A. Cronk	1985	141
171 3/8	Washington County	IL	Robert Schneider	1985	141
171 3/8	Jefferson County	WI	Gary Moyer	1987	141
171 3/8	Sangamon County	IL	Michael R. Vincent	1991	141
171 2/8	Adams County	IA	Gary D. Maatsch	1990	146
171 1/8	Itasca County	MN	John Parmeter	1964	147
171 1/8	Platt County	IL	Ronald E. Waugh	1971	147
171 1/8	Morton County	ND	Tony Schatz	1974	147
171 1/8	Tazewell County	IL	John P. Cordis	1987	147
171 1/8	Clark County	OH	Lafayette Boggs III	1991	147
171 0/8	Belmont County	OH	Charles J. Wilson	1979	152
171 0/8	Parke County	IN	Fred Sills	1985	152
170 7/8	Republic County	KS	Carroll Couture	196	154
170 7/8	Leavenworth County	KS	Jacob W. Dragieff	1987	154
170 7/8	Bureau County	IL	Steve W. Hayes	1990	154
170 6/8	Mitchell County	IA	Dan Block	1981	157
170 6/8	Racine County	WI	Anthony J. Wozniak	1985	157
170 6/8	Jackson County	MI	Richard J. Galicki	1991	157
170 5/8	Vermillion County	IL	Mark Pittman	1980	160
170 5/8	Teton County	MT	James R. Dean	1983	160
170 5/8	Schuyler County	MO	Mike Meinhardt	1989	160
170 4/8	Des Moines County	IA	Bob Fudge	1966	163
170 4/8	Vilas County	WI	Rick R. Lax	1990	163
170 4/8	Rock Island County	IL	Joseph V. de Schepper	1991	163
170 4/8	Cerro Gordo County	IA	Chuck Harris	1991	163
170 4/8	Pawnee County	NE	Kenneth C. Mort	1991	163
170 3/8	Hall County	NE	Gust Bergman	1965	168
170 3/8	Decatur County	IA	Julian Toney	1982	168
170 3/8	Ogle County	IL	John E. Lawson	1985	168
170 3/8	Howard County	IA	Clarence Mincks	1991	168
170 2/8	Lee County	AL	George P. Mann	1980	172
170 2/8	Clayton County	IA	Myles Keller	1989	172
170 1/8	Edwards County	KS	Jay Schaller	1968	174
170 1/8	Winona County	MN	Roger Traxler	1980	174
170 1/8	Mower County	MN	Robert D. Plumb	1984	174
170 1/8	Harford County	MD	Ed Garrison	1987	174
170 1/8	Miami County	KS	Keith Groshong	1968	174
170 1/8	Racine County	WI	Michael H. Poeschel	1989	174
170 1/8	Winnebago County	IA	Matthew Modeland	1990	174
170 1/8	La Crosse County	WI	Scott R. Waura	1991	174
170 0/8	Scott County	KS	Monte L. Baker	1973	182
170 0/8	Puslinch Twp.	ONT	Richard Foss	1980	182
170 0/8	Jo Daviess County	IL	Bart Blocklinger	1982	182
170 0/8	Plymouth County	IA	David Erdmann	1987	182
170 0/8	Battle River	SAS	Gordon Stefanuk	1989	182
170 0/8	Jackson County	MI	Michael D. Fitzgerald	1990	182
170 0/8	Harvey County	KS	Dan Stahl	1991	182
169 6/8	Decatur County	IA	Bruce Jermyn	1979	189

Pope & Young White-Tailed Deer Records, Typical Antlers

Score	Area	State	Hunter's Name	Date	Rank
169 6/8	Coffey County	KS	Jack McCullough	1984	189
169 5/8	Neosho County	KS	Jeff Friederich	1992	191
169 4/8	Charles Mix County	SD	Don Carda	1974	192
169 4/8	Hennepin County	MN	Mark Kirkwold	1989	192
169 4/8	Harvey County	KS	Ron Hershberger	1989	192
169 4/8	Rock Island County	IL	Leo Hoogerwerf	1990	192
169 4/8	Lafayette County	WI	E. Michael Kitral	1991	192
169 3/8	Hamilton County	OH	Christopher J. Ludwig	1990	197
169 2/8	Ashland County	OH	Darrell Huff	1985	198
169 1/8	La Salle County	IL	Dave Mrowicki	1985	199
169 0/8	Warren County	IA	Brad Vonk	1980	200
169 0/8	Marion County	KS	Max Williams	1985	200
169 0/8	Grant County	WI	Richard Hein	1986	200
168 7/8	Jackson County	IA	Al Weidenbacher	1984	203
168 7/8	Washington County	MN	Ronald Jacobson	1985	203
168 7/8	Jefferson County	IL	Rudy Moore	1987	203
168 6/8	Muskingum County	OH	Gerald Shepler	1988	206
168 5/8	Des Moines County	IA	Michael P. Anderson	1977	207
168 5/8	Mahoning County	OH	Jeff J. Hartman	1984	207
168 5/8	Calhoun County	IL	Dennis A. Kendall	1985	207
168 5/8	Taylor County	WI	Bradley Cornell	1986	207
168 5/8	Hancock County	OH	Robert E. Ebert	1988	207
168 5/8	Winnebago County	IA	Jim Orthel	1990	207
168 5/8	Harrison County	KY	Sam Blackburn	1991	207
168 4/8	Lincoln County	KS	Gerald Huehl	1985	214
168 4/8	Grayson County	KY	John David Johnson	1989	214
168 3/8	Jefferson County	IL	Ben Howard	1988	216
168 3/8	Kingsbury County	SD	Donald B. Johnson	1989	216
168 2/8	Cowley County	KS	Larry G. Gann	1975	218
168 2/8	Macon County	IL	Larry D. Smith	1985	218
168 2/8	Lyon County	KS	John R. Clifton	1985	218
168 2/8	Mercer County	KY	Steve Baxter	1989	218
168 1/8	Blue Earth County	MN	Rich Detjen	1984	222
168 0/8	Vinton County	OH	Ronald E. Morgan	1978	223
168 0/8	Amherst County	VA	William Dixon Morgan	1980	223
168 0/8	De Witt County	IL	William R. Henson	1982	223
167 7/8	Brown County	OH	David Grayson	1976	226
167 7/8	Clay County	IL	Tom Corry	1985	226
167 6/8	Monona County	IA	Douglas M. Bonnie	1985	228
167 6/8	Coffey County	KS	Edward L. Bess	1985	228
167 5/8	Chase County	KS	William E. Drummond	1984	230
167 5/8	Meigs County	OH	Rick Bolin	1987	230
167 5/8	Leavenworth County	KS	John W. Garrison	1990	230
167 5/8	Washita County	OK	Alan Cooper	1991	230
167 5/8	Macoupin County	IL	Justin Bonnell	1991	230
167 5/8	Fulton County	IL	Robert A. Hammerich	1991	230
167 4/8	Washington County	KS	Bill R. Mallean	1974	236
167 4/8	Coffey County	KS	Glen Stochs	1987	236
167 4/8	Sawyer County	WI	Gary R. Christman	1989	236
167 4/8	Winneshiek County	IA	Tom Gossman	1990	236
167 4/8	Pike County	IL	Timothy Fulmer	1990	236
167 3/8	Sauk County	WI	Daniel Kaczmar	1985	241
167 3/8	Sumner County	KS	Don Braddy	1986	241

Pope & Young White-Tailed Deer Records, Typical Antlers

Score	Area	State	Hunter's Name	Date	Rank
167 3/8	Coshocton County	OH	Harold E. Frank	1989	241
167 3/8	Dawson County	MT	Jerry Fevold	1992	241
167 1/8	Chase County	KS	Ronald E. Rhodes	1985	245
167 1/8	Dodge County	MN	Myles Keller	1985	245
167 1/8	Reno County	KS	R.D. Loudenback	1987	245
167 1/8	McHenry County	IL	Charlie Rand	1989	245
167 0/8	Clay County	MN	Ryan Hines	1986	246
167 0/8	Montgomery County	IN	Joe W. Woodrow	1988	249
167 0/8	Montgomery County	TN	Larry Lee Murphy	1989	249
167 0/8	Fountain County	IN	Steve McQueen	1991	249
166 7/8	Saline County	NE	Scott Theis	1982	253
166 7/8	Geary County	KS	Dennis L. Gillam	1986	253
166 7/8	Lake County	MN	Mark Hal Tucker	1991	253
166 6/8	Lanigan	SAS	Bob Tempel	1985	256
166 6/8	Allegan County	MI	Larry Deater	1989	256
166 5/8	Lyon County	MN	Gene Gustafson	1982	258
166 5/8	Meade County	KS	Tim Ross	1987	258
166 5/8	Johnson County	IN	Joe F. Heath, Jr.	1989	258
166 5/8	Sarpy County	NE	Roy Symanietz	1990	258
166 4/8	Juniper	NBW	Ron Peterson	1989	262
166 4/8	Pierce County	WI	Garrett L. Fleisha	1991	262
166 3/8	Clarke County	IA	Dwight E. Green	1965	264
166 3/8	Yankton County	SD	Roger Irwin	1985	264
166 3/8	Lake County	MN	Daniel Hall	1991	264
166 2/8	Monona County	IA	G.K. Tuttle	1967	267
166 2/8	Republic County	KS	Virgil Graham	1986	267
166 2/8	Monroe County	IA	Cliff VanZee	1987	267
166 2/8	Mower County	MN	Kerry Schroeder	1988	267
166 2/8	Cane County	IL	Roy Howard	1991	267
166 1/8	Morrison County	MN	Corey Loney	1963	272
166 1/8	Stearns County	MN	Bruce C. Meade	1978	272
166 1/8	Texas County	OK	Max Crocker	1986	262
166 1/8	Chase County	KS	Lee Ayers	1987	272
166 1/8	Bartholomew County	IN	Bryan D. Cook	2989	272
166 1/8	White County	IN	Kerry Dean Morton	1989	272
166 1/8	Wayne County	IL	Ronald Riley	1990	272
166 1/8	Ross County	OH	Keith W. Orr	1991	272
166 0/8	Clinton County	IA	Loy J. Brooker	1964	280
166 0/8	Bon Homme County	SD	Delbert Newman	1964	280
166 0/8	Shelby County	IL	Ernest D. Richardson	1977	280
166 0/8	Anoka County	MN	John A. Cardinal	1979	280
166 0/8	Tazewell County	IL	Jerry W. Kammerer	1981	280
166 0/8	Sedgwick County	KS	Louis Turner	1988	280
166 0/8	Martin County	IN	Terry L. McCrary	1988	280
165 7/8	Wapello County	IA	Richard L. Larsen	1976	287
165 7/8	Licking County	OH	Pat Walker	1978	287
165 7/8	Prowers County	CO	Edward Henson	1980	287
165 7/8	Vermilion County	IL	Dick Bayer	1987	287
165 7/8	Weld County	CO	Mark Houtchens	1991	287
165 6/8	Pottawattamie County	IA	Dan Bowen	1968	292
165 6/8	Darke County	OH	Dean Neff	1988	292
165 6/8	Morrison County	MN	Rodney Mysliwiec	1988	292
165 6/8	Ottawa County	KS	Patrick E. Helget	1988	292

Pope & Young White-Tailed Deer Records, Typical Antlers

Score	Area	State	Hunter's Name	Date	Rank
165 4/8	Kent County	MD	Kent Price	1962	296
165 4/8	Peoria County	IL	Larry T Oppe	1984	296
165 4/8	Buffalo County	WI	Patrick Ryan	1985	296
165 4/8	Will County	IL	Donald R. Spence	1988	296
165 4/8	Cherry County	NE	Jack Joseph	1990	296
165 3/8	Owen County	KY	Joseph Caruso	1977	301
165 3/8	Grundy County	IL	Gary R. Kuriger	1978	301
165 3/8	Victoria	MAN	David Wiklund	1984	301
165 3/8	Guthrie County	IA	Scott C. Kemble	1989	301
165 3/8	Hancock County	IN	Gary Dusang	1991	301
165 3/8	Rock Island County	IL	Roman H. Atnip	1991	301
165 3/8	Baca County	CO	Eddie Claypool	1991	301
165 2/8	McPherson County	KS	Daniel Willems	1981	308
165 2/8	Clemont County	OH	Nick Lung	1985	308
165 2/8	Dubuque County	IA	Paul Kluesner	1988	308
165 2/8	Wapello County	IA	Robert McDowell	1988	308
165 2/8	Dunn County	WI	Lamoine Roatch	1989	308
165 2/8	Harvey County	KS	Bob Stroble	1989	308
165 1/8	Barry County	MI	Jim Birmingham	1977	314
165 1/8	Sawyer County	WI	Robert N. Dale	1980	314
165 1/8	Iowa County	IA	David Roberts	1980	314
165 1/8	Wilson County	KS	Dr. Steven G. Mitchell	1987	314
165 0/8	Stony Plain	ALB	Wayne C. Prier	1983	318
165 0/8	Doniphan County	KS	Richard Williams	1983	318
165 0/8	Jefferson County	KS	Emmet Copeland	1989	318
165 0/8	Montgomery County	IL	Steven L. Traylor	1989	318
165 0/8	Crawford County	IL	Charles E. Guyer	1990	318
165 0/8	Geary County	KS	Philip J. Palmer	1991	318
164 7/8	Kane County	IL	James A. Anderson	1980	324
164 7/8	Peoria County	IL	Joe R. McCord	1983	324
164 7/8	Elkhart County	IN	Joe Leszczynski	1984	324
164 7/8	Gray County	KS	Ralph W. Herron	1984	324
164 7/8	Madison County	MT	Gordan Sampson	1986	324
164 7/8	Coles County	IL	Ralph Garland	1988	324
164 7/8	Richland County	OH	Erwin Merkli	1988	324
164 7/8	Butler County	OH	Will McQueen	1989	324
164 6/8	Shelby County	OH	Jerry Atkinson	1975	332
164 6/8	Highland County	OH	Daniel Henges	1976	332
164 6/8	Sanilac County	MI	Michael J. Wines	1981	332
164 6/8	Macoupin County	IL	John E. Eldred	1985	332
164 6/8	Sullivan County	IN	John W. Hale	1988	332
164 6/8	La Salle County	IL	Randy Hooper	1988	332
164 6/8	Macon County	IL	Cal Heseman	1988	332
164 6/8	Emmet County	IA	Steven L. Reighard, Sr.	1990	332
164 5/8	Sumner County	KS	Archie A. Stralow	1967	340
164 5/8	Fayette County	IA	Jerry Brown	1989	340
164 5/8	Saginaw County	MI	William J. Twarog	1990	340
164 4/8	Morton County	ND	Butch Sammons	1985	343
164 4/8	Trempealeau County	WI	Keith Lynch	1985	343
164 4/8	Bond County	IL	Roger Munie	1987	343
164 4/8	Montgomery County	OH	Michael L. Mrusek	1990	343
164 4/8	Anoka County	MN	Paul Landberg	1991	343
164 3/8	Norman County	MN	Gilbert Guttormson	1953	348

Pope & Young White-Tailed Deer Records, Typical Antlers

Score	Area	State	Hunter's Name	Date	Rank
164 3/8	Wibaux County	MT	Gerald Plesky	1959	348
164 3/8	Trigg County	KY	Charles Stahl	1965	348
164 3/8	Cottonwood County	MN	Jim Hansen	1972	348
164 3/8	Madison County	MT	Jim Schilke	1978	348
164 3/8	Saginaw County	MI	Larry Steinley	1979	348
164 3/8	Hardin County	OH	Anthony A. Krummrey	1982	348
164 3/8	Fayette County	OH	Steven J. Guess	1984	348
164 3/8	Louisa County	IA	Roger Gipple	1984	348
164 3/8	Perth	ONT	Michael Burwell	1986	348
164 3/8	Colfax County	NE	Dennis Indra	1987	348
164 3/8	Rock Island County	IL	Mike Mitten	1989	348
164 3/8	Scotland County	MO	David Westmoreland	1991	348
164 3/8	Van Buren County	MI	Kenneth J. Gillan	1991	348
164 2/8	Grundy County	IL	Jerome M. Fris	1972	362
164 2/8	Buffalo County	WI	Mark Busch	1986	362
164 2/8	Morrison County	MN	Tim Steinhoff	1987	362
164 2/8	Pike County	IL	Roger Pepper	1987	362
164 2/8	Mason County	IL	Richard J. "Buck" Fuller	1988	362
164 2/8	Kendall County	IL	Christopher Kieman	1989	362
164 2/8	Lake County	IL	Steven Tjader	1989	362
164 2/8	Clark County	IL	Cole Lee	1990	362
164 2/8	Guthrie County	IA	Joe Dowell	1991	362
164 1/8	Morrison County	MN	Lloyd Neuman	1971	371
164 1/8	Washington County	OH	Roger Pape	1980	371
164 1/8	Dundy County	NE	John Crump	1983	371
164 1/8	Otoe County	NE	Dale A. Hall	1989	371
164 0/8	Olmsted County	MN	Robert Meyer	1969	375
164 0/8	Morrison County	MN	Bruce Edberg	1977	375
164 0/8	Buffalo County	WI	Gerald Palmer	1986	375
164 0/8	Burnett County	WI	Gary A. Johnson	1989	375
163 7/8	Caldwell County	KY	Daniel R. Keith	1988	379
163 6/8	Fayette County	IA	Bob Nicolay	1981	380
163 6/8	Porter County	IN	Raymond T. Satterblom	1983	380
163 6/8	Graham County	KS	Russell Hull	1987	380
163 6/8	Clark County	IL	Gerald Shaffner	1991	380
163 5/8	Phillips County	KS	Bill Duncan	1969	384
163 5/8	Lawrence County	IL	Larry K. Karns	1975	384
163 5/8	Wright County	MN	Rick Heberling	1978	384
163 5/8	Fulton County	IL	Mike Reatherford	1982	384
163 5/8	Jackson County	MO	Chris Shotton	1985	384
163 5/8	Franklin County	IN	Roger Mullins	1987	384
163 5/8	Carver County	MN	Ryan Jopp	1991	384
163 4/8	Renville County	ND	Bobby Triplett	1958	391
163 4/8	Wright County	MN	Dale Guetzkow	1978	391
163 4/8	Lawrence County	OH	Berkley Pennington, Sr.	1981	391
163 4/8	Racine County	WI	Greg A. Hanson	1991	391
163 3/8	Linn County	IA	Delmar Phillips	1960	395
163 3/8	Morrison County	MN	Alvin A. Diemert	1973	395
163 3/8	Scott County	KY	Garry Hoffman	1982	395
163 3/8	Chase County	KS	John Moore	1983	395
163 3/8	Winnebago County	IL	Bradley S. Conrad	1984	395
163 3/8	Eaton County	MI	Dennis Orr	1987	395

Pope & Young White-Tailed Deer Records, Typical Antlers

Score	Area	State	Hunter's Name	Date	Rank
163 2/8	Brown County	IL	Keith E. Meiser	1981	401
1632/8	Drew County	AR	Larry Standley	1982	401
163 2/8	Mason County	KY	R. Kenton Ring	1982	401
163 2/8	Licking County	OH	Don Conrad	1985	401
163 2/8	Sumner County	KS	Kevin Disney	1985	401
163 2/8	Kiowa County	KS	Jesse Zook	1989	401
163 2/8	Crawford County	KS	Melinda S. Nutt	1981	401
163 2/8	Hennepin County	MN	Larry Watson	1991	401
163 2/8	Ross County	OH	Sam Detty	1992	401
163 1/8	Logan County	WV	Gilbert Sexton	1963	410
163 1/8	Knox County	OH	Robert Hammond	1983	410
163 1/8	Lake County	IL	Andrew Holst	1987	410
163 1/8	Logan County	OH	Jerrod Pooler	1988	410
163 1/8	Clayton County	IA	Daniel J. Brady	1988	410
163 1/8	Wright County	MN	Jerry Goodale	1990	410
163 1/8	Bayfield County	WI	Steve Polkowski	1992	410
163 0/8	Dickinson County	IA	Harold Ehrp	1959	417
163 0/8	Texas County	OK	Edward F. Bryan, Jr.	1976	417
163 0/8	Switzerland County	IN	Richard W. Keebler	1977	417
163 0/8	Ashland County	WI	Sid Kilger	1982	417
163 0/8	Gibson County	IN	Phil Scott	1986	417
163 0/8	Marshall County	KS	Tim Wanklyn	1986	417
163 0/8	Jefferson County	IN	Don Field	1987	417
163 0/8	Clarke County	IA	Gary Cobb	1988	417
163 0/8	Clermont County	OH	Larry W. Van	1990	417
162 7/8	Queen Annes County	MD	L.P. Stephens, Jr.	1962	426
162 7/8	Cowley County	KS	Kenneth Highfill	1968	426
162 7/8	Lee County	IA	Mike Bentler	1983	426
162 7/8	Perry County	IL	Kevin Tate	1989	426
162 7/8	Baltimore County	MD	Bruce Hoover	1991	426
162 7/8	Edmonton	ALB	Mark Daniel Stanley	1991	426
162 6/8	Rice County	MN	Ken Bakken	1957	432
162 6/8	Clayton County	IA	Dale Kartman	1984	432
162 6/8	Ozaukee County	WI	Joe Seaman	1989	432
162 5/8	Marshall County	KS	Gary W. Tobin	1966	435
162 5/8	Saunders County	NE	Robert Parkins	1967	435
162 5/8	Henry County	IL	Lewis E. Burson	1976	435
162 5/8	Lucas County	IA	Bill Brown	1979	435
162 5/8	Crawford County	KS	Fred Geier	1981	435
162 5/8	St. Charles County	MO	Roland Heiliger	1985	435
162 5/8	Buffalo County	WI	Paul Schultz	1986	435
162 5/8	Hubard County	MN	Nick J. Thill, Jr.	1987	435
162 5/8	Pike County	IL	Leroy Leonard	1987	435
162 5/8	Cerro Gordo County	IA	R.C. Field	1989	435
162 5/8	Wyandot County	OH	David Weininger	1991	435
162 4/8	Branch County	MI	Randy Massey	1981	446
162 4/8	Louisa County	IA	Michael Bell	1983	446
162 4/8	Allegheny County	PA	Christopher T. Joyce	1985	446
162 4/8	Dundy County	NE	Bradley Wiese	1985	446
162 4/8	Stearns County	MN	Pat Gross	1986	446
162 4/8	Vermilion County	IL	Sandra Downing	1986	446
162 4/8	Will County	IL	Joseph R. Franco	1986	446

Pope & Young White-Tailed Deer Records, Typical Antlers

Score	Area	State	Hunter's Name	Date	Rank
162 4/8	Anoka County	MN	Kim Van Tassel	1987	446
162 3/8	Barber County	KS	Glen Snell	1982	454
162 3/8	Lake County	IL	Donald M. Hewkin	1986	454
162 3/8	Menard County	IL	Mitchell Coffey	1987	454
162 3/8	Ogle County	IL	Jeffrey S. Burke	1989	454
162 3/8	Morrison County	MN	Edward J. Kastner	1989	454
162 3/8	Edmonton	ALB	Dale Spooner	1992	454
162 2/8	Kingsbury County	SD	Dale Peterson	1972	460
162 2/8	Le Sueur County	MN	Joe Rybus	1981	460
162 2/8	Marion County	KS	Leslie Lalouette	1983	460
162 2/8	Trego County	KS	Craig Doll	1985	460
162 2/8	Hendricks County	IN	Leon Smith	1986	460
162 2/8	Litchfield County	CT	Warren Hensel	1988	460
162 2/8	Miller County	MO	Steve Wyrick	1990	460
162 2/8	Will County	IL	Mike O'Connor	1991	460
162 1/8	Buffalo County	WI	Bruce Curtis	1983	469
162 1/8	Winnebago County	IL	Jeffrey A. Saxby	1984	469
162 1/8	Monroe County	IA	Larry Whitson	1985	469
162 1/8	Lafayette County	WI	Charles D. Potter	1986	469
162 1/8	Clinton County	OH	Mark A. Ross	1988	469
162 1/8	Adams County	IL	Randall Lummer	1990	469
162 0/8	Bond County	IL	Larry Nelson	1976	475
162 0/8	Wabash County	IL	Ron Hawf	1978	475
162 0/8	Edgar County	IL	John J. Dillon	1985	475
162 0/8	Marion County	KS	Don Bredemeier	1987	475
162 0/8	Mahoning County	OH	Mark A. Brooks	1988	475
162 0/8	Anoka County	MN	Dean Smith	1990	475
162 0/8	Tolland County	CT	Bruce Moore	1990	475
162 0/8	Richland County	ND	Tim Poehls	1992	475
161 7/8	Saunders County	NE	David Strimple	1961	483
161 7/8	Douglas County	NE	Noel Miller	1970	483
161 7/8	Fulton County	IL	Bob Neal	1981	483
161 7/8	Greene County	OH	Charles O. Hill	1982	483
161 7/8	Tuscarawas County	OH	Gary Stevens	1982	483
161 7/8	Brandon	MAN	Gary Kaluzniak	1985	483
161 7/8	Winona County	MN	Tim Rislow	1986	483
161 7/8	Jones County	IA	Paul Johnson	1986	483
161 7/8	Marion County	MO	James Schaefer	1987	483
161 7/8	Jefferson County	WI	Adam Achilli	1988	483
161 7/8	Ontario County	NY	Adam T. Kupis	1989	483
161 7/8	Mahoning County	OH	Nicholas Young	1990	483
161 6/8	Lake County	IL	David Mitten	1987	495
161 6/8	Jo Daviess County	IL	Timothy T. Westemeier	1987	495
161 6/8	Pike County	IL	Brad Stamp	1988	495
161 6/9	Montgomery County	TN	Zane Mason	1991	495
161 5/8	Dunn County	WI	Leonard Hines	1970	499
161 5/8	Juneau County	WI	Harlan Steindl	1971	499
161 5/8	Jefferson County	IL	Rick Osborn	1982	499
161 5/8	Butler County	KS	Mike Turner	1982	499
161 5/8	Butler County	KS	Ronald Tilson	1983	499
161 5/8	Franklin County	KS	Dennis Ballweg	1987	499
161 5/8	Woodford County	IL	Lynn Roseman	1989	499
161 5/8	Forest County	WI	Daniel G. Van Hoosen	1990	499

Pope & Young White-Tailed Deer Records, Typical Antlers

Score	Area	State	Hunter's Name	Date	Rank
161 4/8	Bond County	IL	Sam White	1974	507
161 5/8	Jackson Parish	LA	James K. Morgan	1977	507
161 4/8	Sumner County	KS	Phill Allton	1983	507
161 4/8	Jones County	IA	David A. Leuchs	1984	507
161 4/8	Cass County	NE	Ray Brock	1985	507
161 4/8	Crawford County	KS	Fred Geier	1988	507
161 4/8	Oconto County	WI	Jeffery J. Brabant	1989	507
161 4/8	Clinton County	IL	Tracy Hawes	1989	507
161 4/8	Dane County	WI	Greg Berndt	1990	507
161 4/8	Van Buren County	IA	Jim Francois	1990	507
161 4/8	Washburn County	WI	Larry Allen Blaylock	1991	507
161 3/8	Wyandotte County	KS	George F. Bigelow	1967	518
161 3/8	Sumner County	KS	Larry Wycoff	1980	518
161 3/8	Clark County	OH	Kenneth Preston	1982	518
161 3/8	Fayette County	IL	Bill Holman	1983	518
161 3/8	Auglaize County	OH	Lee Atha	1983	518
161 3/8	Butler County	KS	David R. Rogers	1985	518
161 3/8	Grant County	WI	Chris Nelson	1986	518
161 3/8	Anderson County	TN	John Johnson	1987	518
161 3/8	Lake County	IN	David R. Turbin	1988	518
161 3/8	Waukesha County	WI	Dirk Stolz	1989	518
161 3/8	McPherson County	KS	Daniel Willems	1990	518
161 2/8	Muskingum County	OH	Lee E. Wilson	1984	529
161 2/8	Graham Country	KS	Chris Jolly	1984	529
161 2/8	Saulk County	WI	Hank Loncki	1989	529
161 2/8	Cowley County	KS	Dwayne Graham	1990	529
161 1/8	Clark County	IN	Frank Mauk, Jr.	1966	533
161 1/8	Marinette County	WI	Dale J. Hanson	1985	533
161 1/8	Lake County	IL	John Schnider	1987	533
161 1/8	Polk County	IA	Jim Garton, Jr.	1989	533
161 1/8	Wayne County	IL	Will Sapia	1990	533
161 1/8	Butler County	OH	Dale Gross	1990	533
161 0/8	La Cross County	WI	Ray Howell	1977	539
161 0/8	Jefferson County	IN	Donnie Ball	1984	539
161 0/8	Morris County	KS	Craig Johnson	1985	539
161 0/8	Orange County	NC	R.J. Hickeman	1987	539
161 0/8	Lucas County	IA	Gary Goering	1987	539
161 0/8	Butler County	OH	Fred S. Spurlin	1987	539
161 0/8	Fond du Lac County	WI	Dave E. Stubbe	1988	539
161 0/8	Lawrence County	IN	Dale Waldbieser	1988	539
161 0/8	Dakota County	MN	Dave Vomela	1988	539
161 0/8	Day County	SD	Jim Madsen	1990	539
161 0/8	McHenry County	IL	Richard A. Houge	1991	539
161 0/8	Marion County	IA	Dwight T. Robuck	1991	539
161 0/8	Peoria County	IL	Robert E. Grainger	1991	539
160 7/8	Frontier County	NE	Vernon Laverack	1959	552
160 7/8	Smith County	KS	Ron Sturgeon	1965	552
160 7/8	Lincoln County	MN	Bernie Ahlberg	1974	552
160 7/8	Clark County	IL	Wes Romines	1977	552
160 7/8	Saline County	KS	Ray Peterman	1979	552
160 7/8	Pike County	IL	Richard Dewey	1981	552
160 7/8	Leavenworth County	KS	Albert Lyle Karl	1982	552
160 7/8	Rockingham County	VA	JIm Burther	1989	552

Pope & Young White-Tailed Deer Records, Typical Antlers

Score	Area	State	Hunter's Name	Date	Rank
160 7/8	Clark County	OH	Ron McGuire	1989	552
160 7/8	Bond County	IL	James Coleman	1989	552
160 7/8	Sangamon County	IL	David C. Jostes	1990	552
160 7/8	Bulter County	OH	Norman R. Sampson	1991	552
160 7/8	Parkland County	ALB	Sam Halabi	1991	552
160 6/8	Sarpy County	NE	Lawrence A. Klabunde	1968	566
160 6/8	Fillmore County	MN	Doyle Tarrence	1974	566
160 6/8	Alleghany County	VA	Roger O. Wyant	1984	566
160 6/8	Lake County	IL	Charles R. Zradicka	1986	566
160 6/8	Muskegon County	MI	Dave Haack	1988	566
160 6/8	Bayfield County	WI	Jim Peters	1989	566
160 5/8	Lawrence County	IL	Bob Brian	1971	572
150 5/8	Murray County	MN	Paul Beech	1974	572
160 5/8	Montcalm County	MI	Rodney Snyder	1980	572
160 5/8	Hubbard County	MN	Myles Keller	1982	572
160 5/8	Morrison County	MN	Randy Johnson	1986	572
160 5/8	Kenedy County	TX	Cal Adger	1987	572
160 5/8	Waukesha County	WI	Dick Harris	1988	572
160 5/8	Van Buren County	IA	Noel E. Harlan	1988	572
160 5/8	Scott County	MN	Kris Huber	1988	572
160 5/8	Christian County	IL	Richard Krider	1988	572
160 5/8	Allamakee County	IA	Warren W. Woods	1991	572
160 4/8	Williams County	ND	John Bloom	1963	583
160 4/8	Lyon County	IA	Marvin H. Peterson	1970	583
160 4/8	Keith County	NE	Gil Wilkinson	1970	583
160 4/8	Fairfield County	OH	Robert A. Fletcher	1977	583
160 4/8	Dawson County	MT	Frank Legato	1978	583
160 4/8	Trempealeau County	WI	Duane Kupietz	1981	583
160 4/8	Waukesha County	WI	Donald T. Lurvey	1982	583
160 4/8	Daviess County	MO	Sam Boyd	1987	583
160 4/8	Jefferson County	OH	Robert E. Howell	1987	583
150 4/8	Wayne County	MO	Carl Roach	1988	583
160 4/8	Schuyler County	IL	Tom Grover	1991	583
160 4/8	Pike County	IL	Tim Fulmer	1991	583
160 4/8	Olmsted County	MN	Jim Hanson	1992	583
160 3/8	Sheridan County	NE	Wayne Krotz	1975	596
160 3/8	St. Charles County	MO	Dan Schulte	1976	596
160 3/8	Barber County	KS	Herbie M. Landwehr, Jr.	1980	596
160 3/8	Clark County	IL	Gerald Shaffner	1983	596
160 3/8	Hamilton County	IL	Clifford R. Schoolman	1984	596
160 3/8	Jefferson County	IL	Jerry Newell	1986	596
160 3/8	Saskatoon	SAS	Maurice Parent	1987	596
160 3/8	Rock County	WI	Ronald A. Vike, Jr.	1989	596
160 3/8	Clay County	MO	James Wollard	1991	596
160 3/8	Washita County	OK	Larry Snider	1991	596
160 2/8	Nance County	NE	Ralph I. Hansen	1963	606
160 2/8	Cherokee County	IA	Jerry L. Smith	1969	606
160 2/8	Valley County	MT	John 'Rosey' Roseland	1981	606
160 2/8	Mills County	IA	Dale R. Clayton	1983	606
160 2/8	Phelps County	NE	Bruce Nielsen	1984	606
160 2/8	La Salle County	IL	John Thomas	1987	606
160 2/8	Lake County	IL	Woody Scruggs	1987	606

Pope & Young White-Tailed Deer Records, Typical Antlers

Score	Area	State	Hunter's Name	Date	Rank
160 2/8	Ashland County	WI	Steven Roginske	1988	606
160 2/8	Rusk County	WI	Shawn Harris	1991	606
160 2/8	Winnebago County	IL	Douglas R. Greensides	1991	606
160 1/8	Polk County	MN	Scott Gullickson	1985	616
160 1/8	Blue Earth County	MN	Darwin Arndt	1985	616
160 1/8	Ross County	OH	Randall W. Haines	1986	616
160 1/8	Lafayette County	WI	Jeff J. Kahle	1988	616
160 1/8	Clayton County	IA	Wayne M. Lau	1989	616
160 1/8	Washington County	MS	Odis Hill, Jr.	1990	616
160 1/8	Huntington County	IN	Troy Harris	1991	616
160 1/8	Fergus County	MT	John Fleharty	1992	616
160 0/8	Worth County	IA	Terry Lynch	1972	624
160 0/8	Winona County	MN	James Enderson	1973	624
160 0/8	Cooper County	MO	Nancy Smith	1984	624
150 0/8	Stephenson County	IL	Richard K. Kerr	1985	624
160 0/8	Morrill County	NE	Michael A. Brening	1985	624
160 0/8	Ellsworth County	KS	Dave Fisher	1986	624
160 0/8	Charles County	MD	William J. Kovach	1990	624
160 0/8	Sawyer County	WI	Todd Carlson	1990	624
160 0/8	Clemont County	OH	John Fischer	1991	624
160 0/8	Becker County	MN	Kurt Holland	1992	624
159 7/8	Clark County	KS	William Rule	1983	634
159 7/8	Garden County	NE	Wynn Fontenot	1984	634
159 7/8	Brown County	NE	Lorne Allen	1988	634
159 7/8	Alberta Beach	ALB	Joe Hanson	1991	634
159 7/8	Will County	IL	Gene Hagberg	1991	634
159 7/8	Webster County	KS	Ronald Nicholson	1991	634
159 6/8	Vanderburgh County	IN	Floyd Jackson	1977	640
159 6/8	Sherburne County	MN	Allen Hugget	1981	640
159 6/8	Buffalo County	WI	Bill Peterson	1981	640
159 6/8	Miami County	KS	Tom Wiggin	1982	640
159 6/8	Washington County	MS	Steve Nichols	1986	640
159 6/8	Page County	IA	Dave Bayless	1986	640
159 6/8	Rock Island County	IL	Russ Courter	1988	640
159 6/8	Greenwood County	KS	John Porubski	1989	640
159 5/8	Des Moines County	IA	Richard Howard	1964	648
159 5/8	Pittsburg County	OK	John Baumann	1977	648
159 5/8	Reno County	KS	Richard A. Swisher	1978	648
159 5/8	Madison County	IL	Barry Ash	1980	648
159 5/8	Muskingum County	OH	Brent L. Taylor	1981	648
159 5/8	Ogle County	IL	Charles L. Martoglio	1982	648
159 5/8	Watonwan County	MN	Richard Enger	1983	648
159 5/8	Cochrane	ALB	Edward Defrancesco	1984	648
159 5/8	Hamilton County	IA	Stephen L. Cink	1987	648
159 5/8	Hennepin County	MN	John Earl Ford	1988	648
159 4/8	Blue Earth County	MN	Harold Tow	1963	658
159 4/8	Wabash County	IL	Tom J. McRaven	1967	658
159 4/8	Hocking County	OH	James Allen Downs	1980	658
159 4/8	Morris County	KS	Kenneth R. Bryant	1983	658
159 4/8	Dade County	MO	Charles A. Myers	1985	658
159 4/8	Scott County	IA	Albert Perreault	1985	658
159 4/8	Goodhue County	MN	Brad C. Nesseth	1986	658

Pope & Young White-Tailed Deer Records, Typical Antlers

Score	Area	State	Hunter's Name	Date	Rank
159 4/8	Will County	IL	Larry Elumbaugh	1987	658
159 4/8	Linn County	IA	Jim Arp	1989	658
159 4/8	Buffalo County	WI	Ronald Brenner	1990	658
159 4/8	Foster County	ND	Bryon Hallwachs	1990	658
159 4/8	Pike County	IL	Kevin McCallister	1991	658
159 4/8	Randolph County	IN	Roy Patterson	1991	658
159 3/8	Pike County	OH	Ray C. Pritchett, Jr.	1977	671
169 3/8	Washington County	KS	Tony Mann	1985	671
159 3/8	Rock Island County	IL	Mike W. Greeno	1988	671
159 3/8	Pike County	IL	Phil McEuen	1988	671
159 3/8	Houston County	MN	Steve Bjerke	1989	671
159 3/8	Hillsdale County	MI	Dennis L. Burlew	1989	671
159 3/8	Washtenaw County	MI	Gregory Kuhn	1990	671
159 2/8	Hamlin County	SD	John R. Gregory	1975	678
159 2/8	Johnson County	AR	Kenn R. Young	1979	678
159 2/8	Yankton County	SD	Michael L. Tacke	1983	678
159 2/8	Anne Arundel County	MD	Jim Roy	1985	678
159 2/8	Madison County	IA	Tom Arpy	1987	678
159 2/8	Milwaukee County	WI	Terry R. Brandenburg	1989	678
159 1/8	Lucas County	OH	Martin Higley	1962	684
159 1/8	Clayton County	IA	Gary Troester	1978	684
159 1/8	Heard County	GA	Howard E. Taylor	1980	684
159 1/8	Saline County	KS	Raymond Peterman	1984	684
159 1/8	Winona County	MN	Vernon Zachariason	1986	684
159 1/8	Allamakee County	IA	Daniel R. Kennedy	1987	684
159 1/8	Livingston County	MI	Keith Joseph Daniels	1988	684
159 1/8	Vermilion County	IL	Horace E. Marsh	1990	684
159 1/8	Douglas County	KS	Paul Gordon	1991	684
159 0/8	Shelby County	IL	Gary E. Sievers	1971	693
159 0/8	Pulaski County	IN	William F. Bean	1977	693
159 0/8	Sarpy County	NE	Todd W. Steward	1984	693
159 0/8	Switzerland County	IN	Donald R. Barker	1986	693
159 0/8	Lawrence County	OH	Kevin Whitt	1986	693
159 0/8	Jackson County	MN	Ken Bute	1987	693
159 0/8	Pike County	IL	Steven R. Tice	1989	693
159 0/8	Clark County	IL	Ronald E. Pender	1989	693
159 0/8	Adair County	OK	Dan Mallory	1998	693
158 7/8	Pope County	IL	Gary Thomas	1964	782
158 7/8	Blue Earth County	MN	Gordon F. Kopischke	1968	782
158 7/8	Owen County	IN	Steven Collins	1973	782
158 7/8	Sedgwick County	KS	Marion A. Crumm	1974	782
158 7/8	Putnam County	IL	David A. Heath	1975	782
158 7/8	Crawford County	OH	Charles Ellis	1977	782
158 7/8	Charles County	MD	Jim Wright	1966	782
158 7/8	Paulding County	OH	Karl A. Langham	1988	782
158 7/8	Henry County	MO	LaVern Rucker	1988	782
158 7/8	Pottawattamie County	IA	Mike L. Smith	1989	782
158 7/8	Marshall County	IA	Mark A. Hedum	1998	782
158 7/8	Chippewa County	WI	Dennis Johnson	1998	782
158 7/8	Westchester County	NY	Gregg Della Rocca	1991	782
158 6/8	Irion County	TX	John K. Watson	1977	715
158 6/8	Dodge County	MN	Mark A. Lenz	1986	715
158 6/8	Vernon County	WI	Dan Morrison	1988	715

Pope & Young White-Tailed Deer Records, Typical Antlers

Score	Area	State	Hunter's Name	Date	Rank
158 6/8	Brooks County	TX	Billy Ellis III	1989	715
158 6/8	Howard County	IA	Mike Grube	1992	715
158 5/8	Marinette County	WI	Valerie P. Williams	1966	728
158 5/8	Shelby County	IL	Jim Helm	1977	728
158 5/8	Chariton County	MO	Brian Argetsinger	1986	728
158 5/8	Lee County	IA	Jeff Horsey	1989	728
158 5/8	Burlington County	NJ	Thomas Stevenson, Sr.	1989	728
158 5/8	Dane County	WI	Keith Matush	1998	728
158 4/8	Cedar	KS	Gordon Reneberg	1965	726
158 4/8	Des Moines County	IA	Michael P. Anderson	1978	726
158 4/8	Boone County	IA	Chris W. Doran	1984	726
158 4/8	Adair County	MO	Terry Clay	1987	726
158 4/8	Adams County	MS	John Harvey	1989	726
158 4/8	Douglas County	WI	John Lawler	1991	726
158 3/8	Texas County	OK	Edward F. Bryan, Jr.	1988	732
158 3/8	Jackson County	MI	Donald L. O'Dell	1984	732
158 3/8	Douglas County	WI	Gerald Berg	1988	732
158 3/8	La Porte County	IN	Scott Saliwanchik	1988	732
158 3/8	Logan County	IL	Douglas A. Hulinger	1989	732
158 3/8	Jo Daviess County	IL	Michael P. Pickel	1998	732
158 3/8	Euphrasia	ONT	Tom Perks	1998	732
158 3/8	Lake County	IL	James C. Carlson	1991	732
158 2/8	Lee County	IA	Gary Frost	1965	748
158 2/8	Barron County	WI	Gary Kohlmeyer	1989	748
158 1/8	Randolph County	IN	Ron J. Carlin	1973	742
158 1/8	Kossuth County	IA	Steve Rochleau	1981	742
158 1/8	King George County	VA	L.M. 'Ted' Williams	1981	742
158 1/8	Jackson County	IA	Jeff W. Ernst	1984	742
158 1/8	Brown County	OH	Michael W. Babcock	1985	742
158 1/8	Wyandot County	OH	Michael D. Saam	1985	742
158 1/8	Columbiana County	OH	David S. Landsberger	1986	742
158 1/8	Rock Island County	IL	Donald G. Jones	1986	742
158 1/8	Racine County	WI	Joe Spang	1987	742
158 1/8	Allamakee County	IA	Joe Lieb	1988	742
158 1/8	Adams County	IL	Jim Vahle	1988	742
158 1/8	Berkeley County	WV	Robert W. Deeds	1998	742
158 1/8	Bulitt County	KY	Tim Williams	1991	742
158 8/8	Wayne County	IL	Bill Naney	1981	755
158 8/8	Lancaster County	NE	Martin Erickson	1983	755
158 8/8	Jackson County	OH	Jim Ridge	1986	755
158 8/8	Jackson County	IA	Terry Amling	1988	755
158 8/8	Houston County	MN	Michael Val Stevens	1989	755
158 8/8	Webster County	IA	Mike Jones	1989	755
158 8/8	Ogle County	IL	Art Heinze	1998	755
158 8/8	Van Buren County	IA	Gerald Palmer	1998	755
158 8/8	Bremer County	IA	Virgil Marlette	1991	755
157 7/8	Meeker County	MN	Russell T. Nelson	1974	764
157 7/8	Goodhue County	MN	John 'Jack' Cordes	1975	764
157 7/8	Harvey County	KS	P. Bruce Mosiman	1984	764
157 7/8	Boone County	MO	Robert Hagans	1986	764
157 7/8	Calhoun County	MI	Jeff Edward Titus	1986	764
157 7/8	Butler County	KS	Jim P. Smith	1987	764
157 7/8	Sedgwick County	KS	Jim Molitor	1988	764

Pope & Young White-Tailed Deer Records, Typical Antlers

Score	Area	State	Hunter's Name	Date	Rank
157 7/8	Boone County	IA	Jim Humberg	1988	764
157 7/8	Simpson County	KY	Mike Stovall	1998	764
157 6/8	Lyon County	MN	M. Dean Holm	1976	773
157 6/8	Phillips County	KS	Lavern A. Wheaton	1978	773
157 6/8	Des Moines County	IA	David Bollei	1979	773
157 6/8	Geauga County	OH	John A. Suszynski	1981	773
157 6/8	Oconto County	WI	Richard E. Liss	1983	773
157 6/8	Leavenworth County	KS	John Garrison	1983	773
157 6/8	Des Moines County	IA	Ken Thorndyke	1984	773
157 6/8	Genesee County	MI	Alfred L. Allen	1987	773
157 6/8	Martin County	IN	Terry Kirkman	1987	773
157 6/8	Shawnee County	KS	Steven E. Deever	1988	773
157 6/8	Yankton County	SD	Alan Peterson	1988	773
157 6/8	McLean County	IL	Jim Dicken	1991	773
157 6/8	Vermillion	ALB	Glenn Moir	1992	773
157 5/8	Marion County	KS	Ron Hershberger	1982	786
157 5/8	Fulton County	AR	Lynn Luther	1983	786
157 5/8	Saline County	KS	Richard Cockroft	1985	786
157 5/8	Bartholomew County	IN	Jean E. Sneed	1986	786
157 5/8	Atoka County	OK	Patrick C. Patton	1988	786
157 5/8	Morgan County	IL	Roger Smith	1989	786
157 5/8	Wayne County	MO	Rod Bowling	1989	786
157 5/8	McHenry County	IL	Dennis Huhn	1998	786
157 5/8	Wood County	WI	Michael L. Hewitt	1991	786
157 5/8	Du Page County	IL	Ron Knebel	1991	786
157 5/8	Washington County	IA	Chris Davies	1991	786
157 4/8	Marion County	IA	Charles H. Walter	1967	797
157 4/8	Kalamazoo County	MI	Guy Stutzman	1979	797
157 4/8	Webster County	IA	Larry K. Fossen	1988	797
157 4/8	Henry County	VA	Mike Weaver	1986	797
157 4/8	Jackson County	OH	Steven L. Roe	1987	797
157 4/8	Hardin County	IL	Larry Hall	1988	797
157 4/8	Grundy County	IL	Brian Bergmann	1988	797
157 4/8	Hennepin County	MN	Mike Hintzen	1998	797
157 4/8	Crawford County	IL	Steve Parker	1998	797
157 4/8	Sawyer County	WI	Gary Haus	1991	797
157 4/8	Lake County	IL	Russ Tallman	1992	797
157 3/8	Adams County	IL	John Musolino	1966	888
157 3/8	Harrison County	KY	Kevin Poe	1984	888
157 3/8	Yuma County	CO	Chuck Anderson, Sr.	1985	888
157 3/8	Vermillion County	IL	Russell A. Sill	1989	888
157 3/8	Price County	WI	Mike Case	1998	888
157 2/8	Johnson County	IL	Jim Casey	1963	813
157 2/8	Mountrail County	ND	Dean A. Rehak	1963	813
157 2/8	Cottonwood County	MN	Brian Grothe	1978	813
157 2/8	Jessamine County	KY	David Cartwright	1979	813
157 2/8	Argyle	MAN	Russ Snell	1982	813
157 2/8	Westchester County	NY	Ralph Finacchairo	1983	813
157 2/8	Chickasaw County	IA	Theodore J. Steege IV	1987	813
157 2/8	Ashland County	OH	Bert P. Reynolds	1989	813
157 2/8	Elbert County	CO	Tom Kelley	1998	813
157 2/8	Houston County	MN	Rob Larson	1991	813

Pope & Young White-Tailed Deer Records, Typical Antlers

Score	Area	State	Hunter's Name	Date	Rank
157 2/8	Chisago County	MN	Chris Peterson	1991	813
157 1/8	Puslinch Twp.	ONT	Jeff Sinclair	1977	824
157 1/8	Fairfax County	VA	Chris Jackson	1986	824
157 1/8	Eaton County	MI	Bryan Coburn	1998	824
157 1/8	McHenry County	IL	Rich Matras	1991	824
157 8/8	Watonwan County	MN	Dave Ellertson	1973	828
157 8/8	McKenzie County	ND	Donald Olson	1974	828
157 8/8	Ashland County	OH	William Kucic	1985	828
157 8/8	McLean County	IL	Daryle W. Tipsord	1985	828
157 8/8	Kiowa County	KS	Royce E. Frazier	1986	828
157 8/8	Blue Earth County	MN	Tom Lacina	1987	828
157 8/8	Roane County	TN	Larry T. Cook	1988	828
157 8/8	Lake County	IL	Mike Mitten	1988	828
157 8/8	Parke County	IN	Jeff Myers	1989	828
157 8/8	Clayton County	IA	Curt Ferguson	1989	828
157 8/8	Brown County	IL	Larry Grant	1992	828
156 7/8	Chippewa County	MN	Paul D. Lundgren	1969	839
156 7/8	Johnson County	KS	Jim Laybourne	1979	839
156 7/8	Lake County	IL	Dennis P. Schor	1979	839
156 7/8	Clearwater County	MN	Dennis Engerbretson	1988	839
156 7/8	Cherokee County	IA	Dan Roberts	1982	839
156 7/8	Butler County	KS	William D. George	1986	839
156 7/8	Atoka County	OK	Kevin W. Guinn	1987	839
156 7/8	Eugenia	ONT	Ron Lusher	1987	839
156 7/8	Franklin County	IA	Ron Hansen	1998	839
156 7/8	Morrison County	MN	Stephan Felix	1992	839
156 6/8	Lincoln County	WV	Gary Smith	1978	849
156 6/8	Meigs County	OH	Brian Kelley	1982	849
156 6/8	Des Moines County	IA	Don Smith	1986	849
156 6/8	Clark County	IL	Gary Taylor	1986	849
156 6/8	Howard County	IA	Terry Larson	1987	849
156 6/8	Washington County	IL	Bruce Diedrich	1987	849
156 6/8	Walworth County	WI	Brian Strickler	1988	849
156 6/8	Miami County	OH	Gary L. Tipps	1988	849
156 6/8	Lapeer County	MI	Wayne Coulman	1998	849
156 5/8	Grant County	WI	Walter Edge	1957	858
156 5/8	Traverse County	MN	Roland L. Hausman	1968	858
156 5/8	Des Moines County	IA	E.E. Smith	1965	858
156 5/8	Nicollet County	MN	Thomas J. Merkley	1967	858
156 5/8	Queen Annes County	MD	Charles Milford Squires	1969	858
156 5/8	Wabaunsee County	KS	Tom Willard	1983	858
156 5/8	Kossuth County	IA	Ron Burton	1985	858
156 5/8	Johnson County	IA	Larry Hermanstorfer	1987	858
156 5/8	Price County	WI	Larry Halvorson	1998	858
156 5/8	Eaton County	MI	Dudley Miller, Jr.	1998	858
156 4/8	Williamson County	IL	Roy Williams	1968	868
156 4/8	Forest County	WI	Daniel Radder	1968	868
156 4/8	Jones County	IA	Gary McCormick	1977	868
156 4/8	Graham County	KS	Russell Hull	1979	868
156 4/8	Waukeshaw County	WI	Steve Hoelz	1987	868
156 4/8	McLeod County	MN	Craig Hrkal	1988	868
156 4/8	Jackson County	OH	Michel L. Cornett	1988	868
156 4/8	Osage County	KS	Gerald Britschge	1988	868

WHITE-TAILED DEER (Non-Typical Antlers)
Minimum Score: 150

Score	Area	State	Hunter's Name	Date	Rank
279 7/8	Hall County	NE	Del Austin	1962	1
257 0/8	Reno County	KS	Kenneth B. Flowler	1988	3
249 6/8	Greenwood County	KS	Clifford Pickell	1968	3
245 5/8	Vermilion County	IL	Robert E. Chestnut	1981	4
245 4/8	Chase County	KS	Douglas A. Siebert	1988	5
241 2/8	Cochrane	ALB	Dean Dwernuchuk	1984	6
238 6/8	Mahoning County	OH	Ronald K. Osborne	1986	7
237 5/8	Wilson County	KS	Gilbert Boss	1986	8
233 7/8	Greenwood County	KS	Randy Young	1989	9
232 7/8	Kiowa County	KS	Royce E. Frazier	1978	10
231 5/8	Dane County	WI	Dennis Shanks	1979	11
231 4/8	Iroquois County	IL	Sam G. Townsend	1986	12
231 0/8	Phillips County	KS	Virgil Henry	1987	13
230 6/8	Peoria County	IL	Tophil L. Simon	1984	14
229 7/8	Yuma County	CO	David "Jake" Powell	1986	15
227 6/8	Fulton County	IL	Richard Keener	1977	16
225 1/8	Walworth County	WI	F. Dan Dinelli	1992	17
224 3/8	Stevens County	WA	J.C. Baker	1987	18
224 0/8	La Salle County	IL	Ronald R. Lahman, Sr.	1989	19
222 7/8	Coles County	IL	Kim L. Boes	1989	20
222 1/8	Hancock County	IA	J.M. Monson	1977	21
222 0/8	Marion County	KS	Claude Allen	1989	22
220 7/8	Gove County	KS	Mike Shull	1986	23
220 6/8	Rock Island County	IL	John Angel	1979	24
220 3/8	Riley County	KS	Melvin D. Padgett	1989	25
219 3/8	Webster County	IA	David Propst	1987	26
219 0/8	Morrison County	MN	Michael R. Langin	1992	27
218 1/8	Clay County	IA	Blaine R. Salzkom	1970	28
217 0/8	Carroll County	IL	Noel Feather	1982	29
215 6/8	Meeker County	MN	Steve Turck	1982	30
215 5/8	Wayne County	IA	Chris Hackney	1983	31
214 4/8	Parker County	TX	George C. Courtney	1991	32
214 2/8	Lyons County	KS	Gary Dall, Jr.	1992	33
212 5/8	Allamakee County	IA	George A. Smith	1991	34
212 3/8	Martin County	IN	David D. Foote	1988	35
210 7/8	Teton County	MT	Todd Jensen	1986	36
210 6/8	Marion County	KS	Bruce Schroeder	1985	37
210 5/8	Waukesha County	WI	Gerald J. Roethle, Jr.	1991	38
210 3/8	Lac qui Parle County	MN	Steven J. Karels	1974	39
209 7/8	Richardson County	NE	Albert W. Montgomery	1989	40
209 6/8	Pulaski County	KY	Alan Sidewell	1988	41
209 2/8	McPherson County	KS	Lonnie Ensminger	1968	42
208 5/8	Buffalo County	NE	Carl Clements	1985	43
207 7/8	Otter Tail County	MN	Patrick Millard	1986	44
207 0/8	Noble County	IN	Joseph A. Fulford	1987	45
206 7/8	Smoky River	ALB	Kirby Smith	1991	46
206 0/8	Saunders County	NE	Nordean E. Bade	1964	47
205 6/8	Cottonwood County	MN	Larry Gravely	1975	48
205 4/8	Seward County	KS	Lynn Leonard	1988	49
205 3/8	Beltrami County	MN	Matt Stone	1990	50
204 1/8	Dubuque County	IA	Joe Rettenmeier	1987	51

Pope & Young White-Tailed Deer Records, Non-Typical Antlers

Score	Area	State	Hunter's Name	Date	Rank
203 7/8	Union County	OR	Joe Mengore	1982	52
203 5/8	Warren County	IA	Ted Miller	1986	53
203 4/8	Dodge County	MN	Lawrence Sowieja	1955	54
203 3/8	Adams County	IL	Elroy Little	1981	55
203 3/8	Lehigh County	PA	Craig E. Krisher	1988	55
203 08	Geauga County	CH	Rudy Grecar	1969	57
202 2/8	Clay County	SD	Patrick Hudson	1969	58
202 0/8	Clark County	KS	Dennis Rule	1982	59
201 5/8	Kane County	IL	Keith Kampert	1991	60
201 4/8	Rock Island County	IL	Jeff Maier	1989	61
201 2/8	Steams County	MN	Richard D. Berens	1991	62
201 1/8	Carroll County	IL	Mel Landwehr	1991	63
200 7/8	Morgan County	KY	Greg Powers	1989	64
200 7/8	Washington County	KS	Ronald Montague	1990	64
200 5/8	Clayton County	IA	Dorrance Arnold	1977	66
199 6/8	Jackson County	MO	Jack Hollingsworth	1989	67
199 3/8	Atchison County	KS	Kirby A. Clifton	1973	68
199 3/8	Comanche County	KS	Phillip L. Kirkland	1981	68
198 7/8	Logan County	KY	Oscar Howard	1989	70
198 6/8	Peoria County	IL	Roger Woodcock	1989	71
198 5/8	Douglas County	NE	Ivan Masher	1961	72
198 5/8	Montgomery County	IL	Earl W. Law, Jr.	1989	72
198 3/8	Lyon County	MN	Edward Matthys	1966	74
198 3/8	Reno County	KS	Greig Sims	1987	74
198 3/8	Pottawattamie County	IA	Rodney P. Stahlnecker	1991	74
198 2/8	Fulton County	IL	Mike Massingale	1991	77
198 1/8	Hocking County	OH	Hugh Cox	1954	78
197 6/8	Pratt County	KS	Mike Patton	1987	79
197 4/8	Johnson County	IA	Dennis R. Ballard	1971	80
197 4/8	Lyon County	KS	John R. Clifton	1984	80
197 3/8	Faribault County	MN	Randy Lee Sandt	1982	82
197 2/8	Nemaha County	KS	D. Jay Hartter	1990	83
197 1/8	Linn County	IA	Marsha Fairbanks	1974	84
197 1/8	Jackson County	MO	Jim Martin	1984	84
197 1/8	Bullock County	AL	Ronnie Everett	1990	84
197 0/8	Marshall County	IL	Larry Rowe	1975	87
196 7/8	Lake County	IL	Kory Lang	1991	88
196 6/8	Lawrence County	IN	John E. Johnson	1987	89
196 1/8	Edgar County	IL	Jerry R. David	1988	90
195 6/8	Dubuque County	IA	Jim H. Dougherty	1985	91
195 5/8	Martin County	MN	Ben Johnson	1973	92
195 5/8	Waushara County	WI	Randy Chamberlain	1984	92
195 4/8	Putnam County	IN	Chris M. Tanner	1982	94
195 4/8	Crawford County	IA	Larry Sparks	1985	94
195 4/8	Jessamine County	KY	Tony W. Drury	1991	94
195 0/8	Juneau County	WI	Maurice Sterba	1955	97
194 7/8	Warren County	MO	Dennis Jones	1982	98
194 5/8	Guernsey County	OH	Dick Bayer	1985	99
194 5/8	Lake County	IL	Paul H. Woit	1991	99
194 4/8	Miami County	KS	Alfred E. Smith	1990	101
194 4/8	Polk County	IA	Paul Beesley	1990	101
194 2/8	Pike County	MO	William E. Knowles	1980	103
193 7/8	Blaine County	MT	Gene Wensel	1981	104

Pope & Young White-Tailed Deer Records, Non-Typical Antlers

Score	Area	State	Hunter's Name	Date	Rank
193 7/8	Eau Claire County	WI	Greg Miller	1990	104
193 6/8	Lake County	IN	Walter Sobczak	1979	106
193 3/8	Roanoke County	VA	Randy Brookshier	1983	107
193 0/8	Lake County	IL	Steven Derkson	1989	108
192 6/8	Washington County	KS	Jim Snyder	1986	109
192 6/8	Vermilion County	IL	Ed Gudgel	1988	109
192 5/8	Republic County	KS	Don Dejmal	1983	111
192 4/8	Redwood County	MN	Mark A. Steinle	1973	112
192 1/8	Gray County	KS	Randall Koehn	1985	113
192 1/8	Brown County	OH	Paul R. Durbin	1992	113
192 0/8	Day County	SD	Doug Rumpca	1985	115
191 7/8	Du Page County	IL	Pete Heliotis	1986	116
191 6/8	Murray County	MN	Delbert Peck	1956	117
191 6/8	Preble County	OH	Claude Adkins	1989	117
191 3/8	St. Joseph County	IN	Daniel T. Karaszewski	1979	119
191 2/8	Westchester County	NY	Nick Rigano	1987	120
191 2/8	Pike County	IL	Timothy M. Fulmer	1991	120
191 1/8	Crawford County	OH	Michael B. Hoffman	1988	122
191 0/8	Pope County	MN	Ron Johnson	1985	123
190 7/8	Douglas County	KS	Leon J. Bidinger	1983	124
190 5/8	Lee County	IA	Tim Digman	1981	125
190 4/8	Licking County	OH	John McGee	1982	126
190 3/8	Saginaw County	MI	Robert Morey	1975	127
190 2/8	Isanti County	MN	Johnny J. Williams	1982	128
190 2/8	Montgomery County	PA	David S. Krempasky	1985	128
190 0/8	Douglas County	KS	Dan Norris	1977	130
190 0/8	McHenry County	IL	Edward Schultz	1984	130
189 7/8	Logan County	OH	Larry Pooler	1989	132
189 6/8	Chisago County	MN	Reinhold L. Lind	1956	133
189 5/8	Stearns County	MN	Nathan Batzel	1991	134
189 2/8	Clayton County	IA	Jim Monat	1981	135
189 2/8	Buffalo County	WI	Roger Comero	1987	135
189 1/8	Graham County	KS	Don Berry	1970	137
189 1/8	McDowell County	WV	Lonnie Wolfe	1991	137
189 0/8	Scott County	MN	Chris Rivers	1987	139
188 7/8	Marinette County	WI	James Spielvogel	1981	140
188 6/8	Adair County	MO	David C. Reid	1991	141
188 5/8	Ross County	OH	Dan Seymour	1987	142
188 3/8	Benton County	IA	Lyle Miller	1977	143
188 3/8	Rock County	WI	Steven J. Shull	1988	143
188 1/8	Barnes County	ND	William Cruff	1961	145
188 1/8	Dane County	WI	Bill Needham	1983	145
188 0/8	La Salle County	IL	Gary Tabor	1983	147
188 0/8	Buffalo County	WI	Russell G. Goldsmith	1991	147
187 7/8	Shiawassee County	MI	Joseph S. Lunkas	1978	149
187 6/8	Hitchcock County	NE	Tom Chance	1986	150
187 6/8	Bent County	CO	Chris Malden	1991	150
187 5/8	Monroe County	IA	Cecil Dicks	1961	152
187 5/8	Washburn County	WI	Russell Worman	1988	152
187 3/8	Vernon County	WI	Darrell A. Bendel	1986	154
187 2/8	Morrill County	NE	Glenn Schmidt	1975	155
187 2/8	Waupaca County	WI	Timothy J. Dercks	1991	155
186 6/8	Traverse County	MN	Roland L. Hausmann	1964	157

Pope & Young White-Tailed Deer Records, Non-Typical Antlers

Score	Area	State	Hunter's Name	Date	Rank
186 6/8	Mackinac County	MI	Steve Gorsuch	1989	157
186 5/8	Scotland County	MO	Charles Lee Smith	1984	159
186 2/8	Otter Tail County	MN	D.F. Vraspir	1959	160
186 1/8	Lake County	IL	Alan F. Benson	1990	161
186 1/8	Lyon County	KS	Edward Bess	1991	161
185 7/8	Jones County	GA	Wallace Reeves, Jr.	1973	163
185 6/8	Christian County	IL	Donald D. Stiner	1990	164
185 5/8	Anderson County	KS	Wayne Hanna	1991	165
185 4/8	Pickaway County	OH	Jerry R. Forson	1979	166
185 3/8	Allamakee County	IA	LeRoy B. Spiker	1968	167
185 3/8	Rice County	MN	Wayne Jahnke	1975	167
185 2/8	Sedgwick County	KS	Alfred Weaver	1965	169
185 1/8	Lewis County	KY	Jeremie Lee Bretz	1992	170
184 7/8	Monona County	IA	Patrick Salmen	1989	171
184 6/8	Scioto County	OH	Ryan Darnell	1990	172
184 5/8	Vinton County	OH	Dan Davis	1985	173
184 3/8	Texas County	OK	William E. Miller	1983	174
184 3/8	Black Hawk County	IA	Paul Hughson	1985	174
184 1/8	St. Charles County	MO	Larry D. Stelzer	1962	176
184 1/8	Waushara County	WI	Dwight A. Olson	1979	176
183 3/8	Lake County	MN	Christopher Harristhal	1990	178
183 5/8	Lincoln County	SD	Mervin Sterk	1985	179
183 3/8	Morrison County	MN	Ralph Hakel	1974	180
183 3/8	Fillmore County	MN	Michael M. Gehrking	1985	180
183 2/8	Holt County	NE	Lyle Ruff	1967	182
183 2/8	Christian County	MO	Roger J. Newell	1984	182
183 2/8	Riley County	KS	Larry Larson	1985	182
183 2/8	Washburn County	WI	Jerry J. Genson	1989	182
182 7/8	Arkansas County	AR	Tommy Horton	1972	186
182 7/8	Olmsted County	MN	Dan Matheson	1973	186
182 4/8	Will County	IL	Richard Heintz	1971	188
182 4/8	Macoupin County	IL	John Tevini	1991	188
182 3/8	Goodhue County	MN	Jim Danielson	1984	190
182 3/8	Warren County	IN	Gregory S. Zak	1990	190
182 2/8	Pik County	IL	Dennis Kendall	1990	192
182 1/8	Brown County	KS	Bill Butrick	1985	193
182 0/8	Albemarle County	VA	Richard A. Shifflett	1989	194
181 7/8	Marion County	IA	Roger DeMoss	1990	195
181 6/8	Adams County	IL	Festal McCarty	1967	196
181 6/8	Kiowa County	KS	Royce E. Frazier	1985	196
181 5/8	Bureau County	IL	Louis J. Guerrini	1990	198
181 5/8	Pike County	IL	Steven R. Tice	1991	198
181 4/8	Morrison County	MN	Peter De Chaine	1984	200
181 4/8	Wyoming County	WV	Bobby Smith	1985	200
181 4/8	Edgar County	IL	Dennis Gosnell	1991	200
181 3/8	Hardin County	IA	Howard Nelson	1963	203
181 3/8	Sawyer County	WI	Bill "Red" Gilbert	1989	203
181 2/8	Desha County	AR	John T. Greer	1962	205
181 2/8	Darke County	OH	Dean P. Neff	1979	205
181 2/8	Clark County	IA	Larry Bear	1991	205
181 1/8	Coles County	IL	Gerald L. Davis	1973	208
181 0/8	Knox County	OH	Don Quick	1984	209
181 0/8	Pittsburg County	OK	Harold Jones	1986	209

Pope & Young White-Tailed Deer Records, Non-Typical Antlers

Score	Area	State	Hunter's Name	Date	Rank
181 0/8	Clark County	IL	Harold A. Funk	1991	209
180 6/8	Pope County	AR	Johnny Reed	1983	212
180 5/8	Preble County	OH	James R. Whittaker	1978	213
180 5/8	Linn County	IA	Craig Whepard	1980	213
180 4/8	Teton County	MT	James Dean	1981	215
180 4/8	Buffalo County	WI	John L. Smith	1988	215
180 4/8	Butler County	KS	John Parsons	1989	215
180 4/8	Osage County	OK	James H. Farmer	1991	215
180 4/8	Jewel County	KS	Bruce Meyer	1991	215
180 4/8	Price County	WI	John Michalski	1991	215
180 1/8	Winnebago County	IA	Jim Orthel	1983	221
179 6/8	Creek County	OK	Marion Lewis	1975	222
179 6/8	Hamilton County	OH	Lawrence Ashbrook	1981	222
179 5/8	Fillmore County	MN	Wayne Pfremmer	1972	224
179 5/8	Dane County	WI	Kip Kalscheur	1989	224
179 2/8	Marion County	IA	Roger DeMoss	1982	226
179 2/8	Chippewa County	WI	Kip Knez	1986	226
179 1/8	Will County	IL	Michael Suggs	1990	228
178 6/8	Lincoln County	SD	H.L. Tuggle	1975	229
178 6/8	Madison County	IL	Michael B. Fenton	1984	229
178 5/8	Clay County	IN	Jim Tracy	1989	231
178 5/8	Ozaukee County	WI	Robert A. Wallock	1989	231
178 5/8	Ozaukee County	WI	Gerald Berres	1991	231
178 4/8	Keokuk County	IA	Ron Turner	1983	234
178 4/8	St. Croix County	WI	James Walsh	1988	234
178 3/8	Traverse County	MN	Roland L. Hausmann	1953	236
178 3/8	Mineral County	MT	Gene Wensel	1981	236
178 3/8	Finney County	KS	Randy Miller	1984	236
178 1/8	Montgomery County	OH	Jack B. Odum	1990	239
178 0/8	Jefferson County	WI	Mike Leslie	1988	240
178 0/8	Kenedy County	TX	Miguel Mireles	1991	240
177 7/8	Ross County	OH	Robert Elliott	1981	242
177 7/8	Pottawatomie County	KS	Loyd C. Flowers	1983	242
177 6/8	Pope County	MN	Roger Tollefson	1977	244
177 6/8	Delaware County	OH	Ronald Eugene Murphy	1983	244
177 4/8	Flathead County	MT	Jerry Karsky	1972	246
177 3/8	Pike County	IL	Daniel Doran	1992	247
177 1/8	Pope County	MN	Doyle Anderson	1988	248
177 0/8	Rock County	WI	Kirk C. Douglas	1987	249
177 0/8	Boone County	IA	Robert J. Van Roekel	1989	249
177 0/8	Olmsted County	MN	Leo Kuisle	1991	249
176 6/8	Dodge County	WI	Erwin C. Koehler	1957	252
176 5/8	Day County	SD	Lonnie L. Heuer	1987	253
176 5/8	Polk County	WI	Jessee Tonn	1991	253
176 3/8	Greene County	OH	Leroy M. Thompson	1982	255
176 1/8	Brandon	MAN	Larry J. Pollock	1980	256
175 7/8	Guernsey County	OH	Jack Milligan	1971	257
175 7/8	Freeborn County	MN	Douglas Swank	1979	257
175 4/8	Woodbury County	IA	Everett Gothier	1962	259
175 4/8	Belmont County	OH	Dan Clutter	1985	259
175 3/8	Grant County	MN	Lee Offerdahl	1972	261
175 3/8	Buffalo County	WI	Timothy L. Brommer	1984	261
175 3/8	Salem County	NJ	Richard Wendt	1985	261

Pope & Young White-Tailed Deer Records, Non-Typical Antlers

Score	Area	State	Hunter's Name	Date	Rank
175 2/8	McHenry County	IL	Richard G. Hickey	1988	264
175 1/8	Dubuque County	IA	Gregory Klein	1983	265
175 1/8	Cherokee County	KS	Darren Collins	1988	265
175 1/8	Franklin County	KS	Dennis N. Ballweg	1988	265
175 1/8	Wayne County	MO	Jesse Whittley, Jr.	1988	265
175 1/8	Chase County	KS	Greg Windler	1988	265
174 7/8	Waseca County	MN	Robert Barrie	1974	270
174 7/8	Des Moines County	IA	Tom Lappe	1985	270
174 4/8	Otter Tail County	MN	Don Oelschlager	1976	272
174 4/8	Benson County	ND	Curtis A. Ehnert	1977	272
174 4/8	Brown County	IL	Angela Vogel	1988	272
174 3/8	Vinton County	OH	Jack McConnell	1982	275
174 3/8	Winnebago County	IL	Dave Fisher	1986	275
174 2/8	Clay County	IA	Darrell Magnussen	1962	277
174 1/8	Charles County	MD	Robert H. Jones Sr.	1971	278
174 0/8	Delaware County	OH	Michael H. Seamster	1983	279
173 6/8	Spink County	SD	Milton Haag	1959	280
173 6/8	Douglas County	MN	John Duberowski	1980	280
173 5/8	Gray County	KS	Allen D. Bailey	1982	282
173 5/8	Pepin County	WI	Don Linse	1988	282
173 5/8	St. Louis County	MO	Michael M. Branson	1989	282
173 5/8	Chippewa County	WI	George A. Olson	1991	282
173 4/8	Barton County	KS	Norman Kimber	1967	286
173 4/8	Trumbull County	OH	Peter Bradley	1969	286
173 4/8	Renville County	MN	Larry Godejahn	1973	286
173 3/8	Pike County	IL	Ronnie Bauer	1988	289
173 0/8	Lincoln County	KS	Scott Kingery	1988	290
172 7/8	McIntosh County	OK	Clark Utley	1976	291
172 7/8	Morrison County	MN	Harlan Grams	1988	291
172 7/8	Sedgwick County	KS	Cary Renner	1989	291
172 6/8	Washburn County	WI	Clint Atkinson	1986	294
172 5/8	Trumbull County	OH	Dick Keagy	1989	295
172 4/8	Marshall County	MN	James C. Pederson	1992	296
172 3/8	Mississippi County	AR	Dennis Perkins	1990	297
172 3/8	Chariton County	MO	Dennis W. Meyers	1991	297
172 2/8	Calhoun County	MI	Roger W. Hanselman	1989	299
172 2/8	Cadogan	ALB	Howard Schreiber	1991	299
172 1/8	Green County	WI	Dean Dilly	1974	301
172 0/8	Warren County	IA	Dennis R. Jacobe	1988	302
171 7/8	Will County	IL	James Giese	1987	303
171 6/8	Dubuque County	IA	Dick Theis	1975	304
171 6/8	Vermilion County	IL	Gene Maier	1984	304
171 6/8	Leavenworth County	KS	Albert Lyle Karl	1987	304
171 6/8	Montgomery County	TN	Dennis Morris	1991	304
171 5/8	Wapello County	IA	Rex Jones	1983	308
171 5/8	Iroquois County	IL	Frank Snow	1987	308
171 4/8	Butler County	KS	Jeff Stevens	1982	310
171 3/8	Logan County	OK	Billy Wayne McBride	1989	311
171 3/8	Kane County	IL	Matthew Peterson	1991	311
171 2/8	Van Buren County	MI	David Anderson	1979	313
171 2/8	Scotts Bluff County	NE	Doug Hauser	1984	313
171 1/8	Jackson County	MI	Shawn R. Surque	1985	315
171 1/8	Birds Hill	MAN	Daniel Kowalchuk	1991	315

Pope & Young White-Tailed Deer Records, Non-Typical Antlers

Score	Area	State	Hunter's Name	Date	Rank
171 0/8	Dodge County	WI	Dallas Johnson	1955	317
171 0/8	Lee County	IA	Gary Frost	1967	317
170 7/8	Redwood County	MN	Todd G. Gilb	1982	319
170 7/8	Kleberg County	TX	Bradley Peltier	1989	319
170 6/8	Nobles County	MN	David Janssen	1973	321
170 6/8	Washtenaw County	MI	Dennis D. Clarke	1989	321
170 6/8	Anoka County	MN	Wayne Nicholson	1991	321
170 5/8	Oklahoma County	OK	Tim R. Reid	1990	324
170 4/8	Tazewell County	IL	Bret Hamilton	1982	325
170 3/8	Fairfield County	OH	Brian Morrison	1987	326
170 3/8	Fairfield County	OH	Brian Morrison	1987	326
170 2/8	Callaway County	MO	Larry Murphy	1988	328
170 1/8	Lyon County	KS	Russell Reed	1986	329
170 1/8	Cowley County	KS	Aaron Chaplin	1990	329
170 0/8	Van Buren County	IA	Gary W. Schutt	1987	331
169 6/8	Carter County	KY	Timothy Carter	1974	332
169 5/8	Dodge County	MN	Lawrence Sowieja	1973	333
169 5/8	Pike County	MO	Marlin E. Foree	1988	333
169 4/8	Branch County	MI	Roy D. Grigsby	1988	335
169 4/8	Price County	WI	James E. Johnson	1990	335
169 3/8	Emmet County	IA	Paul Love	1992	337
169 2/8	Rice County	MN	Vernon J. Kleve	1972	338
169 2/8	Schuyler	IL	Robert J. Logsdon	1981	338
169 2/8	Washington County	WI	Tony Snow	1991	338
169 0/8	Suffolk County	NY	John Bennett	1991	341
168 7/8	Meeker County	MN	Ralph Hakel	1964	342
168 7/8	Otoe County	NE	Roberto Z. Duran	1990	342
168 6/8	Olmsted County	MN	Jeff Meyer	1974	344
168 5/8	Lyon County	KS	Russell Reed	1984	345
168 5/8	Waukesha County	WI	Jeff Stanton	1991	345
168 4/8	Stearns County	MN	Robert Opatz	1987	347
168 4/8	Fulton County	IN	Dennis Kamp	1988	347
168 4/8	Pend Oreille County	WA	Aaron Coleman	1991	347
168 3/8	Jefferson County	IN	Michael Abston	1987	350
168 2/8	Washington County	OH	Mike Ferrell	1982	351
168 1/8	Ozaukee County	WI	Joe Spata	1991	352
168 0/8	Martin County	MN	Charles Sutphin	1974	353
167 7/8	Cypress River	MAN	Harvey Gagne	1987	354
167 7/8	Greenwood County	KS	Danny Linnebur	1991	354
167 6/8	Scott County	IA	Gordon Vrana	1967	356
167 6/8	Barton County	KS	Lance Hockett	1990	356
167 4/8	Iroquois County	IL	Al Weissbohn	1986	358
167 2/8	Sauk County	WI	Charles Davenport	1969	359
167 1/8	Floyd County	IA	Patrick E. Barrett	1990	360
167 0/8	Wright County	IA	Robert Filbrandt	1974	361
167 0/8	Pawnee County	NE	Ed Baburek	1987	361
166 7/8	Hubbard County	MN	Jack Smythe	1973	363
166 6/8	Kenedy County	TX	Steve Ray Dollar	1990	364
166 5/8	Shelby County	IA	Billy Custer	1968	365
166 5/8	Wabaunsee County	KS	Charles Bisnette	1991	365
166 4/8	Midland County	MI	Michael D. Pretzer	1987	367
166 3/8	Brown County	SD	Frank Bauer	1974	368
166 3/8	Okotoks	ALB	Darren Dale	1980	368

Pope & Young White-Tailed Deer Records, Non-Typical Antlers

Score	Area	State	Hunter's Name	Date	Rank
166 2/8	Linn County	IA	Guy D. Williams, Jr.	1986	370
166 2/8	Cecil County	MD	John E. Kostic	1991	370
166 0/8	Ross County	OH	Randy Johnson	1981	372
166 0/8	Pope County	AR	Donald Alan Barnett	1983	372
166 0/8	Talbot County	MD	Ritchy Eason	1987	372
165 7/8	Arkansas County	AR	Bruce Wiggins	1959	375
165 7/8	Gallatin County	KY	John C. Vetter	1977	375
165 7/8	Brown County	IL	Angela Vogel	1983	375
165 7/8	Sedgwick County	KS	Gary Raney	1988	375
165 5/8	Washington County	MS	James Goss, Jr.	1987	379
165 4/8	Boundary County	ID	Gary Stueve	1991	380
165 2/8	Lee County	IA	Gary Frost	1991	381
165 1/8	Creek County	OK	Gary Roberson	1991	382
165 0/8	Columbia County	WI	Daniel L. Golz	1987	383
165 0/8	Wabaunsee County	KS	Ron Phillips	1991	383
164 7/8	Murray County	MN	Lanny Engler	1975	385
164 7/8	Beltrami County	MN	Kelly O'Brien	1986	385
164 7/8	Bentley	ALB	Gary Bruns	1990	385
164 7/8	Plymouth County	IA	Dale E. Brock	1990	385
164 6/8	Chippewa County	MN	Steven P. Ellingson	1975	389
164 6/8	Will County	IL	Gene R. Francisco	1988	389
164 6/8	Piatt County	IL	Boomer Dolbert	1990	389
164 2/8	Rush County	KS	Shawn McHaley	1988	392
164 2/8	Lawrence County	OH	Pete G. McCloud	1990	392
164 1/8	Winona County	MN	Charles W. Benson	1974	394
164 1/8	Meeker County	MN	Mike Rollinger	1989	394
164 0/8	Guthrie County	IA	Dick Rote	1980	396
164 0/8	Lake County	IL	Ted Hysell	1990	396
164 0/8	Randolph County	IL	Scott Oathout	1991	396
163 7/8	Dickinson County	IA	Eldon L. Kraninger	1969	399
163 6/8	Kenedy County	TX	Miguel Mireles	1987	400
163 5/8	Pepin County	WI	Mike J. Breitung	1988	401
163 4/8	Hancock County	ME	Daniel D. Hardy	1990	402
163 3/8	Wapello County	IA	Rick Grooms	1990	403
163 1/8	Cherry County	NE	Walter Cady	1975	404
163 1/8	Burke County	GA	John A. "Andy" Tisdale	1989	404
163 0/8	Caddo County	OK	Donald Boling	1975	406
162 7/8	Walsh County	ND	Randy Schuster	1985	407
162 6/8	Webb County	TX	James Richter, Jr.	1977	408
162 6/8	Franklin County	OH	Randy Kelley	1991	408
162 5/8	Burnette County	WI	Scott L. Treague	1989	410
162 5/8	Columbia County	PA	Paul Weisser, Jr.	1989	410
162 5/8	Iroquois County	IL	James Albricht	1991	410
162 4/8	Houston County	MN	Russell Craig Kruse	1991	413
162 4/8	Jasper County	MO	Douglas H. Roberts	1991	413
162 2/8	Elma	MAN	Wendell Schatkowsky	1990	415
162 1/8	Jackson County	IA	Larry R. Zirkelbach	1990	416
162 0/8	Coshocton County	OH	Richard Morgan	1987	417
161 7/8	Cascade County	MT	Kits Smith	1980	418
161 7/8	Warren County	IA	Bob R. Branchcomb	1988	418
161 4/8	Butler County	KS	Dave Rogers	1989	420
161 2/8	Des Moines County	IA	Whitey Johnson	1987	421
161 1/8	Marshall County	MN	Richard Hoff	1983	422

Pope & Young White-Tailed Deer Records, Non-Typical Antlers

Score	Area	State	Hunter's Name	Date	Rank
161 0/8	Johnson County	NE	Stan Pfingsten	1988	423
160 7/8	Saginaw County	MI	Marty Massa	1986	424
160 7/8	Roane County	TN	Rodney Maynard	1986	424
160 6/8	Bremer County	IA	Steven Sims	1983	426
160 6/8	Columbiana County	OH	David Tice	1987	426
160 5/8	Adams County	IL	Ray Gedaminski	1967	428
160 5/8	Rice County	KS	Carl Gillespie	1990	428
160 4/8	McDonough County	IL	David S. Irwin	1987	430
160 3/8	Winnebago County	WI	John M. Duchatschek	1980	431
160 3/8	Jackson County	MO	Wendell Hood	1991	431
160 2/8	Lawrence County	IL	Mike Deckard	1978	433
160 2/8	Scott County	IA	Jeffrey R. Coonts	1989	433
160 0/8	Gallatin County	KY	William J. Epeards	1980	435
160 0/8	Rockingham County	NC	Michael R. Chrismon	1987	435
159 7/8	Edmonton	ALB	Brian Bruce	1981	437
159 7/8	Huron County	OH	Donald W. Howard	1984	437
159 7/8	Huron County	OH	John R. Gockstetter	1984	437
159 6/8	Greene County	AR	Randy Ladd	1985	440
159 4/8	McPherson County	KS	Kenneth L. Vogts	1979	441
159 3/8	Vernon County	WI	Daniel F. Malin	1986	442
159 3/8	Brown County	IL	Angela Vogel	1987	442
159 1/8	Scott County	KY	Vic Morrison	1972	444
159 0/8	Lake County	IL	Robert H. Fugett	1976	445
159 0/8	Sullivan County	IN	Steve Hobbs	1980	445
158 7/8	Buffalo County	WI	Ted Bauer	1984	447
158 7/8	Washtenaw County	MI	Larry R. Lange	1984	447
158 7/8	Monroe County	IL	Wayne Doerr	1987	447
158 6/8	Joe Daviess County	IL	Gerald J. Dupasquier	1987	450
158 5/8	Sullivan County	IN	John P. Hale	1986	451
158 4/8	Winona County	MN	Randy SuPalla	1985	452
158 3/8	Morrison County	MN	Duane Rodine	1987	453
158 2/8	La Salle County	IL	John Thomas	1988	454
158 1/8	Jackson County	MI	Kim H. Whittman	1982	455
157 7/8	Dane County	WI	Donald W. Pache	1982	456
157 6/8	Lincoln County	SD	Mac Butler	1987	457
157 5/8	Black Hawk County	IA	Darrell Zacharias	1976	458
157 2/8	Crawford County	IA	Scott Pelino	1990	459
157 2/8	Montgomery County	IL	Charles O. Herman III	1991	459
157 1/8	Rock County	WI	Daniel T. Steinke	1982	461
156 6/8	Prince Georges County	MD	Anthony C. Malpasso	1979	462
156 6/8	Jackson County	MO	Daniel Johnson	1986	462
156 4/8	Winnebago County	IL	Jim Dorney	1975	464
156 4/8	Monroe County	NY	David Stymus	1991	464
156 3/8	Boulder County	CO	Guy-Maurice Algier	1988	466
156 2/8	Holt County	NE	Darrell Clyde	1963	467
156 2/8	Meriwether County	GA	William Clark Brown	1990	467
156 1/8	Cottonwood County	MN	Joe Earl	1959	469
156 1/8	Lake County	IL	Mike Mitten	1984	469
156 1/8	Walworth County	WI	Al Lehman	1988	469
156 0/8	Stewart County	TN	Ronald M. Widner	1974	472
156 0/8	Lake County	SD	Lonnie Iverson	1987	472
155 6/8	Sedgwick County	KS	Keith Jopp	1987	474
155 4/8	Pottawatomie County	KS	Richard L. Ruetti	1970	475

Pope & Young White-Tailed Deer Records, Non-Typical Antlers

Score	Area	State	Hunter's Name	Date	Rank
155 4/8	Douglas County	MN	Al Ratajesak	1986	475
155 4/8	Fayette County	IA	James E. Smith	1991	475
155 3/8	Winona County	MN	John W. Zahrte	1974	478
155 3/8	Morton County	ND	Dennis Simenson	1981	478
155 3/8	Vigo County	IN	Lowell Leturgez	1991	478
155 0/8	McCreary County	KY	Eddie Howard	1985	481
154 7/8	Calhoun County	MI	Norman E. Nuding	1982	482
154 6/8	Marshall County	IN	Sennett Dietl	1965	483
154 4/8	Marinette County	WI	LeRoy Olson	1974	484
154 3/8	Morrow County	OH	Nancy Shade	1982	485
154 1/8	Butler County	KY	Dolores G. Renfrow	1988	486
153 7/8	Bayfield County	WI	Claude B. Butler	1954	487
153 7/8	Branch County	MI	Keith Ackerman	1973	487
153 7/8	Wabasha County	MN	Robert W. Mann	1991	487
153 6/8	Custer County	SD	Bennie Spring	1961	490
153 3/8	Blue Earth County	MN	Maynard L. Nelson	1968	491
153 3/8	Juneau County	WI	Jeffery J. Scott	1991	491
153 2/8	Orleans County	NY	Randy Piedmonte	1987	493
153 1/8	Richland County	ND	Lamarr Van Dame	1992	494
153 0/8	Ripley County	IN	Robert H. Pitt	1970	495
153 0/8	Lee County	AL	Leonard Hochstedler	1975	495
153 0/8	Lake County	IL	Steve E. Menter	1990	495
152 5/8	Mercer County	IL	Kenneth E. Yeater	1990	498
152 3/8	Allegan County	MI	Elwood Snell	1947	499
152 2/8	Clay County	KS	Robert D. Ridley	1987	500
152 2/8	Sauk County	WI	Jane Nelson	1989	500
152 2/8	Westmoreland County	PA	Louis Dodaro	1991	500
151 6/8	Van Buren County	MI	Rex S. Millard	1986	503
151 6/8	Florence County	WI	Carole M. Englebert	1986	503
151 5/8	McIntosh County	ND	Craig Lambrecht	1980	505
151 5/8	Hunterdon County	NJ	Jeff Anderson	1982	505
151 5/8	Barry County	MI	Donald G. Cordray	1989	505
151 3/8	Scott County	KY	Johnny Mulberry	1982	508
151 3/8	Coshocton County	OH	William Randles	1983	508
151 2/8	Anoka County	MN	Mike Hiltner	1988	510
150 7/8	Cumberland County	NJ	Bob Eisele	1980	511
150 5/8	Berkshire County	MA	Chris Lawson	1988	512
150 4/8	Jackson County	IL	Carl D. Todd	1982	513
150 4/8	Suffolk County	NY	John Bennett	1990	513
150 3/8	Harnett County	NC	Neil Vernon Wilson	1989	515
150 2/8	Cottonwood County	MN	Matthew M. Peacock	1989	516

Venison Recipes

Readers of *Deer & Deer Hunting* magazine are as serious about cooking as they are hunting white-tailed deer. A few years ago, readers were asked to send the magazine their favorite venison recipes. The response was tremendous — several hundred readers responded, providing countless tasty recipes, leading to the printing of *301 Venison Recipes: The Ultimate Deer Hunter's Cookbook*.

The next 12 pages include samples of the recipes. Learn how to prepare delicious dishes such as pot roasts, chops, stew, chili, and even venison jerky and sausage!

Salisbury Steak

1-1/2 pounds ground venison
1/2 cup dry bread crumbs
1/4 cup onions, chopped fine
1/2 cup water
2 cans beefy mushroom soup
1 egg, slightly beaten
1/8 teaspoon pepper

Mix thoroughly: 1/4 cup soup, venison, bread crumbs, egg, onion and pepper. Shape firmly into 6 patties. In skillet brown patties; pour off fat. Stir in remaining soup and 1/2 cup water. Cover. Cook over low heat 20 minutes or until done. Stir occasionally. Serve with mashed potatoes and use the soup as gravy for potatoes. Serves 6.

Ed Baugrud
Neenah, WI

Venison Loins In Gravy

1 pound venison cut 1/2-inch to 1-inch thick
1/3 cup margarine
2 tablespoons vegetable oil
3/4 cup flour
1 teaspoon salt
1 tablespoon black pepper
1 teaspoon garlic powder
1 (4 ounce) can mushrooms, drained
1 10- 1/2 ounce can cream of mushroom soup
1 can water

Rinse venison with cold water and drain well.
Mix remaining dry ingredients in a bowl large enough so the venison can be added. Cover bowl and shake well until venison is coated with flour mix. Place in skillet. Brown on medium heat 5 minutes per side. Remove from skillet and brown remaining venison, if necessary. Drain skillet. Place all venison in skillet. Add mushrooms, cream of mushroom soup, and water to venison in that order. Bring to a boil, while stirring soup mix in. Reduce heat to low, cover and simmer 45 minutes to 1 hour. Serve hot.

Barry McCombs, Williamsburg, IA

Venison Pot Roast

3 to 4 pound top round or shoulder roast
Flour
2 tablespoons cooking oil
Pepper
1 clove garlic
1 envelope onion-mushroom soup mix
5 large carrots
5 potatoes with skin, quartered
1 tablespoon cornstarch

Roll roast in flour. Heat oil in a Dutch oven and brown the roast
in oil. Sprinkle roast with pepper. Add garlic and contents of the
soup envelope to the pot, along with 2 cups of hot water. Cover
the Dutch oven and simmer until the meat is nearly tender,
from 1-1/2 to 2 hours. Turn the roast a couple of times during
the cooking. Add vegetables to the pot. Simmer another 30 minutes. Remove the meat and vegetables to a heated platter.
Thicken the sauce with cornstarch dissolved in 1/2 cup of cold
water. Stir and heat until the gravy is thick. Served 4 to 6.

Dutch Oven Venison Roast

6 strips bacon
1 medium to large venison roast
5 cloves, garlic, sliced
Salt and pepper
Browning sauce
Flour
1 large can golden mushroom soup
1/2 can water
1 large onion
1 4-ounce can mushrooms, drained

Cook bacon until crisp in large frying pan. Remove bacon,
crush and set aside. Leave bacon fat in pan. Stick roast with
knife and insert small slivers of garlic. Coat roast with
browning sauce and salt and pepper before dusting with flour.
Heat bacon fat and sear roast on all sides until thoroughly
browned. Then set aside for a moment. Meanwhile, in Dutch
oven or other deep cooking pot, mix your can of mushroom
soup with 1/2 can of water. Remove enough rings from onion
to cover the roast, separate them and set aside. Dice remain-
der of onion and add to mushroom soup; heat, add salt and
pepper to taste. Color this mixture slightly with browning

sauce. At this point, place a rack in the bottom of your Dutch oven or other deep pot and place the roast on the rack. Secure onion rings on top of roast with wooden toothpicks. Sprinkle crushed bacon over top of roast and do the same with mushrooms. Finally, cover and cook very slowly for about 2 hours or until done.

Venison Swiss Steak, Texas Style

2 pounds venison steak or chops, boned
2 cans cream of mushroom soup
2 stalks celery, chopped
Salt & pepper to taste
1 medium onion, chopped fine
1 can water
2 medium carrots, chopped fine

Brown the meat in an iron skillet, using some cooking oil. Add the 2 cans of mushroom soup and one can of water. Add onions, carrots and celery. Cover and let simmer for three hours, stirring occasionally. Salt and pepper to taste. Serve with potatoes or rice. Serves 4.

Paul Heft
Houston, TX

Deer Steak and Gravy

3 pounds deer steak   2 teaspoons salt
1 medium onion   1 teaspoon pepper
1 bell pepper   1 can cream of mushroom soup
1 cup flour   1/2 cup oil

Slice onion and pepper in rings. Brown onion and pepper lightly in oil. Remove and drain. Mix flour, salt and pepper. Pound into trimmed deer steaks. Brown on both sides. Drain off oil.
Place onion and pepper rings on top of steak and spread soup on top of all. Add water to almost cover meat. Simmer adding water as needed until meat is tender.

Everitt Chesser
Springfield, KY

Venison Steak with Mushrooms

2 pounds venison steak   Milk
2 10-ounce cans mushroom soup   Flour
1 cup mushrooms chopped   Oil

Cut venison steak in serving size pieces. Marinate in milk
overnight or at least 4 hours. Dredge in flour; brown in small
amount of oil over medium heat. Remove meat from skillet. Add to
pan drippings; mushroom soup, chopped mushrooms and 2 cans
milk. Stir this mixture well making a rich gravy. Return meat to
skillet and simmer over low heat for approximately 30 minutes or
until meat is tender. Serve with wild rice or mashed potatoes.

Jack Toms, Jr.
Danville, IL

Sauteed Deer Chops

1/4 pound mushrooms thinly sliced
8 deer chops   Sage
1/2 stick butter   Garlic powder
1 medium onion

Shear edges of chops with sharp knife to prevent the meat from
curling when being cooked. Rub meat with sage and sprinkle
with garlic powder. Saute onion and mushrooms in butter until
almost done. Add 4 chops and cook 2 minutes on both sides.
Remove when done and cook remaining 4 chops. When last 4
chops are done, the onions and mushrooms should be done also.

Charles H. Coppage
Church Hill, MD

SAUCES

Smokey B.B.Q. Marinade

1/4 cup vinegar   1/2 cup water
2 tablespoons sugar   1/2 cup catsup
1 teaspoon mustard sauce   1 onion, diced
1/2 teaspoon cayenne pepper   2 tablespoons Worcestershire

Mix all ingredients except catsup and Worcestershire sauce.
Simmer 10 minutes. Add remaining ingredients and bring to a boil.

Sweet-Sour Marinade

1 cup unsweetened pineapple juice
1-1/2 cups sherry wine
1/2 cup red wine vinegar
2 tablespoons granulated garlic
1/2 cup soy sauce
1 cup sugar

Mix and cover meat of choice. Refrigerate. Marinate for 1 day or longer.

SALADS

Marinated Vegetable Salad With Venison

1/2 cauliflower, cut into flowerettes
1 cup cooked green beans
1 cup cooked carrots
1/2 cup sliced green pepper
3/4 cup sliced mushrooms
2 large onions, sliced
1 can black or green pitted olives
1/2 cup sliced mushrooms
1 can sliced pimentos (2 ounces) or 1/2 cup sliced radishes

Dressing

1/3 cup oil
5 tablespoons lemon juice
2 tablespoons cider vinegar
1 teaspoon sugar
1/4 teaspoon cayenne pepper
2 teaspoons salt
1/4 teaspoon black pepper
1/4 teaspoon dried dill leaves
1 pound leftover venison
2 teaspoons dried oregano leaves

Cut the venison into small pieces. Combine in a large bowl all the ingredients for the salad.
Prepare dressing: Mix all ingredients well in a separate bowl.
Pour dressing over the vegetable meat mixture. Cover and chill overnight, stirring once or twice.
Drain dressing if too liquidy; transfer salad to salad bowl and serve well chilled. Serves 4.

SAUSAGE/JERKY

Venison Salami

3 pounds ground venison
3 tablespoons tender quick curing salt
1 teaspoon garlic powder
2 teaspoons liquid smoke
1/4 teaspoon onion powder
1 tablespoon mustard seed
1 cup water-optional
Pepper

In bowl mix venison with seasoning. Add pepper for desired hotness. Make mixture into 2x8x10-inch rolls. If mixture is too dry to roll, add water. Wrap rolls in foil and refrigerate 24 hours. Poke holes in foil with a fork. Put rolls in roaster. Cover with cold water and boil for 1 hour.

Charles Barker
Eagle, MI

Deer Sausage

6 pounds of deer meat (boned and no fat)
3 pork sausages (mild, medium or hot)
6 teaspoons salt
2 teaspoons red pepper
2 teaspoons brown sugar
3 teaspoons allspice
4 teaspoons sage
2 teaspoons black pepper

Combine all ingredients and run through meat grinder. Wrap in plastic and freezer paper, freeze for future use.

Ron Tate
Bartlesville, OK

Italian Venison Sausages

2 pounds venison, ground
1 pound fresh lean pork
3 garlic cloves, minced
2 tablespoons salt
2 tablespoons pepper (continued on next page)

1/2 teaspoon oregano leaves
1 tablespoon Italian seasoning
1-1/2 cups white wine
4 ounces sausage casing

Mix the ingredients and blend well. Stuff venison sausage into
casings and twist into 6-inch-long links. Sausage should be
about 1 inch thick, it will expand when cooking. Sausage can
also be used in patties. Make large amounts of sausage, then
divide it into meal-sized portions, wrap, and freeze. Enjoy
sausages for lunch and dinner meats, or add them to tomato
sauce and serve with pasta. Also try pizza with sliced sausage
and use in recipes.

Deer Jerky

Slice lean meat not more than 1/4-inch thick.
For 1 pound of meat mix:
1/2 teaspoon salt
1/4 teaspoon pepper
1/2 teaspoon onion powder
1/4 teaspoon Worcestershire sauce
1/4 teaspoon garlic powder
3 drops of Tabasco sauce
4 teaspoons vinegar
1 teaspoon liquid smoke

Dissolve in just enough water to cover meat. Weight down and
refrigerate 24 hours. Drain and pat dry with paper towel. Lay
on oven rack and bake at 150 degrees with oven door slightly
ajar. When dry, store in airtight containers. Will keep a year.

Ralph Krepp
Franklin, PA

SOUPS/CHILIS

Venison Vegetable Stew

3 pounds venison stew meat, cut 1-inch thick
3 tablespoons oil or shortening
1-1/2 cups water
1/2 cup beer
2 envelopes (8 ounces each)
onion gravy mix   (continued on next page)

6 parsnips, cut up or small
potatoes
1 bay leaf
1/4 teaspoon ground thyme
6 carrots, cut up
1 tablespoon brown sugar
1 cup frozen peas

Brown venison in oil in large Dutch oven. Combine water, beer, gravy mix, brown sugar, bay leaf and thyme; add to pot. Cover and simmer 1 hour or until almost fork tender, stirring occasionally. Add vegetables, cook 20 minutes. Makes 6 servings.

Hunter's Venison Stew

3 pounds venison, cubed and fried in butter
3 leeks, cut up
4 cloves garlic
2 teaspoons oregano
1/2 bottle hearty red wine
2 small cans tomato paste
8 tablespoons olive oil
2 large cans pitted black olives, sliced
2 red peppers seeded and cut in strips

Heat oil and simmer leeks, peppers and garlic until soft. Add oregano, tomato paste and wine. Simmer until tasty and add venison and sliced olives. Layer over cooked lasagna noodles.

Venison Camp Chili

2 pounds ground venison
1 large onion, diced
1 16-ounce can white beans
1 16-ounce can kidney beans
Dash Tabasco sauce
1 chili pepper
1-2 teaspoons chili powder
1 cup diced celery
3 16-ounce stewed tomatoes
Dash sugar
8 ounce glass of wine

Brown venison and onions in a large kettle. Add Tabasco, chili pepper, celery, stewed tomatoes and sugar. Simmer for 1 hour in large kettle. Add the beans and chili powder and cook at low heat for 10 minutes.

After The Hunt Stew

2 pounds venison, cut into 1 inch cubes
1 tablespoon Worcestershire sauce
2 tablespoons cooking oil   1/4 cup brown sugar
1 cup carrots, sliced   2 tablespoons horseradish
1 cup water   1 teaspoon salt
3 teaspoons corn starch   4 potatoes, sliced
1 cup onions, sliced   5 stalks of celery
1/4 cup white wine

In a skillet, brown meat in cooking oil. Place meat in a slow
cooker (Crockpot). Add all ingredients, cover and cook for 3
hours on high. Before serving, you may need to thicken the stew,
by adding cornstarch. Serve with bread and butter. Serves 4.

Joe Bontke
Long Valley, NJ

Trout's Bow Hunt Deer Stew

1-2 pounds venison (front shoulder or   1 cup ketchup
  neck meat) cut into 1-inch pieces   1 cup tomato juice
1/2 large onion, chopped   1/4 cup lemon juice
3 medium potatoes, chopped   1/4 cup oil
2 large carrots, chopped   2 tablespoons margarine
3 stalks of celery, chopped   3 ounces
                                           Worcestershire sauce
1 green pepper, chopped   3 ounces steak sauce
1 cup white cooking wine   10 drops Tabasco
1 clove garlic   Salt, pepper, chives,
Parsley
1 12-ounce bottle of beer   1 15-ounce can of corn

Heat margarine and oil in stew pot. Add green pepper and
onion. When they get soft add the deer meat, and let cook for 5
minutes without a cover on. Add seasonings, wine,
Worcestershire sauce, A-1 Steak Sauce and Tabasco and cook
for 10 minutes, without a cover.
Next add lemon juice, ketchup, tomato juice, garlic and celery
and cook for 30 minutes with a cover on. Stir occasionally.
Add carrots, potatoes, beer, corn and water, (if needed). Cook
covered for 45 minutes. Continue cooking until meat is tender.
Flour and water to thicken if necessary.

William D. Trout, Jr., Bridgeton, NJ

Forkhorn Stew

2-3 pounds stew meat, cubed
5 large potatoes, cubed
4 cups cabbage, diced
2 cups cauliflower
1 large carrot, sliced
2 sticks celery, sliced
Worcestershire sauce

1 medium onion, diced
1/2 bell pepper, diced
1 teaspoon salt
1 teaspoon pepper
1/4 teaspoon garlic salt
1 tablespoon

Place cubed tenderloin in big stew pot and cover with water, about 1/2 inch over meat. Cook over medium heat until meat is just about done and you have a good broth. Add rest of your ingredients and a cup or two of water. Stir occasionally. Cook until all ingredients are done.

Douglas Carney
Hershey, PA

Venison White Stew

1-1/2 to 2 pounds venison
(1 inch or smaller chunks)
2 pork bones (or beef bones)
2 cans beef broth
2 onions, diced
1 pound of carrots (peel and cut to desired length)

4 bay leaves
1 pint whipping cream
2 garlic cloves, minced (optional)
Salt, pepper, flour
Vinegar (served on the side)
Potatoes or rice

In a large pot (with cover), cook venison chunks, bones, beef broth, and onions approximately 2 hours over medium heat. Add spices as soon as it comes to a boil. After 2 hours, remove the bones and discard. Add cream and flour and obtain desired thickness of gravy. Cook carrots in a separate pot and add after gravy is completed. Simmer for 15 minutes.
Cook potatoes or rice separately (mashed potatoes work well). Serve on bed of mashed potatoes or rice. Add vinegar to taste.

Howard T. Martin
Eau Galle, WI

Venison Chili

4 pounds ground or
1/2- inch cubes venison
2 medium onions chopped

1 green pepper chopped
2 cloves of garlic minced

1 teaspoon jalapeno peppers chopped

6 tablespoons oil

8 tablespoons chili powder
1 tablespoon ground cumin

2 teaspoons garlic salt
1/4 teaspoon Tabasco
or to taste
1 teaspoon oregano
1 28-ounce can whole
tomatoes
1 12-ounce can tomato
sauce
1 6-ounce can tomato
paste
1 4-ounce can diced
green chilies
2 bay leaves
2 cans of beer

Saute vegetables in 2 tablespoons of oil until onions are transparent. Set aside. Brown venison in 4 tablespoons of oil. Combine with vegetables in a large pot. Combine spices and 1 can of beer and let stand a few minutes. Add spice/beer mixture, whole tomatoes, tomato sauce, tomato paste, chilies, bay leaves and another can of beer. Cover and simmer on low for 3 hours, stirring often.

Forty Below Chili

4 pounds venison, ground
1 dash red pepper, crushed
2 medium onions, chopped
2 24-ounce cans tomato paste
2 tablespoons vinegar
1-2 tablespoons chili powder
1 teaspoon Tabasco sauce
1 pound bacon, chopped
2 tablespoons cumin, ground

2 cans beer
1 tablespoon MSG
1-2 cloves garlic, minced
1 tablespoon oregano
1 teaspoon Worcestershire sauce
2 tablespoons bacon drippings
1 tablespoon black pepper
1 can kidney beans

In a large chili pot, combine tomato sauce, tomato paste, beer, chopped peppers, chili powder, vinegar, Tabasco sauce, cumin, crushed red pepper, oregano, Worcestershire sauce, salt and pepper; bring to a simmer. In a large frying pan cook bacon until crisp, add it and 2 tablespoons drippings to chili pot. Brown meat, onions, garlic and MSG a little at a time and add to chili pot. Cover pot and simmer for one hour. Add kidney beans with liquid. Simmer for 1/2 hour more.

Venison Chili Beans

3 slices thick bacon
2 pounds venison, diced
1 pound red kidney beans
2 12-ounce cans of beer
6 large tomatoes, chopped

3 tablespoons chili powder
1 tablespoons ground cumin
1 tablespoons dried oregano
2 teaspoons Worcestershire sauce
1 teaspoon cornmeal

Rinse and cover beans with 2 quarts of water and soak overnight. Boil beans with the liquid, lower heat and simmer for two hours. Cook bacon until crisp, remove bacon from pan and brown venison in bacon drippings. Add beer, tomatoes, chili powder, cumin, oregano and Worcestershire sauce. Add beans to sauce. Bring to a boil, reduce heat and simmer 1 hour. Crumble bacon and add to chili. Then stir cornmeal into three tablespoons of water and add to mix (this thickens chili). Bring to a boil. Reduce heat and simmer 20 minutes more. Ranchers make this in huge quantities for barbecues. We often make double or triple recipes with tougher cuts and trimmings when we butcher deer or other game such as elk, antelope or moose. With careful wrapping, meal-size portions keep nicely for about six months.

Mexican Breakfast

Try this spicy dish for an early morning start.

Leftover cooked venison,
   sliced into thin
strips (1/4 pound for two)
1 onion, chopped
1 pepper, chopped
1 clove garlic

Salt and pepper
2 tablespoons oil
2 tablespoons butter
1/4 cup chopped tomato
4 eggs

Saute peppers, onions and garlic in heated oil until soft. Add meat for 5 minutes. Add tomato, beat eggs with pinch of salt and pepper. Add to pan. Turn up heat, cook 3 to 4 minutes. Check and turn when starting to harden; cook 2 minutes more.

Making Good Sense of Scents

In 1994, *Deer & Deer Hunting* magazine published the results of the first nationwide survey on how and why deer hunters use scents to improve their chances for success.

The findings came from a 40-question survey about scents and scent eliminators. More than 2,200 readers responded to the survey, offering insight into their personal hunting practices. Here's a sample of what has worked for them:

Douglas A. Sutfin, Michigan: "I cut the tarsal glands from bucks I've shot, but I always use them on different land from where the buck was taken. I believe this makes it difficult for deer to identify the buck's smell. I tie these glands near or over the scrape I am hunting. In one instance, the scrape doubled in size overnight the second night after I hung the glands. The brush and trees were torn up badly. On the third night the tarsal glands were missing. I never found them again."

Barry Blanchard, Louisiana: "In the early season I killed a young doe and removed her full bladder. I poured it into a spray bottle, adjusted it for a fine spray, and sprayed it in 15- to 20-inch circles around some rubs I found near a watering hole. When I want the deer to avoid an area, I spray deodorant (Right Guard) along the trail and around the area. This forces them to take a trail that favors my stand site."

Nathan Schuldt, Minnesota: "I spray scents on the tail and nose of my decoy, hoping to make the setup more realistic. I also place scent in canisters set under the decoy, and

around my stand."

Gary Amon, Connecticut: "I cut the tarsal glands from deer I've shot and hang them near my stand the next time I hunt."

Michael J. Mitchell, Wisconsin: "Deer always followed a trail too far from my stand. I put paper toweling under my arms as I walked to the stand, then hung the toweling on their preferred trail. This turned them back onto a trail that went past my stand."

Victor Keam, Ontario, Canada: "I often use doe-in-heat lure in a canister with knitting wool that I have cut into 4- to 6-inch pieces. These pieces are easy to tie to twigs or branches at various levels to lead bucks past me."

Gary Sane, North Carolina: "After finding a fresh scrape, I carefully add a few drops of doe-in-heat scent, and then use a small stick to lightly scrape the dirt. I revisit it and repeat the process in three days, and then two days, and then every day until I harvest the buck. It has yet to fail."

Bryan G. Zeringue, Louisiana: "I have used a string and pulley to put my scent dripper about 100 feet away without walking into the area."

Thomas R. O'Connor, New York: "I attach a paper clip to a (scent-soaked) tampon, and then use unscented dental floss to hang it 2 feet off the ground. I can then store this in a bottle when I'm not using it."

Bill Grieb, New Jersey: "I believe in keeping as scent-free as possible. That's why I wear knee-high rubber boots, and use anti-bacterial soaps and scent-free laundry detergent. I rate spray-on scent-eliminators as ineffective. During bow season I keep a short GI haircut, and don't smoke or drink. I don't grow a beard, and I shave my arm pits to eliminate odors. I spray red fox urine on my boots and at the base of my tree stand. When still-hunting, I keep a stiff turkey feather in my hat with a fox-scented cotton ball tied to its end."

David N. Baxter, Pennsylvania: "When I'm about 15 to 20 yards from my stand I circle it while sprinkling rutting buck and doe-in-heat lure as I walk."

Mike Moutoux, Ohio: "I make scent trails and a mock scrape upwind of me in a shooting lane. This helps to focus the deer's attention away from me."

Terry Whitmer, Nebraska: "I once used apple jelly and a roast

Have you seen deer react negatively to an artificial scent?
Yes 53.6%
No 29.3%
Not sure 17.1%

Have you seen deer react positively to an artificial scent?
Yes 80.5%
No 10.7%
Not sure 8.8%

beef sandwich to attract a doe from 80 yards away. I've also used anise oil, which they sniff without being alerted. In most cases I use cover scents on my clothes, cotton balls for liquid scents, and I hang deer parts for attractants."

Bruce Roeder, Pennsylvania: "During the rut, I put out several glass canisters with cotton balls saturated with full rut doe-in-estrus scent. Sometimes I leave a trail leading to the canisters."

Dave Mauer, Indiana: "I save the urine from any deer I kill, buck or doe, and store it in a clean bottle. I then use it in mock scrapes 20 yards from my tree stand, usually for bow-hunting but sometimes for gun-hunting. I have killed several deer with this method. It causes deer to stop and sniff the scrape, giving me a good bow shot."

Bruce Cline, Michigan: "I like to still-hunt through heavy cover

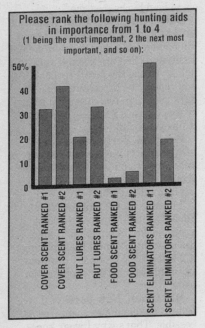

Please rank the following hunting aids in importance from 1 to 4
(1 being the most important, 2 the next most important, and so on):

near known bedding areas while using boot scent pads. I'll then take a stand downwind from my approach and watch my back-trail."

Dave Nelson, New York: "I use an eye dropper to make a trail toward a film canister near my stand. I start off with one drop every two steps and increase the number of drops as I get closer to the canister."

Bill Maves, Wisconsin: "I'll save a tarsal gland from a big buck, freeze it if necessary, and then when I find a good scrape and the conditions are right during the rut, I tie it on a boot. I then visit the scrape, and set up downwind from my trail and the scrape.

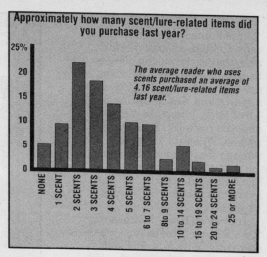

The average reader who uses scents purchased an average of 4.16 scent/lure-related items last year.

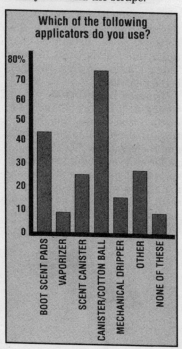

"I once used this technique with the tarsal gland of a 10-pointer. After walking into the scrape, and backing away and setting up downwind, an 8-pointer with an 18-inch spread came in and hit the track. He hit the brakes and wouldn't cross that scent line. He jerked up his head and scanned the area where I had spread the scent. He literally backed right toward me for an easy bow shot."

Dennie Kincaid Jr., West Virginia: "I like to use doe-in-heat lure in film canisters while using calls. I freshen the canisters with new lure each time before I put them out. I distribute them completely around my stand. Besides rattling, the calls I use are bleats, soft buck grunts, doe grunts, and the breeding bellow of a doe. I've used these techniques to call in different-aged bucks and does."

Steve Rathlen, Florida: "I stop about 200 yards from my stand, tie a gauze drag rag to my boot, wet it with doe-in-heat lure, and then finish my walk. When I reach my stand, I hang film canisters in my shooting lanes."

Bradley R. Block, Wisconsin: "I once hunted a buck that always came through an area 50 yards away, but there was no place to hang a stand there. I put some doe-in-heat lure on a rag, tied on a string, and tied the string to a 6-foot stick. I used the stick to drag the rag 6 feet from where I walked. When the buck came through that night and smelled the scent, ... he followed the scent line directly in front of my stand. I shot him through both lungs at 12 yards."

Jeffrey J. Berg, Minnesota: "I walk along an open area where deer cross. With a 12-foot stick and scent-covered rag at the end, I try to walk to where I expect a buck to come out. I drag the scent rag with the stick so that he will cross the scent line before he reaches my trail, and hope he follows the scent. The last time I tried this, I grunted in a big buck (maybe 150s Boone & Crockett) until he was so close I spooked him when I tried to get a shot. It still hurts!"

John W. Miller Jr., Delaware: "I put rut lure on sweat bands and then put them on my boots when walking to my stand. One time, before I reached my stand, I had a buck follow my trail, grunting all the way."

Jimmy Nealey, Alabama: "When bow-hunting, I set out film canisters with rut lure at known yardages. This helps bring deer into range."

Kevin McLaughlin, Wisconsin: "I hang two or three rags with doe-in-heat lure upwind of where I expect deer to pass within good range. I hang the rags head high so deer will step up into them, which usually exposes their heart area. I usually

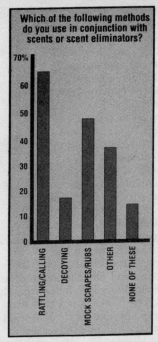

Which of the following methods do you use in conjunction with scents or scent eliminators?

set up so the deer passes between the rags and me. That way, when he stops, he will usually be quartering and looking away from me. This allows me to draw without being detected."

Thomas L. Atkinson, Georgia: "I find a rub line leading to a food source, then back-track it about 400 to 500 yards, and then create a mock scrape under an overhanging branch. I sprinkle the scrape and surrounding bushes with a doe-in-heat scent. This works great in the pre-rut. In 1992 I killed a 9-point buck as he sniffed my trail."

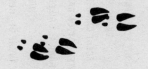

Use Home Remedies to Fool a Whitetail's Nose

The 1994 *Deer & Deer Hunting* scent survey found 22 percent of the respondents make or collect their lures, scent eliminators and cover scents. Here are some home-brewed suggestions:

Carol Eberhard, Arkansas: "I clip cedar sprigs, put them in a pillow case, and throw them in the washer with my clothes without detergent. I also throw the pillow case in the drier afterward. When walking to my stand, I step in cow or horse manure to hide the smell of my boots. Natural scents work best.

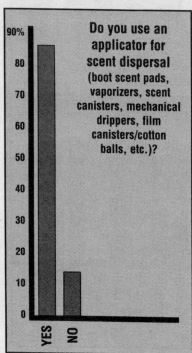

Cedar sprigs and cow flops are free!"

Keith Jones, Pennsylvania: "I remove the tarsal glands from every buck I harvest during the pre-rut or rut, and freeze them for the following year. They usually smell pretty strong by then. I attach them to a tree branch with a clothes pin near a trail or mock scrape. Nothing works better than Mother Nature."

Mike Phillips, Tennessee: "I go to my local slaughterhouse before each weekend during deer season and remove the tarsal glands from deer brought in by other hunters. I hang them around my stand during the rut."

Jimmy Elliston, Texas: "After someone has killed a deer, I rub the hide, especially the tarsal glands, on my clothes. Also, cedar rubbed on your clothes works well."

Brad Johnson, Iowa: "My best success is with cow manure, spreading it up to my waist."

Clarence Wilfong Jr., Michigan: "I collect secretions from the interdigital glands of deer I kill. I also freeze and reuse tarsal glands with scents appropriate to the pre-rut, rut or post-rut. In addition, I've found that peanut butter is irresistible to young deer, and works well as a cover scent."

Butch Heine, Maryland: "I drain the bladder of a freshly killed buck or doe into two clean baby food jars. I then remove both tarsal glands, place one in each jar, and refrigerate. The next time I hunt, I put on rubber gloves, remove the tarsal glands from the jar, and place them around my stand. I always pick up the glands and restore them after each hunt."

Wil J. Erleau, Wisconsin: "After the first deer is down, I remove the metatarsal glands if it's a doe, and the genitals if it's a buck. I then use these on a drag string and circle each of our stands."

Ms. Leslie Randle, Alabama: "I rub native plants and leaves on my clothes and boots on the way to my stand, and tie tarsal glands to my boots. I once applied urine from a road-killed buck to a scrape, and had an 8-point buck run in, looking for a fight."

Greg Poel, Michigan: "I use household ammonia and human urine for making mock scrapes, and I use ammonia as a cover scent.

William Bohnert, Missouri: "One of the best scents I've found is liquid fertilizer that has a urea (manure) base with an ammonia smell. We think the smell attracts deer. It works on does and bucks."

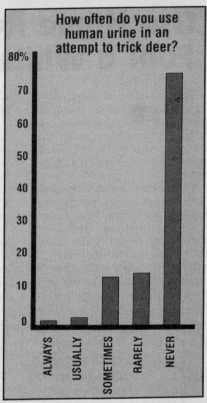

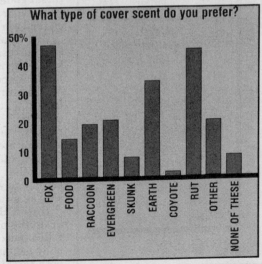

Hunting From High Places

Combine common sense with a good dose of knowledge and you'll have what it takes to stay safe in the deer woods. To underscore how deadly hunting from a tree stand can be, *Deer & Deer Hunting* magazine surveyed its readers and published a series of articles in 1993.

More than 2,300 readers responded to the 27-question survey. The survey revealed a vast amount of information concerning hunters and heights including this fact: More than one in three hunters has taken a fall from a tree stand at some time in his or her life.

The following tips for tree stand safety were compiled from readers, manufacturers and hunter education instructors.

1) After buying a stand or safety equipment, **READ THE INSTRUCTIONS**.

2) Wear a safety belt or harness every possible moment that you're off the ground, including ascending and descending. When in the stand with the belt attached, allow just enough slack in the strap between yourself and the tree so you can sit down and stand up comfortably.

3) Practice with your stand and safety gear before using it in the woods, and understand how your stand works. Almost all stands hold by leverage. The farther your weight is from the tree, the more leverage that is applied. However, the farther out you go, the more torque you apply, which can cause the stand to twist. Practice will show you each stands limitations.

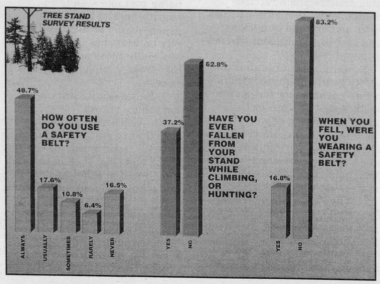

TREE STAND SURVEY RESULTS

HOW OFTEN DO YOU USE A SAFETY BELT?
48.7% ALWAYS
17.6% USUALLY
10.8% SOMETIMES
6.4% RARELY
16.5% NEVER

HAVE YOU EVER FALLEN FROM YOUR STAND WHILE CLIMBING, OR HUNTING?
37.2% YES
62.8% NO

WHEN YOU FELL, WERE YOU WEARING A SAFETY BELT?
16.8% YES
83.2% NO

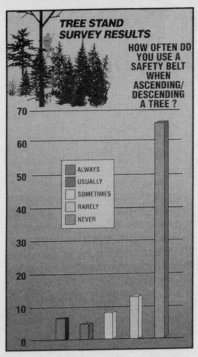

TREE STAND SURVEY RESULTS

HOW OFTEN DO YOU USE A SAFETY BELT WHEN ASCENDING/ DESCENDING A TREE ?

ALWAYS
USUALLY
SOMETIMES
RARELY
NEVER

TREE STAND SURVEY RESULTS

67.1%

DO YOU FAVOR A LAW REQUIR- ING A SAFETY BELT?

32.9%

YES

NO

4) Before buying a stand or safety gear, do your homework and shop carefully. Scour magazine articles and advertisements. Write to manufacturers. Visit archery and gun shops, and test the equipment whenever possible.

5) Maintain your stands and safety gear, and inspect them before each use for flaws and weaknesses. If steps or the stand get muddy or wet, clean them before using them again.

6) Double your precautions when using permanent stands or homemade portables, even if you made them yourself.

7) When choosing a tree for your stand, first check it in daylight for straightness, and irregular shapes, knots and angles. Your first climb should never be made in darkness.

8) Be especially careful when using portable stands on smooth-barked trees — such as aspen, maple or hickory. Don't rely on branches for climbing, especially those on "self-pruning" trees, such as aspen and oak.

9) Be especially wary any time there is rain, snow or ice.

10) With screw-in steps, make sure they're cranked straight into live, solid wood, all the way to the end. The back of the step should rest parallel against the tree trunk when properly seated.

11) Employ the manufacturers' safety pins or fastening straps when reaching your desired height in climbing stands. Don't rely on leverage

AVERAGE TREE STAND HEIGHT

16.55 FEET

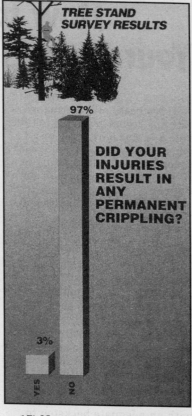

TREE STAND SURVEY RESULTS

97%

DID YOUR INJURIES RESULT IN ANY PERMANENT CRIPPLING?

3%

YES   NO

The majority of falls from permanent tree stands do not result in crippling injuries.

alone to secure the stand.

12) Use a rope to raise and lower equipment, such as your bow or gun.

13) Buy comfortable stands. If a stand isn't comfortable, you will fidget and shift your weight, which can lead to trouble.

14) Take your time and move slowly every moment you're off the ground. This is especially true at the end of the hunt, when you might be cramped and cold from hours of sitting.

15) Use your stand for its intended purpose: hunting. It is not meant for use in trimming trees with a chainsaw.

16) Hunt with a partner who knows your location. If this isn't possible, leave a map and detailed directions with people you trust, and let them know when to expect your return.

17) Never modify a commercially manufactured stand or safety device.

18) Never leave the ground when tired or on medication.

19) Dress carefully. Some clothing — whether bulky, loose or tight — restricts movements.

20) Treat tree stands as you would loaded guns: The minute you stop fearing and respecting them, they'll kill you.

How to Make Your Rifle More Accurate

From Federal Cartridge Co.

The process of "sighting in" or "zeroing" consists of making the rifle and its sight agree on where the bullets strike. With proper procedures, sighting in a rifle is neither mysterious nor difficult.

To sight in your rifle properly, follow these steps:

• The rifle and its sight should be in good condition and properly assembled. Check action screws and scope mounts. Bore sighting, or the use of a collimator, is not a substitute for actually sighting in by shooting on a range.

• Select ammunition for its intended purpose. Be sure to start with enough ammunition to complete the sighting-in process.

• Pick a safe area to shoot with an adequate backstop to stop your bullets. Wear shooting glasses and hearing protection.

• Shoot from a solid rest, such as a bench rest and sand bags. Shoot at close range to get "on paper," but verify the final zero at expected hunting ranges.

• From the solid rest, carefully squeeze off three aimed shots. The center of this group of bullet holes is the rifle's point of impact. Adjusting the sight moves this point of impact to your desired zero. Move open rear sights in the same direction you want the group to move. Adjust scopes following directions on the dials. Continue this process until the group is where you want it.

Do not adjust sights on the basis of single shots. An odd shot can lead to sight adjustment errors and ultimately wastes ammunition.

• Different brands and bullet weights may change the point of impact and necessitate re-sighting. If your rifle gets bumped or dropped, be sure to reverify your zero so you can bag your game with one shot.

Use the chart below to gauge the velocity and distance capabilities of your shotgun loads and rifle cartridges.

Maximum Range

Load	Velocity	Distance
12 gauge 1 oz. slug	1,550 feet per second	1,260 feet / 420 yards
22 long rifle	1,255 feet per second	4,870 feet / 1 mile
.30-30 Winchester 150-grain	2,370 feet per second	9,030 feet / 1.7 miles
.270 Winchester 130-grain	3,050 feet per second	14,380 feet / 2.7 miles
7mm Remington 165-grain	2,940 feet per second	19,790 feet / 3.8 miles

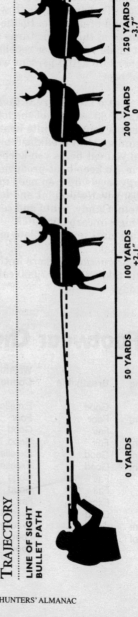

TRAJECTORY

LINE OF SIGHT ------
BULLET PATH ——

| 0 YARDS | 50 YARDS | 100 YARDS +2.1" | 200 YARDS 0 | 250 YARDS -3.7" |

Bullet Trajectory Determined by Velocity, Bullet Design

Trajectory is the arc of the bullet from the firearm's muzzle.

Bullets appear to rise because the barrel is angled up. The bullet's path crosses the line of sight twice — going up near the muzzle and going down through the down-range zero.

The mid-range trajectory is the bullet's highest point above the line

of sight. It usually occurs half way between the muzzle and the zero range.

Velocity and bullet design determine trajectory. Low-velocity cartridges with round-nosed bullets, if sighted for long ranges, will have a very high mid-range trajectory — possibly high enough to cause a miss on close-range targets.

For big game hunting, a trajectory height of 3 to 4 inches is considered acceptable. For small game, about 2 inches is maximum. Consult a ballistic table for velocity, trajectory and appropriate down-range zero for your specific cartridge/bullet.

Secrets to Staying Warm

From Red Wing Shoe Co.

Want to stay warm longer in your tree stand? Sure, we all do, but how?

Use common sense:

Wear a Cap

In cold weather, the body keeps the brain warm by pumping more blood to the head. A bare head may lose up to 50 percent of the body's total heat production at 40°F., and 75 percent of it at 5°F. Old-timers say, "If your feet are cold, put your cap on."

Keep Your Feet Dry

There are three materials that are excellent for keeping your feet dry and warm: waterproof leather, rubber boots, and Gore-Tex® fabric.

Unlike water-repellent oil-tanned leathers, the new high-performance silicone or dry-tanned leathers are 100 percent waterproof. They breathe better than heavily-oiled leathers.

Rubber, of course, is 100 percent waterproof — perfect for standing around in water.

Gore-Tex® fabric is both waterproof and breathable. Booties made from this fabric turns a boot made with water repellent leather into a 100-percent waterproof boot.

Eat a Good Breakfast

About 80 percent of the food we eat is converted into heat. Beginning with breakfast, every meal you eat helps you keep warm. To keep heat-producing energy levels up, you need more carbohydrates and fat and less protein. Candy, fruits and cereals are high in carbohydrates. Butter, nuts and chocolate are high in fat.

Construction workers in the arctic take in about 7,000 calories per day!

The Outdoorsman's Footwear Chart

Boot Style	Comfort Zone	Water Proofing	Breathable	Walking Comfort
Leather boots	Cool	Fair	Good	Excellent
Rubber Boots	Cool	Excellent	Poor	Poor
Shoe-Pacs	Cool	Good	Fair	Good
Gore-Tex®/Pac Boots	Cool	Excellent	Fair	Good
Gore-Tex®/Leather	Cool	Excellent	Good	Excellent
Waterproof Leather	Cool	Excellent	Good	Excellent
Felt Liner Pac Boots	Cold	Good	Fair	Good
Thinsulate™/Pac Boots	Cold	Good	Fair	Good
Mukluks	Dry Cold	Poor	Excellent	Fair
Thinsulate™/Leather	Cold	Fair	Good	Excellent
Double-Boot Leather	Cold	Excellent	Good	Excellent
Insulated Rubber Boots	Ext. Cold	Excellent	Poor	Poor
Double Insulated Pacs	Ext. Cold	Good	Fair	Poor

Tips to Increase Your Arrow Velocity

From New Archery Products

Many bow-hunters today have increased their arrow velocity by reducing the weight of their field points and broadheads. For some, the reduced weight has worked out well. Other archers and bow-hunters, however, have paid the price of reduced accuracy for their increase in arrow speed.

Studies have shown that in order for arrows to fly true, at least 10 percent more weight has to be in the front of the arrow than in the back. The term for this is "percentage front of center," or FOC. Arrows that have less than 10 percent FOC usually do not group as well as arrows having over 10 percent FOC. This problem is usually more noticeable at longer shooting distances.

Here's how to measure the FOC percentage on your arrows:

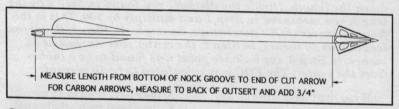

MEASURE LENGTH FROM BOTTOM OF NOCK GROOVE TO END OF CUT ARROW
FOR CARBON ARROWS, MEASURE TO BACK OF OUTSERT AND ADD 3/4"

Step 1. On aluminum arrows, measure the distance between the bottom of the nock groove and the end of the cut arrow. (Note that this does not take the length of the shoulder of the insert, the mounted broadhead or field point into consideration.) For carbon arrows, measure to the back edge of the insert and add 3/4 of an inch. Mark down the length.

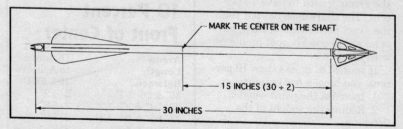

MARK THE CENTER ON THE SHAFT

15 INCHES (30 ÷ 2)

30 INCHES

Step 2. Divide by two the length you calculated in Step 1 and mark the center point on the arrow shaft.

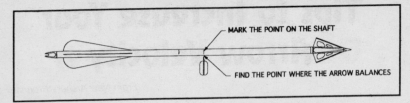

MARK THE POINT ON THE SHAFT

FIND THE POINT WHERE THE ARROW BALANCES

Step 3. Using the sharp edge of a pocketknife, and resting it on a solid surface for safety, find the point on the arrow where it balances nicely. Mark this point on the arrow.

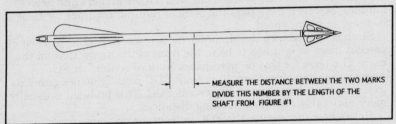

MEASURE THE DISTANCE BETWEEN THE TWO MARKS
DIVIDE THIS NUMBER BY THE LENGTH OF THE
SHAFT FROM FIGURE #1

Step 4. Measure the distance between the two points. Mark down the length. Divide the distance you found in Step 4 by the length you measured in Step 1 and multiply by 100. This is the front of center (FOC) percentage. Example: In Step 1, the arrow length was 30 inches; in Step 2, the center was marked at 15 inches; in Step 3, the balance point was found to be 3 inches from the center. The FOC was calculated to be 10 percent.

If you don't have a calculator, you can use the accompanying chart to figure out if you have at least 10 percent FOC. Follow steps 1, 2, and 3. Look up the arrow length you find in Step 1. The length you get in Step 3 must be at least as great as in the chart for the arrow length to have 10 percent. The chart does not tell you the exact percentage of FOC, but is an aid to quickly spot problems with low FOC.

If your FOC is less than 10 percent, you have a few options:

1. Increase the point weight.
2. Reduce the weight of the fletching.
3. Reduce the length of the arrow, if possible.
4. Switch to non-crested arrows if you use crested arrows.

Arrows having up to 18 percent FOC have been successfully used for hunting and field archery for a number of years.

Determining a Minimum of 10 Percent Front of Center

Arrow Length Between	Distance to Achieve 10% FOC
25" & 26- 1/4"	2- 1/2"
26- 1/4" & 27- 1/2"	2- 5/8"
27- 1/2" & 28- 3/4"	2- 7/8"
28- 3/4" & 30"	3"
30" & 31- 1/4"	3- 1/8"
31- 1/4" & 32- 1/2"	3- 1/4"
32- 1/2" & 33- 3/8"	3- 3/8"

Broadhead Questions & Answers

From Satellite Archery

Q: Why do some broadheads feature carbon steel blades and others stainless steel blades?

A: Carbon blades, with their blue-black finish work nicely in camo patterned broadheads, they are also less costly to shoot.

Carbon blades must be cared for properly or they will corrode. They should be kept away from water, kept clean, and stored with a light oil film on the surface.

Stainless steel blades are virtually non-corrosive and require little maintenance other than being kept clean. They are extremely strong and resist dulling. Their shiny surface reflects sunlight, however, a feature some hunters don't care for.

Q: What should I look for when choosing a broadhead?

A: That depends on a variety of factors, including: type of game hunted, the bow weight, arrows you'll be shooting and the hunting conditions you expect to face. First of all, choose a proven design — radical designs tend to fly erratically. Next, match the broadhead to your needs and equipment.

Consider a light head if you will be shooting a low draw weight (40-55 pounds) or will be taking long shots at, for example, antelope or sheep. Look at heavier heads for heavy bows (70 pounds plus) or on tough, big-game animals like elk or bear. Be sure to get a head with a good amount of cutting edge and that's wide enough in diameter to leave a large hold for blood drainage.

Broadhead strength is also very important. Look for proven lockdown systems and rugged construction materials — you don't want the broadhead coming apart upon impact.

Q: What type of broadheads penetrate best?

A: Generally speaking, broadheads with razor-sharp cutting points penetrate best. These points cut upon entry and, if kept sharp, meet little resistance from hide and muscle.

Broadheads with cutting tips frequently pass completely through big game animals. Broadheads with pencil points and chisel points penetrate less well, but have other redeeming characteristics such as aerodynamic styling (pencil point) and strength (chisel point).

Q: Which types of points are the toughest?

A: Chisel points made of hardened steel are among the toughest. Such points have been tested on sheet steel, bone, wood, and even concrete blocks with excellent results. They cut and

> It pays to experiment with a variety of broadheads before the season, to find out which performs best with your equipment, and under your particular hunting conditions.

split flesh and/or bone upon impact, and if they are large enough, hardened correctly, designed right, and kept sharp, they will give excellent results on the toughest big game animals.

Q: How do broadheads kill?

A: Broadheads kill by causing hemorrhaging. That is why they must be kept razor sharp. But sharp is not enough, they must also fly true to hit the intended spot on the animal, have sufficient cutting surface, and be tough enough to hold together.

Hunters need to also think about game recovery. A dead animal that cannot be recovered is a horrible waste. That is why broadhead manufacturers recommend using large, tough, high-penetration broadheads that will shoot completely through an animal leaving a large, double hole blood trail.

Some hunters, however, like the arrow to "hang up" in mid-body to inflict additional damage. Others prefer the generous blood trail left by a double-holed lung shot.

Q: Which broadheads fly best?

A: Generally speaking, lightweight broadheads with low profile (1 inch to 1-1/8 inches) and aerodynamic styling fly best.

Their light weight and low profile increases arrow speed and minimizes wind resistance. Large diameter heads (over 1-1/8 inches) should be vented to reduce wind resistance. Blade angle is also important. Blades with steep angles generally don't fly well. Most flight problems can be cured with equipment adjustments. A 5-pound reduction in draw weight is a good place to start. If that doesn't work, consider increasing arrow spine. Untrue broadheads will never fly well.

Deal only with reputable manufacturers who use top-quality materials and manufacturing equipment. Beware of inexpensive imported broadheads.

Q: What type of broadhead should I shoot with my over-draw setup?

A: First, you should select a broadhead designed to clear the handle riser of your bow. Then, you should opt for a lightweight head which is both strong and aggressive.

Q: What are the advantages of lightweight broadheads?

A: Lightweight heads can decrease broadhead weight by as much as 15-25 percent, thus increasing speed and flattening trajectory. Lightweight broadheads work well with the lighter, shorter

> **Most hunters probably should choose a broadhead in the 125- to 145-grain range because most game is taken at moderate ranges under moderate conditions.**

shafts commonly in use today.

Q: Do I need to use broadheads for pre-season practice?

A: Absolutely! By shooting field points weighing the same as the broadhead you'll be shooting for most practice. Closer to the hunting season, switch to broadheads to "fine tune" your tackle. You should also wear hunting clothes, mount a full arrow quiver and shoot from a tree stand during this "fine tuning" process. Be sure to practice, practice until you can consistently put your shots where you want them. The best broadhead in the world will not make up for a poor hit. Practice builds confidence; in yourself and in your equipment, and confidence makes good hunters.

Q: What about broadhead price and quality?

A: Price and quality do not always equate when buying broadheads. Some U.S. broadheads are inefficiently made in small shops and in small numbers and grossly overpriced. Many imported heads, while inexpensive, are poor in quality.

Q: Which type of broadhead is best: small and light or big and heavy?

A: Again, that depends upon the individual shooting, the game, and the hunting conditions that will be faced. Light broadheads (equal to or under 130 grains) work better than heavy ones in light bows or where long shots may be taken and flat trajectory is a serious concern. Overdraw setups do well with lighter heads. Heavy heads (equal to over 145 grains) are best for tough game, heavy bows, and short range shooting.

Most hunters probably should choose a broadhead in the 125- to 145-grain range as most game is taken at moderate ranges under moderate conditions. Broadheads in this weight range consistently fly well. Research shows that most whitetail deer are shot at less than 15 yards.

Ultralight and extra-heavy broadheads can be somewhat difficult to shoot. Tests show weight to be much less important than other factors such as aerodynamics, point and blade design on an arrow flight and penetration.

Q: Should I experiment with different broadheads?

A: Yes, different heads perform differently with different bows, arrows, fletchings, etc. and under different conditions. It pays to experiment with a variety of broadheads before the season, to find out which performs best with your equipment, and under your particular hunting conditions.

Q: How should I store my broadheads?

A: In the off-season, apply a thin film of protective oil and store in a covered container in a dry, secure place out of the way of children or others who do not understand the danger of handling broadheads. Sticking the heads into styrofoam will keep them from rattling around and damaging each other.

During the season, always use a quiver which has a broadhead protector and never walk with a nocked arrow or climb with an arrow. Keep extra broadheads in a covered container in your pack, out of the reach of unsuspecting fingers.

Always keep your broadheads clean and try to keep a protective coat of oil on them. Remember, the vast majority of broadhead injuries are self-inflicted.

Q: What are the most common types of broadhead designs?

A: Fixed blade and replaceable blade broadheads. Fixed blade broadheads generally feature heavy resharpenable blades and rock solid construction.

Replaceable blade broadheads feature replaceable blade inserts which can be shot until dull and then discarded. Most modern broadheads feature three or four blade designs and fairly wide diameters (1-1/8"-1-3/8") to maximize cutting capacity.

Q: What are the advantages and disadvantages of each type?

A: Fixed blade broadheads are extremely strong and tough, however, they must be resharpened when they dull.

Replaceable blade broadheads offer bow-hunters the convenience of razor sharp blades which may be inserted in seconds. Some replaceable blade designs are not as strong as fixed blade designs.

Look for proven blade lockdown systems and assemble them carefully.

Q: How do I resharpen my broadheads?

A: A high quality sharpening stone generally works well as do specially constructed broadhead sharpening tools. Fine diamond stones are particularly good.

When using a stone, be sure to consistently hold the blade at one angle — 15 degrees is about right. Changing the angle will only serve to roll the edge over. Surgical clamps are excellent for holding blades while sharpening. Consistency of angle is the key - that's why broadhead sharpening tools work well, they preserve the angle.

It's time to sharpen blades when they can no longer shave hair from your arm.

Arrow Shaft Sizes & Weight Groups

From Easton Inc.

EASTON TARGET & HUNTING SHAFT SIZES GROUPED BY WEIGHT & MODEL

SHAFT MODEL	UltraLite A/C/E	UltraLite Aluminum SuperLite A/C/C SuperLite P/C	SuperLite Aluminum	Lite Aluminum	Standard Aluminum
Models Used for Competition and Recreational Archery					
A/C/E* Aluminum/Carbon/Extreme	1000 780 620 470 920 720 570 430 850 670 520 400 370				
X7* Eclipse™		1511 1711 1912 2312 1512 1712 2012 2512 1611 1811 2112 1612 1812 2212	1514 1714 1914 2114 15+14 17+14 19+14 2214 1614 1814 2014 16+14 18+14 20+14	1516 1716 1916 1616 1816	
E75* Gold			1413	1416 1716 1916 1516 1816 2016 1616 **2115**	
Eagle* Target				1516 1716 1916 1616 1816	
Models Used for Competition, Recreational Archery and Bowhunting					
A/C/C* Aluminum/Carbon/Competiton		2-00 2L-04 3-04 3-39 3L-00 2-04 3L-18 3-49 3-00 3X-04 3-18 3-60 3L-04 3-28 3-71			
P/C* Pure/Carbon		4.5 5.0 5.5 6.1 4.7 5.2 5.7 6.3 4.9 5.4 5.9 **6.5**			
P/C Specter ™		**4.5 5.0 5.5 6.1** **4.7 5.2 5.7 6.3** **4.9 5.4 5.9 6.5**			
XX75* Autumn Orange*			1713 1913 2113 2314 1813 2013 2114 2413 2213 2514	1816 2115 2315 1916 2215 2016 2216	2018 2117 2317 2219 2419
Easton Classic™ PermaGraphic*			2213 2413	1916 2216 2315 2016	2018 2117 2317 2219
Models Used for Bowhunting					
XX78* Super Slam*		2212 2312 2512	2114 2314 2213 2413 2514	2016 2115 2315 2215 2216	2018 2117 2317 2219
XX75 Camo Hunter* — 4-color PermaGraphic w/Super UNI **Bushing**			2013 2113 2314 2114 2413 2213 2514		
XX75 Camo Hunter* — 4-color Standard Camo w/swage			**1913 2113 2314** **2013 2114 2413** **2213 2514**	1816 2115 2315 1916 2215 2016 2216	2018 2117 2317 2219 2419
GameGetter* II				1816 2115 2315 1916 2215 2016 2216	2018 2117 2219
GameGetter				2016 2216	
Eagle Hunter				2016 2216	2018 2117 2219 2018 2117 2219

Determining Correct Arrow Length

From Easton Inc.

Your correct arrow length is determined by drawing back an extra-long arrow and having someone mark the arrow as shown below.

Correct Arrow Length for hunting arrows with broadheads shot from bows with cut-out sight windows (including overdraw). Also for target/field arrows shot from any bow.

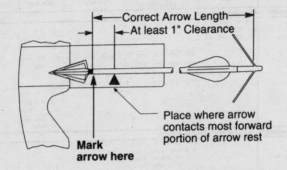

Correct Arrow Length
At least 1" Clearance

Place where arrow contacts most forward portion of arrow rest

Mark arrow here

Correct Arrow Length for hunting arrows with broadheads shot from bows without cut-out sight windows.

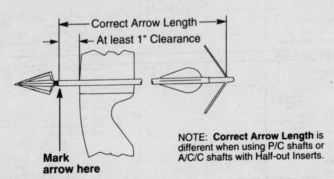

Correct Arrow Length
At least 1" Clearance

Mark arrow here

NOTE: **Correct Arrow Length** is different when using P/C shafts or A/C/C shafts with Half-out Inserts.

Correct Arrow Length is measured from the bottom of the nock groove to the end of the shaft.

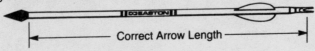

Correct Arrow Length

EASTON. Aluminum Arrow Shafts

EASTON ALUMINUM ARROW SHAFT SPECIFICATIONS AND SIZES

SHAFT MODEL	ALLOY	STRENGTH[2] psi	NOCK TAPER[3]/UNI	NOCK TYPE	WEIGHT TOLERANCE	STRAIGHT-NESS[4]	HARD ANODIZED[3] COLOR/PATTERN	WEIGHT GROUP – SIZES[1] — ULTRALITE	SUPERLITE	LITE	STANDARD
X7* Eclipse*	7178-T9	105,000	UNI or Super UNI System[5]	ACE, Super Nock or Conventional	±3/4%	±.001" (.0005" T.I.R.)	Black	1511 1512 1611 1612, 1711 1712 1811 1812, 1911 1912 2011 2012, 2312 2512	1514 1614 1714 1814, 1914 2014 2114 2214, 16-14 18-14 19-14 20-14	1516 1616, 1716 1816, 1916	2117 2219, 2317 2419
E75* Gold	7075-T9	96,000	Full Diameter Taper	Conventional	±1%	±.003" (.0015" T.I.R.)	Gold	1413		1416 1516 1616, 1716 1816, 1916 2016, 2115	
XX75* Autumn Orange*	7075-T9	96,000	Reduced Diameter Taper[2]	Conventional	±1%	±.002" (.001" T.I.R.)	Autumn Orange		1713 1813 1913 2013, 2113 2114 2213 2214, 2314 2413 2514	1816 1916 2016, 2115 2215 2315	2018, 2117 2219, 2317 2419
Easton Classic* PermaGraphic*	7075-T9	95,000	Full Diameter Taper	Conventional	±1%	±.002" (.001" T.I.R.)	Cedar-grain PermaGraphic		2213 2413	1916 2016, 2216 2315	2018, 2117 2219, 2317 2419
XX78* Super Slam* PermaGraphic*	7178-T9	100,000	Super UNI System[5]	Super Nock or Conventional	±1%	±.0015" (.00075" T.I.R.)	3-Tone PermaGraphic Brown, Tan & Black Camo	2212 2312 2512	2114 2214 2314 2413 2514, 2215 2315 2216	2016, 2115 2215, 2315	2018, 2117 2219, 2317 2419
XX75 Camo Hunter* PermaGraphic*	7075-T9	96,000	Super UNI System[5]	Super Nock or Conventional	±1%	±.002" (.001" T.I.R.)	4-Tone PermaGraphic Green, Brown, Tan & Black Camo	2013	2113 2114 2213 2214, 2314 2413 2514	2013	
XX75 Camo Hunter*	7075-T9	96,000	Reduced Diameter Taper[2]	Conventional	±1%	±.002" (.001" T.I.R.)	4-Tone Black, Brown, Dk. & Lt. Green Camo		1913 2013, 2113 2213	1816 1916 2016, 2115 2215 2315, 2216	2018, 2117 2219, 2317 2419
GameGetter* II	7075-T9	96,000	Full Diameter Taper	Conventional	±1¼%	±.003 (.0015" T.I.R.)	3-Tone Black, Tan & Brown Camo			1816 1916 2016, 2115 2215 2216	2018, 2117 2219
GameGetter*	7075-T9	96,000	Full Diameter Taper	Conventional	±1¼%	±.003" (.0015" T.I.R.)	Dark Green			2016 2216	2018, 2117 2219
Eagle* Target	5086	58,000	Full Diameter Taper	Conventional	±4%	±.006" (.003" T.I.R.)	Red			1516 1716 1916, 1616 1816	
Eagle* Hunter	5086	58,000	Full Diameter Taper	Conventional	±5%	±.010" (.005" T.I.R.)	Light Green				2018, 2117 2219

[1] Shaft sizes in lighter-face type have a full diameter nock taper.

[2] Typical Ultimate Tensile Strength at Final Draw before anodize. Due to variations in aluminum material or manufacturing processes, tensile strength value may vary ± 3%.

[3] All shafts have a hard anodized finish.

[4] Straightness tolerance (T.I.R.=Total Indicator Reading as shaft is rotated 360°)

[5] UNI—Universal Nock Installation System. Shaft sizes in italics use the UNI or Super UNI System.

Rev. 9/94

*=Registered Trademark/Trademark of Jas. D. Easton, Inc.
* Super Slam Registered Trademark of Chuck Adams

BOHNING'S ADHESIVE SELECTION GUIDE FOR ARROW BUILDING

shaft material	application	shaft preparation*	adhesive (s)	compatible thinner
wood	fletching feathers/vanes	Fletch-Lac or Fletch-Tite thinner Fletch-Lac or Fletch-Tite thinner	Fletch-Tite Bond-Tite	Fletch-Tite thinner Fletch-Tite thinner
	fletching feathers	Fletch-Lac or Fletch-Tite thinner	Bohning Feather Fletching Tape	---
	installing hardware	---	Ferr-L-Tite hot melt Stik-Tite hot melt Ferr-L-Tite Epoxy	--- ---
aluminum	fletching feathers/vanes	Prep-Rite II Prep-Rite II	Fletch-Tite Bond-Tite	Fletch-Tite thinner Fletch-Tite thinner
	fletching feathers	Prep-Rite II	Bohning Feather Fletching Tape	---
	installing hardware	---	Ferr-L-Tite hot melt Stik-Tite hot melt Ferr-L-Tite Epoxy	--- ---
carbon graphite	fletching feathers/vanes	Prep-Rite II	Bond-Tite	Fletch-Tite thinner
	fletching feathers	Prep-Rite II	Bohning Feather Fletching Tape	---
	installing hardware	---	Stik-Tite hot melt Ferr-L-Tite Epoxy	--- ---

*For cleaning and degreasing only. Staining, dipping or cresting should also be done prior to fletching. All Bohning stains, lacquers and adhesives are compatible.

Knight Rifles
Muzzleloading Ballistic Information
.50 Caliber Knight Rifle - 100gr. Volume FFg

Bullet Description	Yards	Range Bullet Impact (Inches)	Velocity ft./sec.	Energy ft./lbs.
Knight 240 gr./.44 cal.	0	-	1553	1285
Sabot, Jacketed	50	1059	1488	1159
	100	0	1366	995
	150	-6.21	1260	846
Knight 260 gr./.45 cal.	0	-	1524	1340
Sabot, Jacketed	50	1.65	1461	1233
	100	0	1346	1045
	150	-6.44	1244	894
Knight 300 gr./.45 cal.	0	-	1484	1466
Sabot, Jacketed	50	1.74	1431	1364
	100	0	1333	1183
	150	-6.63	1246	1034
Knight 260 gr./.45 cal.	0	-	1505	1307
Saboted, Lead	50	1.71	1439	1195
	100	0	1319	1004
	150	-6.69	1215	853
Knight 310 gr./.45 cal.	0	-	1447	1441
Sabot, Lead	50	1.85	1394	1338
	100	0	1297	1158
	150	-6.99	1212	1011
385 gr./.50 cal.	0	-	1360	1582
Pure Lead	50	2.26	1294	1431
	100	0	1179	1187
	150	-8.19	1091	1018
410 gr./.50 cal.	0	-	1331	1612
Pure Lead	50	2.34	1263	1452
	100	0	1149	1202
	150	-8.75	1064	1030
180 gr./.490 cal.	0	-	1755	1231
Round Ball (90 grains FFg)	50	2.36	1231	606
100 grains FFg - Not Recommended	100	0	972	378
	150	-1021	843	284

Knight Rifles
Muzzleloading Ballistic Information
.54 Caliber Knight Rifle - 100gr. Volume FFg

Bullet Description	Yards	Range Bullet Impact (Inches)	Velocity ft./sec.	Energy ft./lbs.
Knight 240 gr./.44 cal.	0	-	1553	1285
Sabot, Jacketed	50	1059	1488	1159
	100	0	1366	995
	150	-6.21	1260	846
Knight 260 gr./.45 cal.	0	-	1524	1340
Sabot, Jacketed	50	1.65	1461	1233
	100	0	1346	1045
	150	-6.44	1244	894
Knight 300 gr./.45 cal.	0	-	1484	1466
Sabot, Jacketed	50	1.74	1431	1364
	100	0	1333	1183
	150	-6.63	1246	1034
Knight 260 gr./.45 cal.	0	-	1505	1307
Saboted, Lead	50	1.71	1439	1195
	100	0	1319	1004
	150	-6.69	1215	853
Knight 310 gr./.45 cal.	0	-	1447	1441
Sabot, Lead	50	1.85	1394	1338
	100	0	1297	1158
	150	-6.99	1212	1011
425 gr./.54 cal.	0	-	1277	1539
Pure Lead	50	2.58	1208	1376
	100	0	1096	1134
	150	-9.59	1018	977
215 gr./ .530 cal.	0	-	1765	1487
Round Ball	50	2.44	1207	696
	100	0	951	431
	150	-10.56	820	321

Top numbers: Complete Contender pistols. Bottom numbers: Acessory Contender barrels only.

CONTENDER Selection Chart

CARTRIDGE	10" Octagon Barrel BLUED	10" Bull Barrel BLUED	10" Bull Barrel SST	12" Hunter Barrel Only BLUED	12" Hunter Barrel Only SST	14 BL
.22 LR	No.1010 / No.3010	No.1013 / No.3013	No.2711 / No.4711			
.22 LR MATCH		No.2257 / No.4257	No.2732 / No.4732			
.22 WIN MAG		No.1023 / No.3023				
.17 REM						
.22 HORNET		No.2013 / No.4013	No.2714 / No.4714			
.222 REM						
.223 REM		No.2045 / No.4045	No.2719 / No.4719	N/A / No.4879	N/A / No.4872	No. / No.
7mm TCU*		No.2250 / No.4250	No.2734 / No.4734			
7-30 WATERS				N/A / No.4881	N/A / No.4873	No. / No.
.30/30 WIN		No.2173 / No.4173	No.2727 / No.4727	N/A / No.4882	N/A / No.4875	No. / No.
.32/20 WIN		No.2073 / No.4073				
.357 MAG		No.2093 / No.4093	No.2722 / No.4722			
.357 REM MAX		No.2097 / No.4097				
.35 REM				N/A / No.4884	N/A / No.4876	No. / No.
.375 WIN				N/A / No.4887		No. / No.
.44 MAG		No.2153 / No.4153	No.2726 / No.4726	N/A / No.4885		No. / No.
.45/70 GOV'T				N/A / No.4886	N/A / No.4878	No. / No.
.300 WHISPER		No.2174 / No.4174	No.2728 / No.4728			

‡ = Super 16 Barrel in 45/70 Govt is a Bull Barrel with Muzzle Tamer * = Custom Loaded Cartridge **NOTE:** About the .300 Whisper. Loaded ar

	10" Bull BLUED	10" Bull SST	10" Vent/Rib BLUED	10" Vent/Rib SST	14" Ver Blued
45 COLT / 410 GAUGE	No.2138 / No.4138	No.2724 / No.4724	No.2148 / No.4148	No.2725 / No.4725	No.2547 / No.4547
410 GAUGE SMOOTHBORE	N/A	N/A	N/A	N/A	N/A

The Contender pistol and carbine chart indicates complete guns by the top number which is red. Accessory barrels are indicated by the bottom number which is green.

Super "14"		Super "16"		Contender Carbine Kit		Contender Carbine Youth Model	Contender Carbine 21"	
BLUED	SST	BLUED	SST	Walnut/Blue	Rynite/SST	Walnut/Blue	Walnut/Blue	Rynite/SST
No.2401	No.3201	No.2540				No.1340		
No.4401	No.4201	No.4540				No.4540		
No.2531	No.3218			No. 1113	No. 4313		No.1221	No. 1936
No.4531	No.4218						No.4821	No. 4906
No.2408							No.1208	
No.4408							No.4809	
No.2409	No.3208	No.2545		No.1115	No.4315		No.1215	No.1932
No.4409	No.4208	No.4545					No.4815	No.4902
No.2404								
No.4404								
No.2405	No.3203	No.2544	No.3302	No.1120	No.4320	No.1344	No.1220	No.1933
No.4405	No.4203	No.4544	No.4302			No.4544	No.4820	No.4903
No.2527	No.3214		No.3305				No.1235	No.1938
No.4527	No.4214		No.4305				No.4835	No.4908
No.2502	No.3205	No.2552	No.3306	No.1140	No.4345		No.1240	No.1939
No.4502	No.4205	No.4552	No.4306				No.4840	No.4909
No.2517								
No.4517								
No.2505	No.3206							
No.4505	No.4206							
No.2520	No.3207						No.1251	No.1943
No.4520	No.4207						No.4846	No.4913
No.2508	No.3222							
No.4508	No.4222							
		No.2551‡	No.3304‡			N/A		
		No.4551‡	No.4304‡			No.4551‡		
No.2522								
No.4522								

artridge is available from: COR-BON Bullet Co., 4828 Michigan Ave., Detroit, MI 48201

16 1/4" Vent/Rib		21" Contender Carbine		21" Contender Carbine Kit	
BLUED	SST	BLUED	SST	BLUED	SST
No.2546	No.3303	N/A	N/A	N/A	N/A
No.4546	No.4303				
N/A	N/A	No.1250	No.1942	No.1150	No.4355
		No.4850	No.4912		

NOTE: All Thompson/Center Rifles and Pistols are packaged with complete instructions. These instructions must be read before using the firearm. Consumers who purchase T/C firearms (new or used) and do not receive this material should write to our factory. The proper literature will be sent to them free of charge. Specify serial number.

Hunting Boosts National Economy

When that 10-point buck finally appears and your heart is in your throat, you can be excused for not thinking about hunting's contribution to the nation's economy. But during more relaxed times, that contribution is worth thinking about, and talking about.

Most hunters, and certainly most anti-hunters, will be surprised to learn that the sport of hunting pumps more into our national economy each year than corporate giants like Coca-Cola, RJR Nabisco, Anheuser-Busch and Goodyear Tire and Rubber. In the few minutes that it will take you to read this, you and your fellow hunters will contribute more than $100,000 to the nation's economy. That translates into some $1.6 million an hour, nearly $40 million a day and $14 billion a year, according to the National Shooting Sports Foundation.

Whether it's a young hunter using his paper-route savings to buy his first shotgun, a business executive writing out a $4,000 check for the elk hunt of a lifetime, or a local deer hunter paying $4.50 for breakfast, our hunting heritage fuels the economy at a pace that is rivaled by few sports and few industries.

In this era of layoffs and downsizing government officials may be interested to know that:

•More than 380,000 jobs are directly or indirectly supported by hunting. Each day, hunting produces enough economic activity to support 1,000 jobs. Hunting employs as many people as all Sears Roebuck stores.

•Hunting employs as many people as Northwest Airlines with enough workers left over to staff Delta and USAir.

•The people employed by hunting could fully staff the Turner Broadcasting Company - and 1,000 more companies just like it.

•For each 50 hunters, enough economic activity is generated to create one job.

Put in one place, the people employed by hunting would create a city the size of Minneapolis, Colorado Springs or Sacramento.

According to Bob Delfay, President of The National Shooting Sports Foundation, the NSSF does not maintain that hunting is an acceptable activity merely because it makes a significant contribution to national and local economies.

"Hunting is an acceptable and desirable ingredient of our nation's heritage because wildlife management professionals and our conservation experience over the past century tells us so," Delfay said. " The economic value of hunting is only a bonus to its spiritual, social and environmental worth. If a penny did not change hands, hunting would be no less acceptable or vital to our nation's fabric. But pennies and dollars do change hands. Lots of them."

The average hunter contributes $850 to the economy

> # Hunters spend $7 billion annually on guns, ammunition, scopes, binoculars, clothing, reloading equipment and countless accessories.

each year. *Fortune* magazine recently explained how hunters can afford it. According to the magazine: "A demographic profile of the roughly 20 million Americans who hunt may surprise you! Urbanites may think of hunters as yahoos, but the truth, demographically, is that they get less yahoo-like all the time. Compared with the hunter of five years ago, today's hunter is better educated, more likely to be a professional or manager, and earns more. The average hunter has an income of $43,120 per year, compared to the national average of around $29,000, and 80 percent of all hunters own their homes."

Hunting contributes to the economy in many ways. Among the more obvious are:

•Hunters spend $7 billion annually on guns, ammunition, scopes, binoculars, clothing, reloading equipment and countless accessories.

•Hunters will spend approximately $3 billion annually on food and lodging in association with their hunting trips —be they half-day outings near home or a 10-day hunt of a lifetime.

•Hunters acquire or lease more than $1 billion in real estate for their outdoor pursuits each year.

•Hunters spend $520 million annually on permits, licenses, duck stamps and other government fees directly associated with their sport.

Hunting's economic benefit is often overlooked because the impact is usually concentrated in rural, economically sensitive areas where even modest incremental expenditures by hunters can have a pivotal effect on the success or failure of a local merchant.

As stated in *Fortune*, "The dollars spent by hunters pack special oomph, because they hit small towns, far off the interstate. There, merchants look to hunting season the way Macy's looks to Christmas: it can make or break the year."

Those who are eager to bring an end to hunting in America might consider what substitute they could offer for the $14 billion loss in overall economic value that would result.

According to the NSSF, hunters should not argue that hunting is good or hunting is acceptable in our modern society simply because it provides jobs for 380,000 Americans and funnels $14 billion into the economy.

The foundation does admit, however, that the economic impact is certainly an element that should be factored into the equation when politicians and animal rights activists act on personal beliefs and lobby against hunting.

Calendar of 1996 Outdoor Shows

January

Cincinnati Travel, Sport & Boat
Cincinnati Convention Center
Show Dates: Jan. 12-19

Cincinnati Travel, Sports
& Boat Show
Cincinnati Convention Center
Cincinnati, OH
Show Dates: Jan. 12-21

Greater PA Sports, Travel
& Outdoor Show
Ft. Washington Expo Center
Ft. Washington, PA 19034
Show Dates: Jan. 17-21

Northwest Ohio
Outdoor Expo
Sea Gate Centre
401 Jefferson Ave.
Toledo, OH 43604
Show Dates: Jan. 26-28

West Virginia Hunting
& Fishing Show
Charleston Civic Center
200 Civic Center Drive
Charleston, WV 25301
Show Dates: Jan. 26-28

Mid America Sport & Boat
Kentucky Fair & Expo Center
325 W. Main St., Suite 1408
Louisville, KY 40202
Show Dates: Jan. 27-Feb. 4

Chicagoland Sport Fishing,
Travel & Outdoor Show
Rosemont Convention Center
Rosemont, IL 60018
Show Dates: Jan. 26-Feb. 4

February

Eastern Fishing
& Outdoor Expo
The Centrum
Worcester, MA 01601
Show Dates: Feb. 1-4

Eastern Boat, Camp, Travel
& Outdoor Show
State Fair Show Complex
IIth & MacLay Streets
Harrisburg, PA 17101
Show Dates: Feb. 3-11

Huntin'-Time
Ford Field House
111 Lyon St.
Grand Rapids, MI 48503
Show Dates: Feb. 9, 10, 11

Jamestown Sport & Home Show
Jamestown Civic Center
Jamestown, ND 58401
Show Dates: Feb. 9-11

Great Lakes Fishing
& Outdoor Expo
Buffalo Convention Center
Buffalo, NY 14201
Show Dates: Feb. 15-18

February (cont.)

MI Deer & Turkey Spectacular
Lansing Center
Lansing, MI 48917
Show Dates: Feb. 16-18

Black Hills
Sports Show & Sale
Rushmore Plaza Civic Center
444 Mt Rushmore Road N.
Rapid City, SD 57701
Show Dates: Feb. 16-18

Indianapolis Boat, Sport
& Travel Show
Indianapolis State Fairground
Show Dates: Feb. 16-25

Daniel Boone's Pioneer Classic
Lynchburg City Armory
Main @ 12th St.
Lynchburg, VA 24504
Show Dates: Feb. 17, 18

Capital Sport, Fishing,
Travel & Outdoor Show
The Capital Expo Center
Chantilly, VA 22021
Show Dates: Feb. 22-25

Outdoorama
Novi Expo Center
43700 Expo Center Drive
Novi, MI 48375
Show Dates: Feb. 23-March 5

Southern Outdoorsman
Exposition 1996
Natchez Convention Center
Natchez, MS 39122
Show Dates: Feb. 23, 24, 25

World Fishing & Outdoor Expo
Rockland Community College
Suffern, NY 10901
Show Dates: Feb. 28-March 3

The Springfield
Sportsmen's Show
Big "El" Fairgrounds
W. Springfield, MA 01089
Show Dates: Feb. 22-25

Des Moines Sport Show
Veterans Auditorium
833 5th Ave.
Des Moines, IA 50309
Show Dates: Feb. 27-March 2

March

QCCA Outdoor Show
QCCA Expo Center
2621 4th Ave.
Rock Island, IL 61201
Show Dates: March 1-3

Rochester Sportsmen's Show
The Dome Center
2695 E. Henrietta Rd.
Henrietta, NY 14467
Show Dates: March 7-10

Pennsylvania
Deer & Turkey Expo
Valley Forge Convention Center
King of Prussia, PA 19406
Show Dates: March 8-10

Sioux Empire Sportsmen's Boat
Camping & Vacation Show
Sioux Falls Arena
Sioux Falls, SD 57055
Show Dates: March 14-17

March (cont.)

Northeast Great Outdoors Expo
Convention Center
Empire State Plaza
Albany, NY 12201
Show Dates: Mar 15, 16, 17

Frank Sargeant Outdoors Expo
Florida Expo Park
Florida State Fairgrounds
4800 US Hwy. 301 N.
Tampa, FL 33610
Show Dates: March 1-3

Missouri Deer Classic
Boone County Fairgrounds
Oakland Gravel Drive
Columbia, MO 63502
Show Dates: March 2, 3

Eastern Iowa Sports Show
Cedar Falls, IA 50613
Show Dates: March 7-10

World Fly Fishing Expo
Shriners Auditorium
Wilmington, MA 01887
Show Dates: March 9-10

**Mid America Hunting
& Archery Show**
Dalton Expo Center
14200 Chicago Road
Dalton, IL 61925
Show Dates: March 8, 9, 10

**Ohio Deer & Turkey
Exposition**
State Fairgrounds
Columbus, OH 43215
Show Dates: March 15-17

Palmetto Sportsmen's Classic
SC State Fairgounds
Columbia, SC 29202
Show Dates: March 22, 23, 24

Illinois Deer & Turkey Clasic
Civic Center
Peoria, IL 61601
Show Dates: March 22-24

Wyoming Outdoor Sports
Casper Events Center
No. 1 Events Drive
Casper, WY 82601
Show Dates: March 29-31

Wisconsin Deer & Turkey Expo
New Exhibit Hall Dane County
Madison, WI 53701
Show Dates: March 29-31

June

International Bowhunters Clinic
Anterless Archery Corp.
Grand Ledge, MI 48837
Show Dates: June 14, 15, 16

July

**13th Annual Alabama Deer
Hunters Exhibition**
1 Civic Center Place
Civic Center
Birmingham, AL 35202
Show Dates: July 19, 20, 21

**Gulf Coast
Hunting Show**
1 S. Water St.
Mobile, AL 36602
Show Dates: July 26, 27, 28

July (cont.)

Volunteer State
Hunting Classic
State Fairgrounds
Nashville, TN 37201
Show Dates: July 26-28

Hunter's Extravaganza
George Brown Center
Houston, TX 77010
Show Dates: July 28-30

August

Hunter's Extravaganza
Joe Freeman Coliseum
3201 E. Houston
San Antonio, TX 78219
Show Dates: Aug. 4-6

'96 Kentucky Deer Expo
Exhibition Center
Owensboro, KY 42301
Show Dates: Aug. 9, 10, 11

Knoxville Sports Show
Tennessee Valley Fairgrounds
Knoxville, TN 37914
Show Dates: Aug. 9-11

Will Rogers
Convention Center
123 E. Exchange
Ft. Worth, TX 76106
Show Dates: Aug. 11-13

Virginia Outdoor
Sportsman Show
3000 Mechanicsville Turnpike
Richmond, VA 23201
Show Dates: Aug. 11-13

Buck-A-Rama
Atlanta Expo Center
3650 Jonesboro Road SE
Atlanta, GA 30354
Show Dates: Aug. 15-18

Hoosier Deer Classic
Marion County Fairgrounds
7300 East Troy Ave.
Indianapolis, IN 46227
Show Dates: Aug. 17, 18

Buck-A-Rama
GA National Fairgrounds
401 Larry Walker Pkwy.
Perry, GA 31069
Show Dates: Aug. 23-25

Interactive Sportsmen's
Benefit Shows
Greene County Fairgrounds
Waynesburg, PA 15370
Show Dates: Aug. 24-27

September

Mid America
Hunting & Fishing Show
Kentucky Fair & Expo Center
325 W. Main St., Suite 1408
Louisville, KY 40202
Show Dates: Sept. 6, 7, 8

KEY DEER HUNTING STATISTICS
Descending Numerical Order By State

State 1	Estimated Deer Population 2	State	Total Deer Harvest 3	State	Resident Deer Hunters 4	Non-Resident Deer Hunters 5	Season Bag Limit 6
Texas 8	3,525,000	Texas	476,000	Pennsylvania	1,407,822	29,000	1/day
Mississippi	1,750,000	Pennsylvania	408,557	Michigan	1,248,770	4,351	2
Alabama	1,500,000	Michigan	374,640	Wisconsin	857,756	Unknown	3
Michigan	1,500,000	Georgia	345,100	New York	803,000	2,055	2
Pennsylvania	1,178,368	Mississippi	301,000	Texas	666,000	71,500	1
Minnesota	1,000,000	Alabama	295,000	Ohio	649,000	3,350	11
Wisconsin	1,000,000	Wisconsin	270,592	Missouri	541,488	2,241	2
Georgia	950,000	New York	220,288	Minnesota	516,000	3,813	2/day
Montana 8	910,000	Louisiana	214,900	West Virginia	508,868	23,212	5
New York	900,000	Minnesota	202,000	North Carolina	456,000	21,109	1
North Carolina	900,000	Virginia	201,122	Georgia	445,000	Combined	1
Virginia	900,000	North Carolina	177,000	Virginia	400,452	5,725	10
Louisiana	875,000	Missouri	172,141	Tennessee	366,902	1,200	3
Florida	819,420	West Virginia	169,014	California	337,661	Just Started	4
West Virginia	800,000	Montana	153,928	Indiana	302,900	5,639	2
Tennessee	780,000	South Carolina	142,302	Mississippi	297,000	2,807	6
California 7,8	760,700	Tennessee	138,615	Alabama	290,000	32,635	1
Missouri	760,281	Ohio	135,000	Kentucky	271,600	26,283	6
South Carolina	750,000	Illinois	113,000	Oregon	259,655	1,928	2
Arkansas	700,000	Arkansas	110,401	Oklahoma	246,664	28,153	4
Oregon 7, 8, 9	686,600	Indiana	101,250	Louisiana	244,097	9,658	1
Colorado 7, 8	600,000	Kentucky	95,300	Florida	229,612	28,610	8
Wyoming 7, 8	460,000	Florida	81,942	Illinois	227,325	11,934	4
Kentucky	400,000	Iowa	78,000	Washington	199,330	23,000	4
Washington 7, 8, 9	398,000	Wyoming	70,450	Maryland	199,000	2,369	2
Ohio	350,000	North Dakota	70,293	Iowa	184,353	10,520	1
South Dakota 8	340,000	Oregon	70,000	New Jersey	178,801	16,664	2
Oklahoma 8	322,500	South Dakota	66,800	Idaho	177,600	4,796	20+
Kansas 8	320,000	Colorado	61,500	Maine	177,250	6,433	1
Iowa	300,000	Idaho	61,200	South Carolina	172,500	35,900	6
Indiana	290,000	Oklahoma	58,125	Montana	160,000	24,554	5
Maine	275,000	Washington	55,297	Utah	135,407	1,338	6
New Mexico	260,000	Maryland	51,209	Vermont	125,821	6,000	3
Utah 7,8	250,000	New Jersey	49,942	Colorado	117,300	1,211	5
Arizona 7,8,10	243,000	California	45,000	New Hampshire	105,284	3,394	1
North Dakota 8	230,000	Nebraska	37,277	North Dakota	101,737	104,182	8
Nebraska 8	210,000	Kansas	36,600	Massachusetts	100,000	650	8
Maryland	200,000	Utah	30,733	Arizona	82,708	34,500	10
New Jersey	150,000	Maine	27,402	Wyoming	80,383	4,100	32
Nevada 7,8	149,000	Arizona	18,565	South Dakota	75,000	15,684	20+
Vermont	105,000	New Mexico	17,597	Nebraska	72,963	14,000	6
Massachusetts	70,000	Vermont	13,333	Kansas	70,179	11,910	1
New Hampshire	67,662	Connecticut	10,360	New Mexico	69,041	24,263	3
Connecticut	65,000	New Hampshire	9,889	Nevada	48,154	20,233	3
Delaware	20,000	Massachusetts	8,200	Connecticut	43,000	1,307	1
Rhode Island	5,500	Delaware	7,424	Delaware	31,527	71,490	7
Idaho 7,8	Unknown	Nevada	6,276	Rhode Island	16,058	32,141	1
Illinois	Unknown	Rhode Island	1,322	Arkansas	Unknown	52,786	9
TOTAL	**29,026,031**		**5,861,886**		**14,296,786**	**838,628**	

156

Leading Deer Hunting States
Licensed Resident Deer Hunters

Pennsylvania
1,407,822

Michigan
1,248,770

Wisconsin
857,756

New York
803,000

Texas
666,000

Leading White-tailed Deer States
Estimated Whitetail Populations

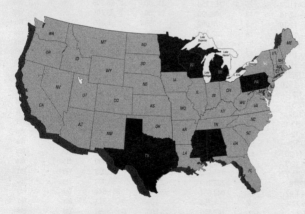

Texas
3,525,000

Mississippi
1,750,000

Alabama
1,500,000

Michigan
1,500,000

Pennsylvania
1,178,368

Minnesota
1,000,000

Wisconsin
1,000,000

1. *Several western states that have more than one species of deer usually allow hunters to buy one license that will allow them to hunt multiple deer species within that state.*
2. *Deer population numbers listed here are the best estimates of state Game & Fish Departments.*
3. *Deer harvest is the actual registered harvest recorded, or the best estimates by the respective state Game & Fish Departments based on a combination of license sales and hunter surveys.*
4. *Resident Deer Hunter numbers are based on actual license sales, or best estimates by the respective state Game & Fish Departments based on a combination of license sales and hunter surveys. Note: Numbers based on license sales are not "weapon specific" and may count a hunter more than once.*
5. *Non-resident hunter numbers are unknown in some states. Some states provide this data "combined" with the resident hunter numbers.*
   Note: Numbers based on license sales are not "weapon specific" and may count a hunter more than once.
6. *Season bag limit is defined here as the general statewide bag limit, or that which is available for the majority of hunters within that state for the year.*
7. *There is a limited number of white-tailed deer, if any, in the state.*
8. *Mule deer are present and included in the estimated deer population figures and/or the deer harvest figures.*
9. *Black-tailed deer are present and included in the estimated deer population figures and/or the deer harvest figures.*
10. *Coues deer are present and included in the estimated deer population figures and/or the deer harvest figures.*

FIREARM HUNTING INFORMATION
In Alphabetical Order By State

State	Firearm Season Dates[1]	Number Of Firearm Season Days[2]	How Many Resident Firearms Hunters?	How Many Non-Resident Firearms Hunters?[3]	Number Of Deer Harvested By Firearms	Are Rifles Permitted?[4]	Are Handguns Permitted?[4]
Alabama	11/20 - 1/31	83	205,000	20,500	270,000	Yes	Yes
Arizona	10/29 - 12/31	46	63,066	3,670	17,519	Yes	Yes
Arkansas	11/13 - 12/18	36	Unknown	Unknown	79,385	Yes	Yes
California	8/13 - 10/9	58	303,720	Combined	27,553	Yes	Yes
Colorado	8/28 - 12/31	122	96,500	61,100	54,100	Yes	Yes
Connecticut	11/21 - 12/10	18	24,000	1,100	6,629	Yes	No
Delaware	11/11 - 1/21	11	17,450	1,236	5,872	No	No
Florida	10/30 - 2/16	72	184,910	3,061	Combined	Yes	Yes
Georgia	10/22 - 1/8	79	330,000	20,000	345,100	Yes	Yes
Idaho	9/15 - 11/20	65	142,000	16,877	61,200	Yes	Yes
Illinois	11/18 - 1/15	13	143,308	Combined	92,000	No	Yes
Indiana	11/13 - 11/28	16	165,000	4,000	74,800	No	Yes
Iowa	12/3 - 12/18	16	131,188	700	61,663	No	No
Kansas	12/1 - 12/12	12	52,604	Just Started	30,000	Yes	Yes
Kentucky	11/12 - 11/21	10	141,960	2,839	68,000	Yes	Yes
Louisiana	10/30 - 1/17	68	189,100	2,142	189,100	Yes	Yes
Maine	10/30 - 11/27	25	160,250	31,300	26,608	Yes	Yes
Maryland	11/26 - 12/10	13	106,000	14,000	33,785	Yes	Yes
Massachusetts	11/28 - 12/10	13	70,000	1,350	6,300	No	No
Michigan	11/15 - 11/30	16	738,200	17,800	251,410	Yes	Yes
Minnesota	11/6 - 11/26	21	443,000	8,500	188,109	Yes	Yes
Mississippi	11/20 - 1/19	47	175,000	16,858	220,000	Yes	Yes
Missouri	11/12 - 11/20	9	436,341	10,390	154,159	Yes	Yes
Montana 5	9/15 - 12/31	36	143,100	15,000	153,928	Yes	Yes
Nebraska	11/12 - 11/20	9	53,967	1,621	30,767	Yes	Yes
Nevada	9/11 - 1/2	97	45,000	10,000	5,991	Yes	Yes
New Hampshire	11/10 - 12/5	26	66,872	10,028	6,643	Yes	Yes
New Jersey	12/6 - 1/22	9	108,116	2,358	27,197	No	No
New Mexico	10/17 - 11/15	22	59,000	5,100	16,820	Yes	Yes
New York	10/22 - 12/13	53	600,000	30,000	Combined	Yes	Yes
North Carolina	10/17 - 1/2	67	260,000	14,000	150,000	Yes	Yes
North Dakota	11/4 - 11/20	17	89,691	669	65,375	Yes	Yes
Ohio	11/28 - 12/3	6	350,000	3,000	104,400	No	Yes
Oklahoma	11/19 - 11/27	9	151,002	606	40,033	Yes	Yes
Oregon 5	9/3 - 12/18	91	233,100	2,086	64,000	Yes	Yes
Pennsylvania	11/29 - 1/22	42	1,044,634	75,777	351,544	Yes	Yes
Rhode Island	11/26 - 12/4	9	7,758	200	313	No	No
South Carolina 5	8/15 - 1/2	141	147,500	29,500	Combined	Yes	Yes
South Dakota 5,6	9/18 - 12/19	56	Combined	Combined	63,100	Yes	Yes
Tennessee	11/20 - 1/9	34	190,200	5,228	85,568	Yes	Yes
Texas 5	11/6 - 1/30	85	588,000	12,000	456,000	Yes	Yes
Utah	10/17 - 10/23	7	97,000	9,500	21,822	Yes	Yes
Vermont	11/12 - 11/27	16	89,423	17,082	10,043	Yes	Yes
Virginia	11/21 - 1/7	42	278,562	14,307	158,361	Yes	Yes
Washington	9/15 - 11/20	48	168,156	1,083	47,701	Yes	Yes
West Virginia	11/21 - 12/17	21	329,472	46,065	132,820	Yes	Yes
Wisconsin	11/20 - 11/28	9	639,964	26,606	217,584	Yes	Yes
Wyoming 5	9/10 - 11/30	52	72,272	50,117	69,415	Yes	Yes
TOTALS			**10,131,386**	**619,356**	**4,542,717**		

Leading Firearm Hunting States
Licensed Gun Hunters

Pennsylvania
1,044,634

Michigan
738,200

Wisconsin
639,964

New York
600,000

Texas
588,000

Leading Firearm Deer Kill States
Total Whitetail Kill Using Gun

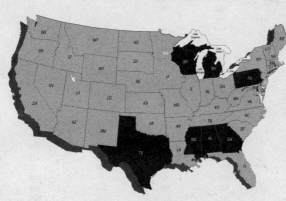

Texas
456,000

Pennsylvania
351,544

Georgia
345,100

Michigan
251,410

Alabama
270,000

Mississippi
220,000

1. Dates for the firearm season as listed here are in the broadest context due to space limitations. These dates reflect the first day to the last day of firearm activity within the state. While some states have statewide seasons, others have varying seasons for different management units within the state. Some of the dates listed were for the 1993 - 1994 season, and some are for the 1994 - 1995 season.

2. The number of firearm season days is the total number of available firearm hunting days in each state. Some states do not allow hunting on Sundays, while some states break seasons into "early" and "late" seasons.

3. "Combined" means that the non-resident hunter figure is included with the resident hunter figure.

4. Indicates types of weapons that may be used to hunt deer at some time period during the year. "Yes" signifies that the firearm is allowed in at least some parts of the state, but not necessarily all parts. Check regulations for restrictions.

5. The number of resident firearm hunters, non-resident firearm hunters, and total deer harvested by firearms includes both the firearm totals and the muzzleloader totals.

6. Refer to the "State Deer Hunting Statistics" chart for hunter numbers.

STATE DEER HUNTING REGULATIONS
In Alphabetical Order By State

State	Minimum Hunting Age	Is General Hunter Education Mandatory?	Is Bow-Hunting Education Mandatory?	Is A Separate Bow-Hunting Education Class Offered?	Is Bow-Hunting From Tree Stand Allowed?
Alabama	None	Yes	No	No	Yes
Arizona	10	No	No	No	Yess
Arkansas	None	Yes	No	No	Yes
California	12	Yes	No	No	Yes
Colorado	14	Yes	No	Yes	Yes
Connecticut	12	Yes	Yes	Yes	Yes
Delaware	None	Yes	No	Yes	Yes
Florida	None	Yes	Yes	Yes	Yes
Georgia	None	Yes	No	No	Yes
Idaho	12	Yes	Yes	Yes	Yes
Illinois	None	Yes	No	No	Yes
Indiana	None	Yes	No	No	Yes
Iowa	None	Yes	No	Yes	Yes
Kansas	14	Yes	No	No	Yes
Kentucky	None	Yes	No	No	Yes
Louisiana	None	Yes	No	Yes	Yes
Maine	10	Yes	Yes	No	Yes
Maryland	None	Yes	No	No	Yes
Massachusetts	12	No	No	Yes	Yes
Michigan	12	Yes	No	No	Yes
Minnesota	12	Yes	No	Yes	Yes
Mississippi	None	Yes	No	No	Yes
Missouri	11	Yes	No	No	Yes
Montana	12	Yes	Yes	Yes	Yes
Nebraska	14	Yes	Yes	Yes	Yes
Nevada	12	Yes	No	No	Yes
New Hampshire	None	Yes	No	Yes	Yes
New Jersey	10	Yes	Yes	Yes	Yes
New Mexico	12	Yes	No	Yes	Yes
New York	14	Yes	Yes	Yes	Yes
North Carolina	None	Yes	No	No	Yes
North Dakota	14	Yes	Yes	Yes	Yes
Ohio	None	Yes	No	No	Yes
Oklahoma	None	Yes	No	No	Yes
Oregon	12	Yes	No	No	Yes
Pennsylvania	12	Yes	No	No	Yes
Rhode Island	12	Yes	Yes	Yes	Yes
South Carolina	None	Yes	No	No	Yes
South Dakota	12	Yes	Yes	Yes	Yes
Tennessee	None	Yes	No	Yes	Yes
Texas	None	Yes	No	No	Yes
Utah	14	Yes	No	No	Yes
Vermont	None	Yes	No	No	Yes
Virginia	None	Yes	No	No	Yes
Washington	None	Yes	No	No	Yes
West Virginia	None	Yes	No	No	Yes
Wisconsin	12	Yes	No	Yes	Yes
Wyoming	14	Yes	No	No	Yes

State Deer Hunting Regulations
In Alphabetical Order By State

State	Is Gun Hunting From Tree Stand Allowed?	Is Blaze Orange Required?	May Food Bait Be Used?	May You Hunt Over Salt Or Minerals?	May Dogs Be Used To Trail Wounded Deer?[4]	May Dogs Be Used To Hunt Deer?[4]
Alabama	Yes	Yes	No	Yes	Yes	Yes
Arizona	Yes	No	No	Yes	No	No
Arkansas	Yes	Yes	Yes	Yes	Yes	Yes
California	Yes	No	No	No	Yes	Yes
Colorado	Yes	Yes	No	No	No	No
Connecticut	Yes	Yes	No	No	No	No
Delaware	Yes	Yes	No	No	No	No
Florida	Yes	Yes	Yes	Yes	Yes	Yes
Georgia	Yes	Yes	No	No	Yes	Yes
Idaho	Yes	No	No	No	No	No
Illinois	Yes	Yes	No	No	No	No
Indiana	Yes	Yes	No	No	No	No
Iowa	Yes	Yes	No	No	No	No
Kansas	Yes	Yes	Yes	Yes	No	No
Kentucky	Yes	Yes	Yes	Yes	No	No
Louisiana	Yes	Yes	Yes	Yes	Yes	Yes
Maine	Yes	Yes	No	No	No	No
Maryland	Yes	Yes	Yes	Yes	No	No
Massachusetts	Yes	Yes	No	No	No	No
Michigan	No	Yes	Yes	Yes	No	No
Minnesota	Yes	Yes	No	Yes	No	No
Mississippi	Yes	Yes	No	No	Yes	Yes
Missouri	Yes	Yes	No	Yes	No	No
Montana	Yes	Yes	No	No	No	No
Nebraska	Yes	Yes	Yes	Yes	Yes	Yes
Nevada	Yes	No	No	No	No	No
New Hampshire	Yes	No	Yes	No	No	No
New Jersey	Yes	Yes	Yes	Yes	No	No
New Mexico	No	No	No	No	No	No
New York	Yes	No	No	No	Yes	No
North Carolina	Yes	Yes	Yes	Yes	Yes	Yes
North Dakota	Yes	Yes	Yes	Yes	No	No
Ohio	Yes	Yes	Yes	Yes	No	No
Oklahoma	Yes	Yes	Yes	Yes	No	No
Oregon	Yes	No	Yes	Yes	No	No
Pennsylvania	Yes	Yes	No	No	No	No
Rhode Island	Yes	Yes	No	No	No	No
South Carolina	Yes	Yes	Yes	Yes	Yes	Yes
South Dakota	Yes	Yes	No	No	Yes	No
Tennessee	Yes	Yes	No	Yes	No	No
Texas	Yes	No	Yes	Yes	Yes	No
Utah	Yes	Yes	Yes	Yes	No	No
Vermont	Yes	No	Yes	No	No	No
Virginia	Yes	Yes	No	No	Yes	Yes
Washington	Yes	Yes	Yes	Yes	No	No
West Virginia	Yes	Yes	Yes	Yes	No	No
Wisconsin	Yes	Yes	Yes	Yes	No	No
Wyoming	Yes	Yes	Yes	Yes	No	No

BOW-HUNTING INFORMATION

In Alphabetical Order By State

State	Bow Season Dates (1)	Bow Season Days (2)	How Many Resident Bow-Hunters?	How Many Non-Resident Bow-Hunters? (3)	Number Of Deer Harvested By Bow (4)	May General Public Hunt Deer With A Crossbow?(5)
Alabama	10/15 - 1/31	108	62,000	6,200	32,000	No
Arizona	8/20 - 1/31	74	18,262	621	758	Yes
Arkansas	10/1 - 2/28	151	Unknown	Unknown	14,797	Yes
California	7/9 - 9/11	65	31,870	Combined	1,682	Yes
Colorado	8/28 - 11/26	30	14,300	9,100	4,900	Yes
Connecticut	9/15 - 12/31	108	13,000	2,000	2,165	No
Delaware	9/1 - 1/31	107	6,725	402	507	Yes
Florida	9/11 - 11/14	75	30,613	515	Combined	Yes
Georgia	9/17 - 10/21	35	95,000	2,000	21,450	No
Idaho	8/30 - 12/19	26	23,000	2,734	3,000	Yes
Illinois	10/1 - 1/12	104	81,000	Combined	21,000	No
Indiana	10/1 - 12/31	87	92,500	1,500	23,933	No
Iowa	10/1 - 1/10	86	34,165	450	8,814	No
Kansas	10/1 - 12/31	81	15,000	Just Started	5,500	Yes
Kentucky	10/1 - 1/15	107	94,640	1,800	8,400	No
Louisiana	10/1 - 1/20	112	50,800	345	22,600	No
Maine	9/30 - 10/29	26	12,000	1,175	682	No
Maryland	9/15 - 1/31	118	46,000	7,000	11,043	No
Massachusetts	11/7 - 11/26	20	17,500	337	1,370	No
Michigan	10/1 - 1/1	77	338,320	6,200	99,990	No
Minnesota	9/18 - 12/31	104	70,000	1,100	12,730	No
Mississippi	10/1 - 1/31	62	58,000	5,587	41,000	No
Missouri	10/1 - 12/31	92	92,031	1,544	14,696	Yes
Montana (8)	9/3 - 10/16	44	16,900	8,000	3,473	No
Nebraska	9/15 - 12/31	99	13,177	621	3,581	No
Nevada	8/14 - 1/2	42	1,954	320	285	No
New Hampshire	9/15 - 12/15	91	17,804	3,761	877	No
New Jersey	10/2 - 1/26	76	50,685	2,002	17,006	No
New Mexico	9/1 - 1/15	96	5,314	511	755	No
New York	9/27 - 12/31	96	160,000	5,000	20,048	No
North Carolina	9/12 - 11/19	54	100,000	5,385	10,000	No
North Dakota	9/3 - 12/31	121	11,400	669	4,473	Yes
Ohio	10/2 - 1/31	122	192,000	2,000	23,160	No
Oklahoma	10/1 - 12/31	78	53,106	403	7,837	No
Oregon	8/27 - 12/4	53	26,555	1,308	5,391	No
Pennsylvania	10/2 - 1/8	49	292,247	22,857	49,407	No
Rhode Island	10/1 - 1/31	123	3,800	200	378	No
South Carolina (8)	8/15 - 10/10	41	25,000	5,000	Combined	Yes
South Dakota	10/1 - 12/31	92	Combined	Combined	3,400	No
Tennessee	9/25 - 11/14	44	82,040	5,228	18,691	No
Texas	10/1 - 10/31	31	78,000	2,000	19,500	No
Utah	8/21 - 9/17	28	22,332	1,390	4,704	No
Vermont	10/1 - 12/11	32	23,110	5,592	2,999	No
Virginia	10/1 - 1/7	43	63,273	2,287	15,900	No
Washington	9/15 - 12/15	51	22,013	155	4,856	No
West Virginia	10/15 - 12/31	67	107,160	18,047	26,425	No
Wisconsin	9/18 - 12/31	86	215,292	5,535	52,623	No
Wyoming	9/1 - 9/30	30	8,111	2,669	1,538	Yes
TOTALS			**2,887,999**	**151,550**	**650,324**	

Leading Bow-Hunting States
Licensed Resident Bow Hunters

Michigan
338,320

Pennsylvania
292,247

Wisconsin
215,292

Ohio
192,000

New York
160,000

Leading Bow Deer Kill States
Total Whitetail Kill Using Bow

Michigan
99,990

Wisconsin
52,623

Pennsylvania
49,407

Mississippi
41,000

Alabama
32,000

1. Dates for the bow hunting season as listed here are in the broadest context due to space limitations. These dates reflect the first day to the last day of bow hunting activity within the state. While some states have statewide seasons, others have varying seasons for different management units within the state. Some of the dates listed were for the 1993 - 1994 season, and some are for the 1994 - 1995 season.
2. The number of bow season days is the total number of available bow hunting days in each state. Some states do not allow hunting on Sundays, while some states break seasons into "early" and "late" seasons.
3. "Combined" means that the non-resident hunter figure is included with the resident hunter figure.
4. "Combined" means that the deer harvested by bow are included with the number of deer harvested by regular firearms. The total may be found in the chart entitled "State Deer Hunting Statistics."
5. Indicates states that allow the use of a crossbow to hunt deer. Some states classify a crossbow as a firearm, some as a bow, and others outlaw them.
6. Indicates the general statewide bag limit for the majority of bow hunters in the state.
7. "Yes" signifies that a special bow hunting license, stamp, or tag is required to go bowhunting in the state.
8. The general population may use a crossbow during the firearms season, but there are no special archery permits available for the handicapped.
9. Rules of the regular firearms season will usually apply in these states during the bow season. Use of blaze orange, and getting a special permit may be required, among other restrictions.

MUZZLELOADER HUNTING INFORMATION

In Alphabetical Order By State

State	Muzzle-loader Season Dates (1)	Special Muzzle-loader Season Days (2)	Are There Special Muzzle-loader Restrictions? (5)	How Many Resident Muzzle-loader Hunters? (6)	How Many Non-Resident Muzzle-loader Hunters? (7)	Number Of Deer Harvested By Muzzle-loaders (8)
Alabama	11/20 - 1/31	0	Yes	23,000	2,300	Combined
Arizona	10/29 - 12/31	32	Yes	1,380	60	288
Arkansas	10/23 - 1/2	21	Yes	Unknown	Unknown	16,219
California	10/22 - 1/29	48	Yes	2,071	Combined	86
Colorado	9/11 - 9/19	9	Yes	6,500	1,300	2,500
Connecticut	12/12 - 12/24	12	Yes	6,000	250	367
Delaware	10/10 - 1/25	9	Yes	7,352	603	1,045
Florida	10/15 - 2/27	20	Yes	14,089	237	Combined
Georgia	9/23 - 1/12	57	Yes	20,000	1,212	Combined
Idaho	11/10 - 12/9	20	Yes	12,600	1,498	6,000
Illinois	12/9 - 12/11	3	Yes	3,017	Combined	Combined
Indiana	11/13 - 12/19	16	Yes	45,400	225	13,621
Iowa	10/15 - 1/10	32	Yes	19,000	50	6,564
Kansas	9/18 - 12/12	21	Yes	2,575	Just Started	1,100
Kentucky	10/15 - 12/16	9	No	35,000	1,000	8,200
Louisiana	12/6 - 12/10	5	Yes	4,197	50	3,200
Maine	11/29 - 12/4	6	No	5,000	160	112
Maryland	10/20 - 12/31	16	Yes	34,717	5,283	5,174
Massachusetts	12/19 - 12/21	3	Yes	12,500	241	580
Michigan	12/3 - 12/19	17	Yes	172,250	4,153	23,240
Minnesota	11/27 - 12/12	16	Yes	3,000	58	1,097
Mississippi	12/2 - 12/15	14	Yes	64,000	6,165	39,000
Missouri	11/12 - 12/11	9	Yes	13,116	Just Started	2,566
Montana	9/15 - 12/31	0	Yes	Combined	Combined	Combined
Nebraska	12/4 - 12/19	16	Yes	5,819	127	2,282
Nevada	9/11 - 1/2	0	Yes	1,200	200	139
New Hampshire	10/30 - 11/9	11	No	20,608	2,875	2,369
New Jersey	12/13 - 1/1	14	Yes	20,000	436	5,739
New Mexico	9/10 - 9/20	11	Yes	4,727	822	1,692
New York	10/15 - 12/20	14	Yes	43,000	900	3,407
North Carolina	10/10 - 11/19	18	No	96,000	5,169	13,000
North Dakota	11/26 - 12/6	11	Yes	646	0	299
Ohio	1/5 - 1/7	3	Yes	107,000	1,000	10,396
Oklahoma	10/22 - 10/30	9	Yes	42,556	202	10,255
Oregon	10/1 - 12/11	72	Yes	Combined	Combined	868
Pennsylvania	12/27 - 1/8	12	Yes	70,941	5,548	7,606
Rhode Island	10/31 - 12/24	36	Yes	4,500	250	624
South Carolina 9	10/1 - 10/10	10	Yes	Combined	Combined	Combined
South Dakota 9	10/27 - 12/19	42	Yes	Combined	Combined	300
Tennessee	10/16 - 12/12	30	Yes	94,662	5,228	27,858
Texas	1/7 - 1/15	9	No	Combined	Combined	Combined
Utah	11/6 - 11/15	10	Yes	16,075	1,020	3,442
Vermont	12/3 - 12/11	9	Yes	13,288	1,589	291
Virginia	11/7 - 1/7	29	Yes	58,617	3,639	25,995
Washington	10/1 - 12/15	34	Yes	9,161	69	2,740
West Virginia	11/21 - 12/17	6	Yes	72,236	7,378	9,769
Wisconsin	11/29 - 12/5	7	Yes	2,500	Combined	385
Wyoming	9/10 - 11/30	0	Yes	Combined	Combined	Combined
			TOTALS	**1,190,300**	**61,297**	**260,415**

STATE DEER HUNTING TRENDS

In Alphabetical Order By State

State	Deer Vehicle Collisions	Deer Crop Damage	Number Of Youth Hunters	Total Number Of Hunters	Number Of Male Hunters	Number Of Female Hunters	Hunting With Rifles
Alabama	U	I	D	D	D	D	D
Arizona	C	C	U	I	I	I	I
Arkansas	U	C	U	U	U	U	C
California	U	U	U	D	U	U	C
Colorado	U	D	U	C	U	U	C
Connecticut	C	C	C	C	C	C	C
Delaware	I	I	U	I	I	I	NA
Florida	U	C	U	D	U	U	U
Georgia	I	C	U	C	C	I	C
Idaho	U	D	I	I	I	U	I
Illinois	I	U	U	I	U	U	U
Indiana	D	U	U	I	I	I	NA
Iowa	C	C	C	C	U	U	NA
Kansas	C	D	U	C	U	U	C
Kentucky	D	C	D	C	C	C	C
Louisiana	U	D	U	C	U	U	C
Maine	C	U	D	C	U	U	C
Maryland	C	C	D	C	U	U	C
Massachusetts	U	U	U	U	U	U	NA
Michigan	D	D	I	D	D	D	D
Minnesota	U	U	U	C	U	U	U
Mississippi	I	I	U	C	U	U	C
Missouri	D	D	U	I	U	U	C
Montana	U	D	U	C	U	U	U
Nebraska	C	D	U	C	U	U	C
Nevada	U	D	U	D	U	U	D
New Hampshire	D	C	C	C	U	U	C
New Jersey	C	C	D	D	U	U	NA
New Mexico	U	U	U	D	U	U	D
New York	D	C	I	D	U	U	U
North Carolina	C	C	C	C	C	C	I
North Dakota	I	I	I	I	U	U	I
Ohio	I	I	U	I	U	U	NA
Oklahoma	C	I	U	I	U	U	I
Oregon	U	U	D	D	U	U	D
Pennsylvania	I	D	I	D	U	U	D
Rhode Island	I	I	U	I	I	C	I
South Carolina	I	C	C	I	U	U	I
South Dakota	U	I	I	I	I	U	I
Tennessee	U	I	U	C	U	U	C
Texas	U	U	U	I	I	I	U
Utah	D	D	C	D	D	D	D
Vermont	I	I	U	D	U	U	D
Virginia	D	U	I	C	U	U	U
Washington	I	U	D	D	D	C	D
West Virginia	D	D	I	I	I	I	I
Wisconsin	C	C	U	C	U	U	C
Wyoming	D	U	I	D	D	D	D

C = CONSTANT   I = INCREASED   D = DECREASED   U = UNKNOWN   NA = NOT ALLOWED

STATE DEER HUNTING TRENDS
In Alphabetical Order By State

State	Hunting With Shotguns	Hunting With Handguns	Hunting With Muzzle-loaders	Hunting With Bows	Coyote Pressure On Deer Herd	Anti-Hunting Pressure	Problems With Poaching
Alabama	D	D	D	I	I	U	C
Arizona	I	I	I	C	C	C	U
Arkansas	C	C	C	C	U	U	U
California	C	C	C	I	U	C	U
Colorado	U	U	C	I	U	I	C
Connecticut	C	NA	C	I	C	C	C
Delaware	I	NA	I	I	U	I	C
Florida	U	U	D	D	C	I	C
Georgia	C	C	C	C	U	I	C
Idaho	U	U	I	I	U	C	U
Illinois	I	I	C	I	U	C	U
Indiana	I	D	I	I	I	U	U
Iowa	C	NA	C	C	U	U	U
Kansas	C	C	I	C	U	C	C
Kentucky	D	C	I	C	I	C	C
Louisiana	C	I	C	I	U	U	D
Maine	U	U	I	I	C	C	C
Maryland	C	C	I	I	U	I	C
Massachusetts	U	NA	I	I	U	C	U
Michigan	D	D	D	D	I	D	I
Minnesota	U	U	U	C	U	C	C
Mississippi	C	C	I	I	C	C	C
Missouri	C	C	I	I	U	C	U
Montana	U	U	U	U	I	C	C
Nebraska	U	U	I	C	U	C	U
Nevada	U	U	D	D	U	I	C
New Hampshire	C	C	I	I	I	C	I
New Jersey	D	NA	I	I	I	C	C
New Mexico	D	D	I	I	U	I	U
New York	U	U	I	I	C	C	U
North Carolina	D	I	I	C	U	C	C
North Dakota	I	I	I	I	U	I	C
Ohio	I	I	I	I	U	C	C
Oklahoma	C	C	C	C	I	C	C
Oregon	D	C	I	I	I	I	U
Pennsylvania	C	C	D	I	I	C	D
Rhode Island	C	NA	I	I	U	C	C
South Carolina	C	C	D	I	U	I	C
South Dakota	C	C	I	D	C	C	D
Tennessee	C	C	I	C	U	C	C
Texas	U	U	U	U	I	I	U
Utah	D	C	D	D	I	I	D
Vermont	U	U	I	I	C	I	C
Virginia	U	U	I	I	U	U	U
Washington	D	D	D	D	C	I	C
West Virginia	C	C	I	I	U	U	D
Wisconsin	C	I	I	I	C	I	C
Wyoming	C	C	C	C	D	I	C

C = CONSTANT   I = INCREASED   D = DECREASED   U = UNKNOWN   NA = NOT ALLOWED

Wounded Deer Behavior

A. Broken Foreleg

A deer with broken foreleg will leave drag marks in the snow or dirt. A drag mark might not be evident at first. Another sign of a broken foreleg is the evidence of only three hoofprints in the tracks (see figure on next page).

B. Broken Hind Leg

A deer with broken hind leg will also leave drag marks in the snow or dirt. Tracks from a deer with this wound will only include three hoofprints: the two forelegs and one hind leg. (see figure on next page).

C. Bullet Through Lungs, Liver, or Intestines

Deer shot through the intestines, liver, or lungs often leave tracks that are bunched in twos. (see figure on next page).

Wounded Deer Behavior

D. Bullet Through Intestines or Liver

A cross jump track results from a bullet through the intestines or liver with the animal standing broadside to the shooter. (see figure below).

Tracking Patterns of Wounded Deer

TRACKING GUIDE

The myth of the waiting game

REASONS FOR WAITING:

1. Deer will lie down and "stiffen up."

2. Hunter needs pipeful of tobacco.

3. Deer will get the "blind staggers."

REASONS FOR NOT WAITING:

1. It's snowing.

2. It's raining.

3. You're in an area of high hunter density.

4. Darkness is approaching and you can't hunt in the morning.

5. Tracking takes place freely in warm weather.

6. Deer bleed freely in warm weather.

7. Trailing wounded deer with dogs permitted in the area you hunt.

8. Rigor mortis does not occur until three to six hours after death.

9. A running deer has three times the heart rate of a bedded deer.

10. Movement creates greater and more rapid blood loss, thus inhibiting coagulation.

HOW FAR WILL A DEER TRAVEL WHEN HIT THROUGH THE HEART?

Every fall around the evening fires in the deer camps the old question has come up as to how it is possible for a deer to run from fifty to 200 yards after his heart had been perforated by a bullet. We all know he does this but to date no answer has really explained how. We usually wound up the evening in agreement on but two points: 1) The deer should drop when circulation ceases and the brain … suffocates." This should happen almost immediately after the heart is perforated, for, of course, it is taken for granted the heart stops instantly. 2) As we know deer have run 200 yards after a heart shot, this explanation cannot be true and there is something phony about it somewhere. So the question has never been logically answered as far as the deer hunters are concerned.

Then, on October 31, 1928, murderer John W. Deering was placed before a stone wall in Utah State Prison with an electro cardiograph attached to his person. He was outwardly calm. The prison doctor placed a target over his heart. Five picked riflemen fired at that target at short range and four bullets simultaneously pierced his heart. Yet Deering's heart did not stop when pierced by four bullets but continued to beat for 15.6 seconds thereafter. The cardiograph record also showed that a few moments before the shots were fired, through fear, Deering's heart beats, normally seventy-two per minute, were increased to 180 per minute.

Now I cannot say that the effect of a heart shot on a deer and a man are in any way similar. But let us see what would happen if we suppose this might have a bearing on the deer question.

If the deer is frightened before the shot, his heart beats would increase tremendously, also increasing circulation of blood to the brain and muscles. And how far would he run in the 15.6 seconds before his heart stopped? At Anticosti Island I timed a mature white-tailed deer over a measured course with a stopwatch. It was shot at but purposely missed, Its speed was eighteen miles per hour.

The highest speed when another deer was fully extended and had to run, was about thirty miles per hour. At eighteen miles per hour, the deer could travel 137 yards in 15.6 seconds. At twenty-five miles per hour the deer could travel about 152 yards. At thirty miles per hour the deer could travel about 229 yards.

Doesn't it sound to you a little bit as if John Deering may have solved the riddle and that the deer's heart does not stop when perforated?

— *William Monypeny Newsom*

Tracking Responsibilities

Anyone who hunts has a responsibility to the game pursued, to the person or persons who own the land, to other hunters and to him or herself. A good hunter tries to learn all that is possible about the species hunted. Shots should be planned and carefully taken, and if a hit is made the game should be trailed until found or until it is reasonable to believe it was not vitally hit. Once the game is found, it should be properly handled so it will not be wasted. This ranges from correct field dressing to preparation of the meat and/or the trophy.

Hunters should consider the landowner by treating the landowner as a friend, and the land as if it were their own home. Mutual consideration between hunters and landowners can do much to keep hunting available.

Hunters are conspicuous because of their clothes, hunting devices, and other features. For this reason it is important to realize that the behavior of one hunter will be identified with all hunters. Good field behavior and courtesy will reflect well on the whole sport. Discourteous, illegal and irresponsible behavior of one or a few individuals can prejudice people against all hunters. Realize that hunters are in the minority in this country and that many people who are not hunters are watching. The future laws on hunting and hunting devices may depend on these people. Act accordingly.

There are several procedures recommended when a hit is made on a big game animal:

• After a shot, stay put and try to remember where the hit was made on the animal. Wounded deer usually run with their tail down.

• Take compass readings on the last sighting and/or sound of the game. If no compass is available, carefully note direction the animal traveled.

• With binoculars check the details of the place where the game was last seen. Try to identify some landmark to aid in locating correct trail.

• Wait for at least an hour before starting to trail. Wait at least six hours before starting to trail an animal hit in the guts, weather and circumstances permitting. Gut-shot animals almost always die from the wound. Gut-shot animals often 'hump' their back when hit.

• A string tracking device attached to the bow and arrow is sometimes useful in recovering game. However the string does affect the arrow flight on long shots so practice is required.

When the trailing begins:

• Move to the place where the animal was standing at the time of the shot and check for blood, arrow, hair or other signs to verify a hit. Trail very quietly. Avoid talking. Use hand signals or soft whistles if with companion.

• Even if there is no blood, mark the beginning of the trail with surveyors tape or other easily visible material, placed high enough to be easily seen from a distance. All tape should be removed once the animal is found or the trail is lost. Some people use colored crepe paper or toilet paper to mark a trail.

• Move in the direction the animal traveled checking constantly for blood sign. When first block is found mark the location with tape. Note location of blood; i.e., in a foot print, on bushes, grasses or other vertical objects, right or left side of trail, etc. (See special note on blood sign.)

• Look for different or abnormal scuff marks or hoof prints that would identify a wounded animal.

• If trailing alone, mark location of every blood sign until the quantity becomes so great that there is no need for further marking or the sign disappears.

• Be careful not to disturb the trail and sign by staying just to the side.

• If trailing with another person, mark occasional blood sign locations to give direction of travel. The person who locates sign stays put while the partner looks for next sign.

• Three people should be the maximum number trailing. Even with this number, trailing should be silent.

• If the blood trail is lost make sure the last blood sign is conspicuously marked. From this point check all main trail lanes or trails for at least half a mile.

• If no more blood sign shows on trails come back to last sign and start walking in concentric circles outward around the last sign. Animals often double back on a trail, or stagger off of regular trails shortly before they die.

• Some people have difficulty walking circles, particularly on varying levels of ground. Another method of search is to walk a grid pattern using compass readings: if the grid is tight, 3 to 5 feet in

grass and brush, this a good method of searching for more blood signs or a downed animal.

• If no blood or animal can be found but you feel the hit was a lethal one sit down and listen. Often crows, ravens, magpies or jays will be attracted to a downed animal. Listen for their calls.

• Game, after being hit, will often circle back to where it came from. If there is a problem locating a good blood sign, check along the trail on which the animal first appeared.

• Check all major crossing points on human trails, back roads or stream banks for possible sign.

• Vitally hit animals often go downhill rather than climb.

• Be sure to check in streams or swamps for a downed deer if the trail leads in that direction. Gutshot animals become thirsty and often head towards water.

• Heart-shot animals may travel surprising distances and show little external bleeding.

• Deer, particularly in northern areas, have thick layers of tallow along the back and below the brisket. This can plug wounds preventing a good blood trail. Avoid straight-down shots from tree stands for this reason.

• Do not start to follow big game hit in the gut for six to eight hours if daylight permits.

• An exception to the rule about waiting before starting to trail a wounded deer is when the hunter knows the only hit was in the leg. If the animal is kept walking the wound may stay open.

• If there is a threat of rain or snow then it may be necessary to start trailing sooner than preferred. Always trail quietly, even more than when stalking uninjured game.

• In blood trailing sometimes it is necessary to actually rub reddish spots with the fingers to verify that it is not just autumn colors on a leaf. Sometimes getting down to almost ground level will help a hunter spot blood sign that otherwise might be missed.

• When blood trailing, look at specific objects such as stones, twigs and leaves, rather than the whole trail.

• Women are often excellent at trailing because they notice detail and fewer are color blind.

• Practice blood trailing on a simulated trail with artificial blood.

• When near populated areas, remove viscera as well as deer from woods. Rotting guts are poor public relations.

Types of Blood Sign

• Blood that is frothy with bubbles usually indicates a lung hit.

• Very dark blood may indicate a liver or kidney hit.

• Blood mixed with vegetable material often greenish in color indicates a "gut" or viscera shot.

• Blood with bubbles may indicate a neck hit where the arrow has cut the neck arteries and windpipe. The arrow may show almost no sign of blood.

• Blood in spattered pattern may indicate a rapidly moving animal or one in which major blood vessels have been cut.

• Blood on both sides of the trail usually indicates a pass-through wound. In some instances a one-opening wound may produce this sign if the animal doubles back on trail.

• The height of blood sign is an indication of wound location.

• Blood-spatter drops usually point direction of travel of a rapidly moving animal like the fingers of a hand.

• No blood sign doesn't always mean a miss. Bleeding may be internal.

Increasing the "L" Grid

• Pick a length unit (e.g. 10 paces)

• Walk ahead this distance, looking for sign of deer.

• Make a right corner turn and search the same distance. This completes the first "L."

• Now make another tight angle, turn and search two lengths (20 paces).

• Turn again (always to the right) and search two lengths again, completing "L" No. 2.

• Turn again to start "L" No. 3, which will be three lengths (30 paces) on both sides.

• Continue making "L", each one unit longer than the last.

• Continue enlarging the grid unit the game is found or the trail is definitely lost.

• Another effective search pattern, also using the compass, is the U-shape. However this would miss deer that back-track.

• If a hit is made late in the day, and the weather is cool, wait until morning, unless there are a lot of coyotes, wild dogs, raccoons or bears around that might destroy the game.

• If a late hit is made and there is a threat of rain or snow, get good lights, gas or kerosene lantern, leave the bows or guns in camp or vehicle, and trail the game.

Sometimes it is even easier to

trail at night. Be sure to mark trail for two reasons. If the blood trail is lost, there's a better chance of locating it again if tape is tied in conspicuous spots. Also it is very easy to get lost at night while trailing. A well-marked trail will at least get the hunter back to where the trailing started. Reflector tape is a good addition for night trailing.

• If there is no blood, look for compressed or disturbed leaves or vegetation.

• Look for flattened plants with leading edge disturbed. Deer prints are usually narrow and tapered, even in leaves and grass. A running deer tends to scatter leaves to the side of the trail.

Approaching Downed Game

When game is found, approach cautiously and quietly and, if possible, from the back of the animal. Sometimes a wounded animal will suddenly spring to its feet and run. Try to watch the eyes. If they are glazed or unblinking the animal is safe to approach. If the animal is down but still obviously alive try to get close enough for another shot. Bow-hunters should try to place a shot in the rib cage then either quietly back off and wait at a distance or wait silently in place so as not to further "spook" the animal. It's better to have an extra hole in the skin than lose a wounded animal.

Reprinted from Big Game Recovery Guide. Courtesy of National Bowhunter Education Foundation.

DRESSING DEER

Field-Dressing Deer

1) With the deer on its back, carefully open the deer's abdomen.

2) Place a small log under the rump to get it off the ground. Cut

deeply around the rectum, being careful not to cut off or puncture the intestine. Pull to make sure the rectum is separated from tissue connecting it to the pelvic canal. Do not split the pelvic bone. Lift the animal's back quarters a bit, reach into the front of the pelvic canal, and pull the intestine and connected rectum into the stomach area.

3) If you want to make a full shoulder mount, do not cut open the chest cavity. Reach into the forward chest, find the esophagus, cut it off as far up as possible, and pull it down through the chest. If the buck won't be mounted, split the chest and sever the esophagus at its lower end. Or, simply cut into the deer's throat patch deeply enough to sever the esophagus. After it's cut, reach into the chest cavity, find the lower end of the esophagus and pull it through.

4) Roll the deer onto one side and cut the diaphragm away from the ribs all the way to the back-bone area. Roll the deer onto its other side and finish cutting away the diaphragm.

5) Leaving the deer on its side, grab the esophagus with one hand and the rectum/intestine with the other. Pull hard. The deer's innards will come out in one big package with a minimum of mess.

CAPING DEER

Caping A Trophy

Caping — the process of skinning out a trophy deer's shoulder and head — is best left to the taxidermist. In a remote setting, however, storage problems may require you to cape a deer if you want to preserve it as a full shoulder mount. Follow the illustration above when making your cuts.

1) With a short, sharp knife, slit the skin from the top of the withers, up the back of the neck to the midpoint between the ears. Now, going back to the withers, circle the body with another cut. This should leave plenty of hide for the taxidermist.

2) Peel the skin forward up to the ears and jaws, exposing the point where you want to cut through the neck. The easiest way to separate the head from the neck is to make an encircling cut through the neck to the atlas joint, the first vertebra under the skull. This is the only joint on the neck that has no interlocking bones.

3) Remember, when field-dressing a trophy to be mounted, don't cut into the chest or neck area. If blood gets on the area to be mounted, wash it off with snow or water as soon as possible. Also, when taking the deer out of the woods, place it on a sled or rickshaw. All it takes is one sharply broken branch on a deadfall to damage the hide.

SKINNING DEER

Skinning Your Trophy

Skinning deer does not have to be a laborious chore that leaves hair all over the meat. Using a car, truck or come-along, you can winch off the hide in about five minutes of work.

1) With the deer hanging by its neck, slice the hide around the neck as close to the head as possible. (Don't cut into the meat. The neck muscles bear much force later as the hide is pulled off.)

2) Cut down the front of the neck to the opening made during field-dressing.

3) Saw off the legs slightly above the knee joints.

4) Pull the neck hide down until about one foot of it is free. Take a golf-ball sized rock or 1.5-inch section of 2-by-2 and wrap it into the hide's end. Make a tight package and cinch it off with high-quality nylon rope of about 3/8-inch thickness. A double half-hitch works well.

5) Tie the rope's other end to a car, truck or come-along hook. Back up the vehicle until the hide is pulled to the brisket and shoulders. It will bind slightly here. If necessary, have someone work the hide around the brisket. With tension on the rope, the hide will slide over fairly easily.

Weights and Heart Girth

To calculate live or hog-dressed weight, first measure heart girth, the circumference of the body just behind the front legs. Then consult this chart to convert girth into a close estimate of weight.

Heart girth inches (cm)	Hog-dressed weight Adults pounds (kg)	Live weight Adults pounds (kg)
26 (66.0)	46 (20.9)	69 (27.2)
27 (68.6)	52 (23.6)	68 (30.8)
28 (71.1)	58 (26.3)	75 (34.0)
29 (73.7)	64 (29.0)	83 (37.6)
30 (76.2)	70 (31.8)	90 (40.8)
31 (78.7)	76 (34.5)	98 (44.5)
32 (81.3)	82 (37.2)	106 (48.1)
33 (83.8)	88 (39.9)	113 (51.3)
34 (86.4)	94 (42.6)	121 (54.9)
35 (88.9)	101 (45.8)	128 (58.1)
36 (91.4)	107 (48.5)	136 (61.7)
37 (94.0)	113 (51.3)	144 (65.3)
38 (96.5)	119 (54.0)	151 (68.5)
39 (99.1)	125 (56.7)	159 (72.1)
40 (101.6)	131 (59.2)	166 (75.3)
41 (104.1)	137 (62.1)	174 (78.9)
42 (106.7)	143 (64.9)	182 (82.6)
43 (109.2)	149 (67.6)	190 (86.2)
44 (111.8)	155 (70.3)	197 (89.4)
45 (114.3)	161 (73.0)	205 (93.0)

Virginia Polytechnic Institute & State University

Charles J. Alsheimer

Midwestern and Northeastern whitetails tend to have big bodies with shorter limbs.

Whitetail Subspecies: How Many are There?

Most deer texts list 38 subspecies of white-tailed deer in North, Central, and South America. Seventeen of these are found in North America. What has all the mixing and shuffling of subspecies done to affect the genetics of deer in restocked areas? We don't know exactly. However, we do know that, to some extent, the idea of 17 distinct subspecies in North America is impractical.

A subspecies is just another way of identifying subpopulations of a particular species. The formal definition, according to Professor Brian Chapman at the University of Georgia, is "a geographically adapted population that is statistically different from other populations." The "statistical difference" in this instance refers to differences in actual physical measurements, such as body length and skull measurements.

In fact, the subspecies of white-tailed deer have all been distinguished by comparing characteristics such as coat color, external dimensions, cranial details, and antler tine-size and spread. Most of the whitetail's subspecies were described before the 1940s, a decade before the peak of restocking efforts in the mid-1950s.

The movement of deer from state to state often introduced subspecies from diverse regions of North America. This raises questions about the original concept of 17 distinct subspecies in North America, and the possibility that currently accepted subspecies distribution maps might be less valid today.

Subspecies of whitetails were often introduced into areas where they had not occurred before. Some of these areas were void of deer, and others had only small remnant populations. It is conceivable that if new studies were undertaken to define geographic distributions of these subspecies using the same characteristics mentioned earlier, a distribution map would show great overlap or islands of subspecies. It's also possible that entirely new intergrades or "hybrids" of subspecies would be described.

As we all know, the whitetail's appearance differs from one region of the country to another. For example, deer from the Northeast and Midwest contain the borealis subspecies, and tend to have big, blocky bodies with short, stocky limbs. By contrast, deer of the texanus subspecies typically have smaller, sleeker bodies with longer limbs.

These variances in physical appearance suggest genetic differences between the subspecies. Although the genetic basis has not been documented, it's true that warm-blooded animals in colder environments tend to be larger in size. This is known as "Bergmann's Rule." The increased size results in a smaller surface area to body-volume ratio, which helps to retain heat. Conversely, a higher ratio helps dissipate heat. This biological principle seems to be true for most subspecies of white-tailed deer.

While genetic factors play an important role in the expression of Bergmann's Rule, there also is an environmental basis for this phenomenon. Work at the University of Georgia suggests that Southern areas that were restocked with Northern deer produce larger animals in areas with good habitat.

However, in overpopulated areas or areas of poor habitat, deer tend to be smaller regardless of the stocking source. Poor management or poor habitat can eliminate any size advantage the Northern stock might have.

That same research points out that proper management of the animal's environment is vitally important in an animal's ability to reach its genetic potential.

"Hey Dad. I Got A Buck!"

Earl L. Little

I have hunted Wisconsin deer for a lifetime, since the age of 12. First, I was allowed only to follow others and my father into the woods. Then came shotgun slugs, the rifle, and bow and arrows. Good years and bad years for the deer, and good and bad years for the hunters. For this hunter, the hunting years were good, but the procuring of venison for the pot was not so good. And, thanks to Hunters' Choice Permits, only a button buck to fill that category. It seems almost impossible to have so many deer seasons gone by with so little deer meat in the freezer to stave off a genuine liking for venison steak. There was also much discouragement.

I have hunted in many parts of Wisconsin, and with many different hunters — hunters with various degrees of expertise. When my luck stayed bad, other men took pity on me and put me on favorite stands, or sent me to secret places. Some made drives for me. Others offered endless advice.

As the years passed, the once serious nature of genuine helpfulness turned to humor. My deer hunting became the joke of many, and still is. And, my family learned to savor what little venison made it to our table.

When my two boys became old enough to go deer hunting and wanted to go deer hunting, I was more than just a little worried that I could not, or would not teach them the right things. Although my wife Joan hunted with me when she could, the boys would make it an exceptional and very special gun-deer season. Little's Rest, the family cottage on a lake in Langlade County, would be our base. I picked the stands while I was bird hunting before the deer season.

When Scott shot on opening morning, I was sure it was him, but with a father's impatience, I waited for his call. When the call came, I crossed the ridge I was on, stumbled through a little valley and made it through the light snow to Scott around the side of another ridge in record time. The little doe, Scott's first deer, was field-dressed and we (the whole family) were happy, and even when it was the only deer we took home.

The next season, Mark had most of the shooting, but being the youngest, he had been given the shotgun and the deer seemed to know the accurate range of shotguns. I was overjoyed that he had seen deer, but disappointed that he did not take his first.

The season that followed found Mark with a severely broken finger in a cast, which covered his whole hand and had to be supported by a sling. His feeling for deer hunting had grown between seasons, and a new rifle had come at Christmas time.

A new rifle that he fired, sighted in and cared for without having to be reminded. A new rifle that brought dreams of fantastic outdoor experiences. But then, in early fall, Mark looked one way while his bicycle went the other way, and he lay sprawled across the neighbor's parked car. He had used a hand to break his fall. The doctor said, "Don't go," but even the doctor knew his warning fell on deaf ears. When opening morning came, we bundled the hand and Mark cradled his new rifle across the sling. Luckily for a worried family, I saw the only deer and Mark did not have a chance to redo the injury. Mark did not take his chanceless season so well, but his efforts made me proud.

Then came the year of the rain. The family again took their stands, but in a driving wet and cold rain. It must have been the adverse conditions — I connected with the Hunter's Choice deer. We were all (including the deer) cold and soaked through when the deer finally hung from the old maple tree at the cottage. After that, we hunted for a while and dried out for a while. The deer hid in some unknown dry place.

My run-down of the deer seasons has finally come to the point where I wanted to start this story. Blame it on wanderlust, the uncontrollable urge to see what is over the next ridge, or whatever you please, Mark and I started looking for another area to hunt. It was not bad where we were, but we looked anyhow. Where do you go when

you go looking for new or different deer country? You go the end of the road, of course. To us, an old unused logging road.

The overgrown tracks of another era crossed along the high ground over the ridge and parallel to the Town Road. With the exception of a small clearcut now dense in young popple, the mature hardwoods seemed to be never-ending. We walked slowly and tried to keep the hunt, but the day was pleasant and we found ourselves strolling in the glory of late fall. When we came to the fork in the ancient ruts, it was on top of one of Wisconsin's biggest hills, at least it seemed that way. The leading edge of the ridge ended here with a descent into pine, spruce, and hemlock, and then alder and the river. The rest of the ridge gave way to rolling ground and a new ridge back toward the big woods and east. We took the west fork.

Walking between the hardwoods and lower evergreens, we seemed to descend farther and farther along this ridge until the river valley allowed a feeling — however, untrue — of level ground.

Deer after deer had come to this same path. The distinct cloven hooves joined together now, crossed a low wet spot, and then separated again. The deer had come here when the first shots were fired, but they moved in an orderly unhurried way.

Our road, now a single lone path, stopped in a little clearing surrounded by old and new cuttings. Huge remnants of old stumps were here and there among chest high popple and various heights of second growth. Deer had come here, too. They rested and grazed on lush grass and legumes, and their sign was everywhere. We went beyond the road to find the river and new popple bordered with spruce and hemlock around small clearings on the west, and a heavy, beautiful, mature spruce stand on the east. Between the end of the path in the clearing to the river, we stopped and marveled many times at deer tracks, rubs, and scrapes, and other fresh sign.

We set up shop then. For two and one-half days, Mark and I left to hunt northern Wisconsin. This natural yet unnatural place became our ground. We hunted there; we listened and watched there; we dreamed there; and we fretted on leaving. We did not see deer there, except in the deep thoughts of anticipation, but we had no second thoughts about coming back.

Somehow, as in-betweens go, the time between discovery and the next deer season did not take us back to what we had found. We saved and savored the time and the place in our minds' eye, and we did not violate the image until it was the first day again.

When the first day came, Mark followed the road to the end. Scott, Joan, and I went to the old stands. I wanted to go with Mark, but the old stands were now familiar and easier to get to. Mark was also old enough now, and wanted that special personal adventure. It was time to let him go. It was that terrible hard time for parents when the cord must be severed, or at least stretched.

When the worry became too heavy, the morning too long, and the distance seemed to widen too much, I could stand it no longer. I told Joan and Scott where I was going and went toward Mark's stand. I had the apprehension of a father, and the pride of a father when Mark disappeared in the morning's dark woods. I knew where he would be, but followed his tracks in the fresh snow, over and along the high ridge, up and down the old ruts to their convergence into a path, and through the young popple toward the edge of the dark green spruce.

One hundred yards from his stand by the river, Mark called to me. He was standing on the edge of the dense spruce growth. Green spruce boughs partially obscured bright blaze orange clothing. Mark is not an emotionally readable person; thoughts and feelings cannot be ciphered from body language; humor and humorous things do not elicit laughs, but various degrees of grins. Even then, they are quiet, back-in-the-corner grins. He was grinning now.

The eight-point buck had suddenly appeared through spruce and the hemlock that made up the edge of the sparse hardwood clearing. Cautious, the deer had only shown head and front shoulders. Then, the animal faced him. Mark had to control the excitement of seeing a buck that size. For some, it would be easy, for others too much. He had to shift his attention from "all I could see was horns", to making a killing shot. The .30-30 round entered the base of the buck's neck. The deer had turned back into spruce trees, and fallen there. Mark had field dressed his first deer, and dragged it about 20 yards before I came along.

I stood and looked at the beautiful animal, and then at my son. I shook his hand. He relived the events which led to this moment, and we started the long drag to the truck. The fresh snow was appreciated now, but varying sizes of second growth and old slashings, are just wonderful to drag a trophy size (trophy to us) 8-pointer through. We changed off with the rope for about half a mile, and then decided it was time to go for help. Mark would go for the rest of the family, especially Scott. I would wait and maybe drag a little more.

Mark disappeared around a big deadfall, and I stood trying to catch my breath. It must have been all those heavy hunting clothes that made me sweat and breathe like this, or were there too many years simply covered by the clothes? Not waiting, or wanting to know the answer, I started another drag.

That buck and I got on intimate terms after that. By the time we made it to the incoming path, I had called that deer everything except a deer. Those eight-points found their way under, over, and into slashings, large deadfalls, trees, brush, and the good earth. I sweated and worse, grunted and cursed, and even begged once or twice. Happiness was seeing orange jackets coming down along the big ridge. Although exclamations about the deer followed by cheery statements like, "Why are you sweating and puffing like that?", fell on a somewhat adverse disposition.

I found Mark with his deer about 11:30 in the morning. Even Mom had helped drag, but most of her help had come in the "direction" department. We hung the buck from the big maple at Little's Rest about 3 p.m. The worst forgotten. The whole family happy.

I started this story talking about my deer hunting, my quest, and my buck. Well, I have now taken my buck through my son. I have now had the best of all deer seasons in a few hours. The discovery with my son of the place. The speculation and anticipation about deer there. The deer which came from there. All of these events have made me feel as though the magnificent animal hanging from a maple tree was a large part mine.

There have since been other deer — bucks and does — taken from the same stand — Mark's stand. For all, except one, I have been there to see the grin, and help. I would never take away from any of my son's deer hunting, especially that first deer, but I will be eternally grateful for my part in the taking of those deer, and for being allowed to share the emotion and the experience.

Who Would Know?

Laurie Lee Dovey

When the 180- to 190-class Boone & Crockett whitetail stepped into sight 80 yards away, I instinctively placed my scope's cross-hairs on his vitals. The buck's antlers spread far beyond his ears. The bases of his main beams were easily half again as big around as my wrists. The ivory-tipped tines of his symmetrical, 14-point rack glowed in the burnt-orange evening sun.

My record-book buck of a lifetime stood before me. My .270's safety was off, and I knew my aim was true. The deer was mine, all right.

But I couldn't shoot.

Thirty minutes before rattling in this huge-racked king, I had shot at a smaller 10-point buck. I saw the 10-pointer bow up under the impact of my shot, yet watched it, out of reflex, jump a barbed wire fence. The deer ran only 30 yards before it dropped out of sight. I believed I had hit the deer, but I couldn't hop the fence to look for its blood trail. When the owners of the Mexican ranch where I was hunting dropped me off, they had told me not to cross that fence no matter what happened. If I crossed, I would have to walk across a county road that bordered another rancher's land. If Mexican officials spotted me, big trouble was certain.

I desperately wanted to see that 10-pointer lying in the brush just over the knoll on the other side of the road. But although it was just a few yards,

it might as well have been a continent away. This was the final hour of a five-day hunt and 12-day road trip. I had been hunting hard, and was now exhausted. I had passed up numerous big deer, mainly heavy-racked 8-pointers, waiting for a super deer. I wanted desperately to return home successful. After shooting at the 10-pointer, I left my setup position and walked along the fence to where the deer had stood when I shot. I didn't find blood.

Immediately, I began doubting everything I had seen. Because the deer was moving toward the fence when I fired, I thought I might have misjudged either my timing or shot placement. After reassessing everything, I decided my chances of a hit were 50-50.

But two events continued to nag me. I clearly saw the deer bow up immediately after the shot, and I saw it disappear 30 yards away as if it had fallen. The buck could be lying just a short distance from where I now stood.

But I had no way to tell. There were no trees to climb for a better view, and the knoll in front of me impeded my line of sight. Frustrated, I retreated to my set-up site and waited for my companions to pick me up. I knew we could then search for the buck because they had permission to go onto the other land.

While I waited, I decided to try a new rattling box I had picked up just six days earlier. Besides,

> The buck's ivory-tipped tines glowed in the burnt-orange evening sun. My .270's safety was off, and I knew my aim was true. The deer was mine, all right. But I couldn't shoot.

I had nothing else to do but wait, and only 30 minutes of daylight remained. I also knew I didn't have anything to lose by trying a new hunting product.

So I rattled the box. Unfortunately for me, it worked like a dream. A magnificent whitetail raged out of the brush along a drainage 100 yards upwind of me. The huge buck was stomping, grunting and snorting, looking for his inferiors.

I gasped at the sight. Never before had I seen an animal equal to this buck. Not even the mounted head on the ranch-house wall that measured 26-plus inches across the main beams could compare. The buck created such excitement and intensity that I felt I was in a trance. He was mine! I began to squeeze the rifle's trigger when reality gripped me.

"You can't shoot," I whispered to myself. "You might have hit the 10-pointer. It might be lying 30 yards past the fence. The law says one deer per hunter. If you kill this buck, too, you're breaking the law. But look at him! You'll never get this chance again!"

Instantly, the corners of my mind engaged in an ethical battle I'll never forget. In retrospect, some of my thoughts not only embarrass me, they shame me. Here's a synopsis of the struggle between my ethics and desires:

I missed that 10-pointer. He jumped the fence. No deer hit by a .270 bullet would or could jump a fence. But wait! Remember the conversation last night with Judd Cooney. He said a wounded deer can, out of reflex, jump a fence. He knows what he's talking about. He's been hunting forever. He's right.

But there isn't any blood. I missed. I can squeeze on this deer and take him without a problem. He's still standing there. He's calmed down. Heck, he's starting to feed along the fence line. This is the surest shot I've ever had on a whitetail!

I start to squeeze. I back off again.

NO! I won't be able to live with myself if I illegally kill two deer.

But I can easily lie about what happened. This is THE deer I've always dreamed of. When they come to get me, if anyone heard two shots, I can say the buck was the first shot, and a coyote I missed was the second shot. That's believable. I simply won't mention the other deer. Who would know the truth? No one.

Am I crazy? Now I'm thinking about lying to myself and to friends. Maybe I don't have to lie. With a buck like this, everyone would understand why I shot. Heck, any other hunter would shoot, right?

I was possessed. I considered every side of the situation as my mental skirmish continued for nearly 15 minutes. All the while, the record-book deer sauntered closer while my cross-hairs followed. With the buck at 65 yards, I could wait no longer. The sun was on the horizon, and darkness was moments away. I had to decide now! My hands shook. I was sweating and breathing heavily.

I knew I couldn't live with a lie. I knew I'd never be able to look at the beautifully mounted deer hanging on my wall without remembering the circumstances of its death. I sighed as I dropped the butt of my rifle to my knee. I was disappointed, distraught and highly emotional. The buck hadn't moved. Again, it taunted me.

I begged: "Lord, if I'm the person who's supposed to take this deer, have it stand there a few more minutes. If I'm not the hunter who's to take him, please make something happen."

Instantly, the buck took three steps, just enough to move behind thick brush and out of sight.

He was gone.

Still, my disappointment deepened, even though I knew I had done right.

After dark, five of us searched for the 10-pointer without luck. We searched again the next morning. We found tracks down a deep drainage, but no blood trail.

Reality sliced my heart. I had cleanly missed the 10-pointer. I could have shot the 14-pointer without breaking any man-made laws. And the clarity of hindsight would have even cleared up any lingering ethical questions.

Or would it? What good is hindsight to ethics? It is ethics, after all, that guide us through pressures of the moment, and tell us to shoot or flip the safety back on.

Yes, I came close to killing that buck. And I've had dozens of other hunters more experienced than I say they would have had no internal debates. They say with conviction that they would have killed that buck. But they're making their judgments in retrospect, knowing the first deer wasn't down. I listen to them, but say you can't know how you'll react until you're living the situation, weighing uncertainties, both legal and ethical.

Two years later, that Mexican buck haunts me continuously. I close my eyes and see him in vivid detail. I wish he were a trophy hanging in my office over the computer recording this story.

Yes, I wish my name were in the record books. But if I had taken the shot, and I had never told another soul the whole story, I would have been stuck with a lie I could never reveal. And every time I looked at the majesty of that incredible buck, I would be living a lie.

I would know the truth. The record-book entry would mock me.

And I could never escape my own stare.

Note: I recently received word from my Mexican hosts that a buck they believe to be the same 14-pointer was shot in 1993. He scored 186.

Era of the Anti's

Al Cornell

Thirty years ago I was a farm boy toting a borrowed 20-gauge and hunting grouse, fox or deer till the cows needed to be milked. It was simple. Everyone approved. Several could exhort with colorful stories of trips north to hunt deer and of encounters with bears and wildcats. My rare successful outings were met with unanimous approval and encouragement. Hunting was natural, easy and compelling. Of course I hunted.

The first wind of change was the "No Trespassing" signs that appeared two miles down the road. I was a little slow adjusting to them, because I knew it couldn't mean me. Eventually, new landowners in the area let me know that indeed I was not welcome to hunt on their land. Through this time hunting changed some but remained highly accepted. The curtain had fallen on the first act, but the stage still offered its high adventure. Of course I continued to hunt.

I'm not sure when I first heard that some people disapproved of hunting. Though the concept seemed unnatural, I wasn't concerned. I was not fond of golf and thought it was a comparable sort of thing. If they didn't like it, certainly no one was pressuring them to do it. I'll pursue a buck, someone else will pursue a par, and we'll all be happy.

Time revealed another secret. Opposition to hunting was a more serious problem than I had thought. All people have a right to voice an opinion toward wildlife and its protection and/or use. Even the indifferent make economic and cultural decisions that affect this great resource. But among those who rise up with sincere concern, a significant number are misdirected.

The profound, and once highly accepted, privilege to hunt now must endure the fiery test of dedicated human opposition. There exists no swift frontal attack by which we can conquer this enemy. The tactics are guerrilla and the duration looms as lengthy. While we must strategically win battles to preserve this privilege, we can't expect our victories to change the mind of the opponent. They will regroup and seek any available weakness for their next attack.

Only a carefully followed plan will ensure continued victories. We must start to look unto ourselves to grasp the image we portray. This is discomforting. There has always been a certain rugged freedom associated with this highest form of outdoor recreation. Can one hunter stand up to his buddies and say, "I won't violate, and I wish you wouldn't"? Wildlife agencies and ethical hunter organizations have long encouraged us to report violators. We should.

Maybe it is time to see ourselves in a new way. Wildlife

> The time has come to hone razor heads and good image, to target vital areas and decent character, and to hunt respectfully and with dignity.

offers many values to our society. We accept the consumptive value of certain species as valid and significant. Anti-hunters abhor this use of the resource. Wildlife also has some negative effects in our society. Deer become a concern when large numbers cause increasing crop damage and car-deer accidents, and stifle forest regeneration. They may also be implicated in the spread of some livestock and human diseases. Anti-hunters offer no reasonable solution to this problem.

So we can solve a problem they can't. Before patting ourselves on the back, we must learn to view this as an obligation to be performed and not a privilege to do with as we like. When we look again to our role, hunters have become a tool of modern wildlife management. Our relation to wildlife populations, especially deer, is a responsibility to that resource and to society.

Many people of urban areas are removed from the problem. Some of them fall to the influence of the anti-hunting philosophy. Also hunters who lobby for a deer behind every tree must somehow come to realize the problems they create. Promoting an unreasonably large deer herd may offer us a couple of short-term benefits. Yet such a view works against hunters and the deer herd. The deer become a plight to their own habitat

when hunters reject their role in management. Our strongest justification used to influence the large non-hunting public revolves around a problem for which we offer a solution. We can wisely choose to be a tool in maintaining a reasonable and healthy deer herd.

Not many forms of recreation fulfill a need to non-participating members of society. Ours does. It keeps the deer herd within acceptable bounds, reducing accidents and crop damage, and promotes desirable ecosystems with diverse life forms. The non-hunting public must be educated to perceive these values of hunting. Then the fights will be easier to win, and the future of hunting will become more firmly entrenched as an important tradition.

When things were simpler, I hunted. I still hunt. The complexity of society challenges but does not overwhelm. The time has come to hone razor heads and good image, to target vital areas and decent character, and to hunt respectfully and with dignity.

The Promise

Dan Bertalan

As Pete brushed the snow from his arrow, he realized he had never loved or hated the woods more. He wished he could be anywhere else, yet knew there was no other place he could be. He had promised he would hunt the deer. So he stared blankly into the swirling snow, his thoughts drifting back to last spring.

"Hey Petey," Dave had called. "Check out this magnum rub." Dave had stood grinning next to a 5-inch cedar stripped bare to the sapwood. "Looks like The Rake made a rub line along this thicket last fall. See how his burr tines have gouged this cedar? I bet other bucks tuck their tails when they see this dude coming."

Raising his eyebrows, Pete smiled at Dave before running his fingers over the scarred tree. Sure enough, the deep marks looked like the work of The Rake. They had spotted the deer one evening last season while driving back to the cabin. It stood frozen in the glow of their headlights, its massive rack sporting clusters of gnarled burr tines and rows of closely packed points, looking more like a giant garden rake than antlers. The buck's image was etched into their minds before the deer loped into the darkness.

Pete had peered deeper into the tangle of Lostlogger Swamp. "Look, more rubs along that alder patch. They weren't there in November when I hunted near the creek. You s'pose he ruts late here?"

Dave looked over Pete's shoulder. "Probably makes his rounds through the swamp during mid-December looking for doe-fawns in their first heat. The guy's a real cradle-robber."

They snickered.

"Then he probably made it through gun season and might be back in the fall."

"More like next December," said Dave. "He ruts later than most bucks. We can catch him here after the snow drives him from those aspen hills. He's made it through lots of gun seasons. He'll be back. I'd bet a dozen arrows on it."

During their spring scouting, Dave always found the best spots. He always found the biggest sheds, too. But Pete didn't mind. Not one bit, because Dave's discoveries were always partly his. They shared everything: campfires, rub lines, sheds, scrapes, hunting gear — all the good stuff in life. They had since the day they left their mother's womb just minutes apart: twin brothers, magically bonded. They could read each other's thoughts, and feel each other's joys, excitement and sorrows.

Sometimes Pete wished the bond wasn't so strong — like now when he could also feel the pain. It hurt, bad, and wouldn't go away. After the spring scouting trip, Dave returned home unusually tired. Pete noticed first. His brother looked pale, especially for a rugged 20-year-old who was always blazing his trail through life. For him the promise of another spring didn't bloom. Dave was diagnosed with leukemia.

Summer swept by like an ashen dream: new doctors, more tests, barely a thread of hope — stuff that was only supposed to happen to someone else, people in movies, not his brother. And when the thread of hope snapped, an unsuccessful bone marrow transplant, Pete couldn't shake the guilt. He had failed Dave miserably. With hope all but gone, Dave faded like fall's colors.

By mid-December he appeared a thin reflection of his brother. Pete hovered near Dave's bedside like a shadow until two days ago when he had left with an unfilled promise. "Come on Petey, please. Please do it for me. We spent way too much time patterning The Rake to let him slip away now. The way it's snowing outside he's gotta be in Lostlogger Swamp. Dad already said he'd go to the cabin with you."

Shaking his head, Pete tried to break free the "Not without you" stuck in his throat.

Dave cut him off. "Look, I'm not asking you to have fun. Just go sit in the stand. It's my only chance to feel the thrill of bow hunting again — through you. Wherever you go, part of me goes. It's always been that way, always will be. For us, Petey; go get The Rake. Say you will. Promise."

Pete saw a shine in Dave's eyes he hadn't seen for months. "OK, I'll go," he said, his words crackling at first, gaining resolve as he spoke. "I'll go for us. And you get ready to feast on Rake steaks when I get back. And that's a promise."

He had left while the fire in Dave's eyes burned bright with a new kind of hope. Now, 200 miles north in the frozen recesses of Lostlogger Swamp, Pete looked down from his jack-pine stand. Dave had been right about the buck. Fresh rubs marked the Rake's old travel lane. Dave had also been right about sharing in the hunt. Looking at the quiver full of cedar arrows they had made together, Pete knew he wasn't alone in the stand. He gripped the recurve they sometimes shared and clenched his jaw. Dave was there all right. Together, maybe they really could fulfill the promise. The snow turned into stinging needles of ice as the final hour of daylight faded into grayness. Pete was gazing at the simple lines of his broadhead when he noticed a distant shadow drifting in the cedars. At first he thought it was another snow swirl. But there it was again, closer, grayer than the icy backdrop. Suddenly the realization struck him. It was The Rake.

Pete barely had time to shake himself free of the cold before The Rake sauntered into the shooting lane. As Pete drew, everything clicked into slow-motion. Ice crystals drifted lazily past his face. The Rake floated into the opening like a gray cloud. Pete's fingers slipped from the string. The arrow leaped, feathers pinwheeling through the cold air. The dull thump of broadhead biting buckskin snapped Pete's senses back.

The buck flinched and spun hard, snow spraying in his path. In a flash The Rake was gone. The tangle of cedars swallowed it with barely a sound. Only the whisper of a raw wind filled the evening.

By the time Pete gathered his gear and took up the trail, darkness and a bitter cold had settled over the swamp. With his flash-

> "Wherever you go, I go. Whatever you do, I do. That's what will always be special about us. I'm part you, you're part me. We're one heck of a deer hunting team; always will be."

light beam knifing the night, Pete plowed through the knee-deep snow, following crimson specks. A hundred yards into the swamp, The Rake burst from under a dead-fall and bolted across a creek. Pete fumbled for an arrow. But the buck melted quickly into the night. Pete pushed deeper into the swamp.

He jumped the buck twice more before it crossed the creek again. An inner voice told him to give up the trail until morning. But another told him he had a promise to keep. Besides, the buck's trail showed it wouldn't last long. Pete headed for the creek. As he leaped for a log near the far bank, his foot slipped, throwing him sideways into the water. Soaking his forearms and legs, Pete clamored up the bank, cursing the cold. He wrung out his gloves and continued on. A hundred yards from the creek, he spotted The Rake lying near a fallen cedar. Pete nocked an arrow. He watched the great buck a long time but it didn't stir, didn't breathe. The Rake was his. He'd kept the promise.

The buck's hot insides stung Pete's numbed hands. He let out a long groan then looked skyward. The clouds had cleared. Stars twinkled overhead. "This one's for you, Dave," he whispered, his breath gathering in a steamy cloud. The temperature was dropping fast.

By the time Pete finished dressing the deer, the crusted snow on his damp jacket and pants had frozen. He tried pulling on his gloves and found them stiff. He jammed his hands inside them anyway and began dragging the buck toward an old logging trail — a shortcut he thought would save time. But after an hour of stumbling through the snowy swamp, he came to another creek. This one looked deep and Pete couldn't remember seeing it before. He wasn't about to get wet again, so he began backtracking his swath in the snow. Even though it was easier dragging the huge buck on a broken trail, cold and exhaustion soon began taking their toll. Pete's damp arms and legs felt prickly numb. His breath came in heaving gasps as he began floundering with the buck. And finally, when each step became a painful struggle, Pete abandoned the buck and plodded on.

When he stopped to rub his hands together sometime later, he realized he no longer carried his bow. Anger quickly turned into despair, then panic. He charged frantically back on his tracks, lurching through the snow. Panting and cursing, he finally found his bow only a short ways from the buck. He crawled over and sat on the now-frozen whitetail and began to sob. Soon he curled up. Moments later a great sleep overtook him.

"Hey Petey," a voice echoed in

his ears. "Get your backside up before you become another legend of Lostlogger Swamp. You and The Rake deserve a better end than this!"

Pete cracked open an eyelid and peered into the darkness. Only ghostly shapes of snow-draped cedars surrounded him. "Who's there?" he mumbled, his voice hoarse and weak.

"Don't give me that old, 'I'm sleepy routine,'" rang Dave's voice. "It's time to celebrate our harvesting of The Rake."

Pete propped himself up on an elbow and tried clicking on his flashlight. No use. The cold had sapped its life. He unfolded his stiff body and stood. His senses felt dull and achy. "Where are you, Dave?"

"Over here behind the wall of cedars. I've found a great place to camp. Come on and start a fire."

Pete stumbled toward Dave's voice. Plowing through the matting of cedars he discovered a giant pile of dead-falls criss-crossed together. "In here Petey, it's open under here like the brush forts we built when we were kids, remember?"

Pete stooped and entered an opening in the tangled mass of trees. Inside it was black, but he wasn't afraid. Dave was there somewhere. "Where are you Dave? How'd you get here?" Pete's words came in an incoherent slur, yet they were answered.

"I'm right next to you. Now get a fire going. It's colder than a chickadee's butt in February in here."

Pete struggled to clear his mind. "I can't make a fire. The only matches I brought won't light. Already tried them earlier. It's no use. They're too damp. It's too cold."

"Then it's a damned good thing you're wearing my lucky jacket," Dave said. "You never could keep from grabbing the wrong one. Just reach inside the rear zipper pouch. There's a disposable lighter and a fire-starter stick in there. These dry birch and cedar branches in here ought to burn like blazes."

With nearly frozen hands, Pete fumbled in the darkness for minutes before finally flicking the lighter to life and lighting the fire starter. He added handfuls of cedar twigs that quickly crackled into bright flames. The fire's glow filled the small fortress. In one corner sat a snowshoe hare, a few weeks short of reaching its full all-white phase, its eyes reflecting back the fire's light. In the other corner sat Dave.

"Pretty neat in here, hey Petey?"

Pete squinted into the smoke and shook his head. His mind ached with a dull buzz. There on a log sat Dave, the same Dave whom Pete had known last spring. He appeared full of life and vigor. Pete sank to his knees and held his hands over the fire. As he wiggled warmth back into his fingers, Dave leaned close to the fire. The smile on his face beamed brighter than ever.

"Great shot, Petey, but you trailed him too soon. You should have waited until morning and let Dad help. He'll be mad that you got lost and spent the night out."

"How did you know I was lost? How did you know I got The Rake?" "Remember Petey? Wherever you go, I go. Whatever you do, I do. That's what will always be special about us. I'm part you, you're part me. We're

Pete jammed his hands inside his gloves and began dragging the buck toward an old logging trail — a shortcut he thought would save time. But after an hour of stumbling through the snowy swamp, he came to another creek. This one looked deep and Pete couldn't remember seeing it before.

one heck of a deer hunting team; always will be. Now what do you say we get down to some real celebrating. Go strip out those buck fillets and let's have some campfire venison like the old days."

Long into the night the two ate roast deer meat and talked around the fire, its warmth filling the snow-blanketed shelter. They sang campfire songs and reminisced about hunts past, and planned hunts anew. Sometime in the night a great sleep overcame them. Pete woke to the cold dripping of melting snow on his forehead and a voice outside. Slivers of light poked through several small openings in the dead-fall maze. He turned and looked around, but Dave wasn't there. He realized suddenly that Dave never had been really, yet deep inside knew with a certainty he always would be — wherever Pete hunted.

He stumbled outside and squinted against a brilliant sun. His Dad's frantic voice cut through the still air.

"I'm over here, Dad. Over here!"

His Dad burst through the wall of cedars, his eyes ringed and red, his face haggard. "For the love of God, Pete, I thought we lost you."

"I'm OK, Dad. We spent the night just fine. Me and Dave even had roast ..."

Pete stopped short when he saw the stab of pain in his Dad's eyes at the mention of Dave. He knew what was coming.

"I'm sorry son, Dave's gone. I got word from the sheriff last night after dark. I drove to town and was on the phone with your mother half the night. Spent the other half looking for you. The wind and snow covered most of your tracks. It was a good thing I found that orange flagging you left marking your way into the swamp."

Pete reached deep into one of his jacket pockets, Dave's pocket he realized, and pulled out a half roll of fluorescent surveyor's ribbon he didn't know was there.

He put his arms around his dad and they quietly held each other for a long time.

Then the three of them dragged The Rake from Lostlogger Swamp.

Christmas Day

Bryce M. Towsley

Jeff felt guilty. He was trying to conceal the disappointment as he polished the silver for his mom. He knew he had no right to feel this way, but he couldn't help it.

The room was filled with the aroma of the cooking dinner. He liked that because this dinner was the wild turkey shot a few weeks before. Dad's was a 17-pound gobbler that had been called in with the raspy yelps that imitated a fellow bachelor. Jeff had shot the other bird, a 12-pound tom that had poked its head over the rise in front of the 12-gauge. Jeff was as proud of his first turkey as any 15-year-old could be.

It had been a good year, the turkey and six partridge falling to his shotgun, and a mess of squirrels to his .22 rifle. He used the .22 because it was more sporting, and good practice for deer.

To top off the autumn hunts, Jeff shot a 6-point buck on opening morning. The buck came the right way and Jeff felt good about outsmarting him. He had scouted his territory and picked his ambush site all by himself.

He had placed his dad's portable tree stand 15 feet up a poplar tree on the trail between the buck's feeding and bedding areas. At 8:30 a.m., a doe came by, stopping often and looking back. Jeff had a doe permit but he waited. He had killed a doe last year, but when he went to dress it out, a buck charged off. He hadn't forgotten the lesson.

Not long after the doe walked by, the buck came along with his nose in her trail. After making the shot, Jeff wanted to do the rest of the job alone. But the buck weighed more than he did and, after dressing it out, he got his uncle to help drag.

The hunting seasons were now over except for rabbit hunting. Today was Christmas, and Jeff was glad it was Dad's turn to play host to the family. It was OK when Uncle Bob had it at his house — the guys still talked hunting and guns almost all day — but his uncle lived in town and, of course, you couldn't shoot there.

When Dad's turn came, they went to the range out back, which had a bench, an automatic trap machine, and steel gongs all the way to 300 yards. To reach the range you stepped out the back door of the heated garage. With the wood stove roaring and sweet cider mulling on top, they had a grand time each Christmas. The shoots were with shotgun, rifle and handgun. They made up the rules as they went along, each taking a turn at inventing a new game.

Grandpa still was the best rifle shot, and Uncle Bob pointed a handgun the best of any (except maybe Dad), but Jeff won more than his share of shotgun matches. Two years ago Jeff won all but one shotgun match. Grandpa insisted he was the most natural shotgun shooter he had ever seen. Jeff thought they were letting him win because he was a

> The gun he craved was a Remington Model 7 in 7mm-08 caliber. He had prayed for it this Christmas, but it wasn't under the tree.

kid, but Dad insisted they didn't. Jeff finally felt like one of the men that day.

Today, though, he felt like a left-out kid again. He had received many nice presents: a new compass, and a Buck knife from Mom and Dad. They also bought him school clothes, a pair of wool hunting pants, and several record albums, some of which he liked.

But the one thing he had wanted most never materialized. He wanted a deer rifle, but not just any rifle. Jeff had killed two deer with Dad's old .32 Special, but a man needed his own rifle. Jeff studied catalogs and gun magazines, and knew exactly what he wanted. He could quote ballistics tables for all his favorite calibers, and even knew which bullets were available for reloading. The gun he craved was a Remington Model 7 in 7mm-08 caliber. He had prayed for it this Christmas, but it wasn't under the tree.

Dad popped his head into the kitchen, saw Jeff working on the silver, and said: "Jeff, your uncle will be here any minute, and I am not about to let him beat me again this year. I need a little warmup. Go down to the reloading bench and get me some 44s."

Trying not to look as glum as he felt, Jeff walked off to the cellar room he and Dad had fixed up into a reloading area last winter. When he turned on the light, there on the bench was a new Remington Model 7 and a note. It said:

"The owner of this gun must be responsible and must act like a man, but he should never forget how to be a kid. To own a gun is a serious responsibility and must be taken as such, but life must never be taken too seriously. Therefore the owner should never forget how to have fun, no matter how old he gets. Use this gun safely and remember the power over life and death it represents. Never kill something just to kill, and always put back into the sport more than you take out. Use this gun and remember to pass on the thrill of the hunt, the sadness of the kill, and the joy of nature to your own children some day. Merry Christmas, Jeff.

— Love, Dad.

P.S. Mom and I decided that next year you can come to deer camp and hunt, not just on the weekends, but the first week of the season. But you must square it with your teachers and make up all the lost work. Also, you must have a "B" or better average, or the deal is off!"

Jeff ran up the stairs and burst into the den. "Even algebra"? he cried.

Dad grinned.

"Especially algebra!"

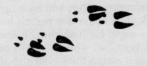

Toward Winter

Joel M. Spring

The thought that we might see deer was probably less important than the simple fact that we were there. I leaned against my unused ladder stand, waiting for John to get into position at the opposite side of the woodlot. The stand hadn't been touched. In fact it looked like no one had been in the area since I last visited it in early October.

On several occasions during small-game season, I had seen two, possibly three big bucks in this part of the woods. Twice, I jumped one of the big 8-pointers while walking across the field on my way to the hardwoods to hunt September squirrels. I had planned to bow-hunt the Catskill mountains on opening week of the season, some six hours away. But in case my schedule fell through, I decided to set up a few stands in these woods, not 10 miles from my house.

In late September, I quit small-game hunting to do some serious scouting. I was rewarded by finding some heavily used runways that led from the thick tangle of vines and beech saplings to a huge cornfield. I placed two stands, one at each end of the woods, that could be used under any wind conditions.

As the season and my scouting wore on, I sighted two of the bucks more frequently. Once two friends and I tried pheasant hunting the field during midday and saw one of the huge bucks running along a small hedgerow. He was a good 200 yards from cover and had been bedded in the field close to where we parked my truck. When he finally entered the woods, he was 50 yards from one of my stands.

My anticipation of archery season was high because I hadn't taken a deer with the bow in three years. Thoughts of big bucks in the woodlot drifted in and out of my mind day and night. I thought about canceling my trip to the mountains, where deer are more plentiful but smaller. Big-antlered bucks like the two I had seen are rare there.

In the end, though, the temptation of hunting monster bucks lost out to the Catskills trip. I began my hunting days there, and I guess I hadn't realized how firmly my heart was rooted in that place and its deer. On the third day of hunting, after moving my portable stand four times and seeing six different bucks, I arrowed a 5-pointer I had spooked the night before while drawing on him. I shot him in the same old abandoned orchard where I took my first bow-killed buck, a small spike. There was great satisfaction in that 5-pointer, and I didn't regret hunting those familiar old woods in the least. But still, I found myself wondering about the big bucks back home.

I spent November's rifle season entirely in the mountains. There had never been any doubt I would be there. The once-a-year meeting of friends and family is traditional, and means more than an "iffy" shot at a big buck in flat farmlands. I left the stands in the woodlot just in case our tags weren't filled in the mountains. Opening week was above average, with three of our five hunters killing bucks on opening day. I managed to kill a big 6-pointer while walking on a small drive. I would help the others get their deer, but the season was over for me.

That simple, indescribable feeling that it was over for another year had overcome me. How many nights had I laid awake, plotting and planning, wishing and dreaming? How many bullets and arrows had sailed through the air at an imaginary 10-pointer in preparation for the season? Too many to count. The practice had paid off in a successful season that now, quite simply, was over.

When I returned home, there was still a week of gun season left, and I thought about the big deer in the woodlot. But I didn't go afield. Although I hoped nobody else would be in that secluded spot hunting those deer, I didn't want to blow anybody's chance at one, either. The last eight days of the season were busy at work, and I found myself thinking less about the bucks.

When the last day of the season came, I barely noticed, until my friend John asked if I wanted to go out and hunt the two remaining hours of daylight after work. John had hunted New York, West Virginia and Pennsylvania this year, and still hadn't filled a tag. He wanted to try some two-man drives in the thick tangle of brush behind his house. He had seen some sign there — not much, he said, but enough to make it worth a try. John is a good friend and has shared more than one secret trout hole with me, so I told him I would take him someplace better. He had actually told me about the woodlot two years ago when I was looking for a new place to squirrel hunt. But I don't think he knew how closely I had been watching its deer.

We walked quickly across the now muddy field toward the woods. To my astonishment, there wasn't a single set of boot tracks to be found.

Deer tracks in the field showed the whitetails were entering and leaving the woodlot at the same spots as early October. And this was December! The reason? The wet autumn had produced such muddy conditions that the farmers were forced to leave the huge cornfield standing. The deer were obviously taking advantage of this.

I sent John to still-hunt around the edge, telling him I would parallel him at the opposite side of the woods. Upon reaching a certain point, he was to sit and wait, looking south.

I would circle through the center of the thick bedding area in hopes of pushing something out to him. Conditions were right.

Two inches of fresh snow on the crisp leaves would make sneaking quietly through the woods easy. The woodlot is small and it wouldn't take much commotion to get the deer moving. As I waited for John to get into position, I noted how much the woods had changed in two months. The thick leaves that had so successfully concealed the gray squirrels from my .22 rifle had now fallen, even from the hardy oaks. The little bushytails could be seen scurrying everywhere now. This first real snow had apparently gotten them moving in search of food. Orange flagging tape that led from the edge of the woods to my stand looked gaudily out of place on the bare trees. I would have to come back next week and pull all of that down. It was sad to see the season go.

When I thought the time was right (because I forgot my watch) I headed out. The snow revealed a few fresh deer tracks, but they were headed out of the bedding area. Earlier in the season, I had seen a huge coyote chasing rabbits in the field. I wondered if I would cross his tracks today as I had so many times in September.

I checked my bearings and adjusted my course. In a moment I spotted my other tree stand, and was happy to see it hadn't been stolen or vandalized. This one was near the edge of the woods and, with the leaves off, would be easily visible from the pasture it faced. I would have to get it out of there soon. The guy who owns the adjoining pasture holds no fondness for hunters and would probably be happy to permanently store it for me.

The sun was getting ready to dip behind the snow clouds that hung threateningly over Lake Ontario, and I knew it would be dark soon. I decided it was time to cut through the bedding area. I just hoped John was in place.

What had been quiet going suddenly turned noisy as I plunged into the head-high tangle of vines, saplings and downed trees. Pushing through the thickest brush, I emerged into a small clearing. It was a fortress. Surrounded on all sides by brush, the 20-foot clearing offered impenetrable security. While I fought my way in from one side, a deer could have easily slipped out the other. But as it was, there were no fresh tracks in this spot where I had twice followed fresh tracks in the fall. I was disappointed, thinking that if I were to push a buck to John, it would have probably been from here.

I fought my way noisily back out the other side of the thicket and stopped short. When I emerged, I thought I saw the hind quarter of a deer protruding from a downed beech top. I froze, staring at this round spot of brown, fringed by white. The thing didn't move. Surely if it were a deer, it would have bro-

> **John and I stood and talked a moment, inspecting the warm bed in the fallen tree top before heading back to the truck. Although it was still daylight, deer season ended there in the woods.**

ken and run as I crashed through the brush, not 20 yards away. I stared, finally taking a few tentative steps in the direction of this brown mystery. My heart raced, and I found myself back in full Deer Mode, which I hadn't expected to be in again for a good six months. I took another step and stopped. I let out a breath, which I'd been holding an eternity, and suddenly a deer's face replaced the brown circle.

The doe was lying down and launched herself straight into the air. She didn't run, but rather looked behind and then back at me. In a moment, instead of dashing for the cover of the woods, she ran straight for the cornfield. I watched as she covered the length of the field and disappeared across the road.

I looked back to where she had come from, not 15 feet from where I was standing. She had held tight until I almost stepped on her. I called to John, knowing if he hadn't shot yet, there were no other deer, or at least no decent ones.

I was shocked when, at the sound of my voice, John appeared.

He was no more than 35 yards away. I asked if he had heard the deer, thinking that was why he gotten there so fast.

It turns out he had been sitting just on the other side of a thick brush patch when I called.

That doe had watched him come in and sit down, and had never moved. When I approached, she was pinned down in between us and had decided to wait it out. If I had been 20 feet one way or the other, we would probably have never known she was there.

John and I stood and talked a moment, inspecting the warm bed in the beech top before heading back to the truck. Although it was still daylight, deer season ended there in the woods. There was time for one more short drive, maybe, but not for us. On the way out, we noticed the plentiful tracks along the edge of the cornfield. One set was particularly large.

We speculated on the whereabouts of the big bucks and decided they were probably safely tucked away in the corn, laughing to themselves as we talked.

The sun finally sank behind the gray clouds that promised more snow. On the way home, in the warmth of the truck, the talk turned to deer and strategies and next year.

The things dreams are made of.

Contacts for Hunting Information

STATE
DEPT/ADDRESS

**STATE
DEPT/ADDRESS**

Alabama
Dept. of Conservation
64 North Union Street
Montgomery, AL 36130

Alaska
Dept. of Fish & Game
Div. of Fish & Wildlife Protection
Box 3-2000
Juneau, AK 99802

Arizona
Game & Fish Dept.
2221 W. Greenway Road
Phoenix, AZ 85023

Arkansas
Game & Fish Commission
No. 2 Natural Resources Drive
Little Rock, AR 72205

California
California Fish & Game
Box 944209
Sacramento, CA 94244

Colorado
Dept. of Natural Resources
Division of Wildlife
6060 Broadway
Denver, CO 80216

Connecticut
Dept. of Environment Protection
391 Route 32
North Franklin, CT 06254

Delaware
Dept. of Natural Resources
89 Kings Hwy.
Box 1401
Dover, DE 19903

Florida
Game & Fresh Water Fish Comm.
Bureau Staff Office
620 S. Meridian
Farris Bryant Blvd.
Tallahassee, FL 32399

Georgia
Dept. of Natural Resources
Wildlife Resources Division
Game Management Section
2070 US Hwy. 278 SE
Social Circle, GA 30279

Hawaii
Dept. of Land & Natural
Resources
Div. of Forestry & Wildlife
1151 Punchbowl Street
Honolulu, HI 96813

Idaho
Dept. of Fish & Game
600 S Walnut Street
Box 25
Boise, ID 83707

Illinois
Dept. of Conservation
524 S Second Street
Springfield, IL 62701

Indiana
Dept. of Natural Resources
402 W. Washington
Room 255D
Indianapolis, IN 46204

Iowa
Dept. of Natural Resources
Wallace State Office Bldg.
Des Moines, IA 50319

STATE DEPT/ADDRESS

Kansas
Dept. of Wildlife & Parks
Route 2 Box 54A
Pratt, KS 67124

Kentucky
Dept. of Fish & Wildlife
#1 Game Farm Road
Frankfort, KY 40601

Louisiana
Dept. of Wildlife & Fisheries
Box 98000
Baton Rouge, LA 70898

Maine
Dept. of Inland Fisheries
284 State Street
State House Station 41
Augusta, ME 04333

Maryland
Department of
Natural Resources
3 Pershing Street, Room 110
Cumberland, MD 21502

Massachusetts
Division of Fisheries
& Wildlife
100 Nashua Street
Boston, MA 02114

Michigan
Department of
Natural Resources
Wildlife Division
Box 30028
Lansing, MI 48909

Minnesota
Dept. of Natural Resources
Division of Fish & Wildlife
Box 7 DNR Bldg.
500 Lafayette
St Paul, MN 55155

STATE DEPT/ADDRESS

Mississippi
Dept. of Wildlife Conservation
Southport Mall
Box 451
Jackson, MS 39205

Missouri
Dept. of Conservation
1110 S College Avenue
Columbia, MO 65203

Montana
Department of Wildlife
1420 E. 6th Avenue
Helena, MT 59620

Nebraska
Game & Parks Commission
2200 N 33rd Street
Box 30370
Lincoln, NE 68508

Nevada
Department of Wildlife
Box 10678
1100 Valley Road
Reno, NV 89520

New Hampshire
Fish & Game Dept.
Region 1 Ofc, Rd 2
Route 3N
Box 241
Lancaster, NH 03584

New Jersey
Division of Fish,
Game &Wildlife
5 Station Plaza CN400
Trenton, NJ 08625

New Mexico
Department of
Natural Resources
Villagra Bldg 408 Galisteo
Santa Fe, NM 87503

STATE DEPT/ADDRESS	STATE DEPT/ADDRESS
New York Dept. of Environ. Conservation 50 Wolf Road Albany, NY 12233	**South Dakota** Division of Wildlife Bldg. 445 E Capital Pierre, SD 57501
North Carolina Wildlife Resources Commission 1328 Valley Road Sanford, NC 27330	**Tennessee** Wildlife Resources Box 40747 Nashville, TN 37204
North Dakota Game & Fish Dept. 100 N. Bismarck Expy. Bismarck, ND 58501	**Texas** Parks & Wildlife Dept. 4200 Smith School Road Austin, TX 78744
Ohio Dept. of Natural Resources 1840 Belcher Drive Columbus, OH 43224	**Utah** Division of Wildlife Resources 1596 W. N. Temple Salt Lake City, UT 84116
Oklahoma Dept. of Wildlife Conservation 1801 N. Lincoln Box 53465 Oklahoma City, OK 73105	**Vermont** Dept. of Fish & Wildlife 103 S. Main Street, 10 S. Waterbury, VT 05671
Oregon Dept. of Fish & Wildlife 400 Public Service Bldg. Salem, OR 97310	**Virginia** VA Dept. of Game&Inland Fish. 4010 W. Broad Street PO Box 11104 Richmond, VA 23230
Pennsylvania Pennsylvania Game Commission Enforcement 2001 Elmerton Avenue Harrisburg, PA 17110	**Washington** Dept. of Wildlife 600 Capitol Way N. Olympia, WA 98501
Rhode Island Dept. of Environmental Mgmt. 83 Park Street Providence, RI 02903	**West Virginia** Wildlife Resources State Capital Complex Bldg. 3 Charleston, WV 25305
South Carolina Dept. of Natural Resources Box 167 Columbia, SC 29202	**Wisconsin** Dept. of Natural Resources 101 S. Webster Street Madison, WI 53707

STATE DEPT/ADDRESS	STATE DEPT/ADDRESS
Wyoming Game & Fish Department 5400 Bishop Blvd. Cheyenne, WY 82002	QUEBEC Wildlife Federation Castelneau St. La Tuque PQ G9X 2P4 CANADA
Canada Alberta Fish & Wildlife Bramalea Building 9920 108th Street Edmonton AB T5K 2M4 CANADA	Energy & Natural Resources Mail Floor, N. Tower 9945-108 St. Edmonton AB T5K 2G6 CANADA
Dept. of Natural Resources Box 6000 Fredericton NB E3B 5H1 CANADA	Wildlife Branch Dept. of Natural Resources Box 24 1495 St James Street Winnipeg MB R3H OW9 CANADA
Quebec Jean-Yves Desbiens 150 Blvd. Rene LaVefque E. 5th Floor Quebec City PQ G1R 4Y1 CANADA	ON Federation of Anglers & Hunters 2740 Queensview Drive Ottawa ON K2B 1A2 CANADA
British Columbia Fish & Wildlife Branch Parliament Bldgs. Victoria BC V8V 1X5 CANADA	SK Dept. of Environment & Resource Management Box 3003 Prince Albert, SK S6V 6G1 CANADA
Provincial Building 136 Exhibition St. Kentville, King Country Novia Scotia B4N 4E5	

Deer Sightings & Notes

Date	Time	Buck/Doe	Area	Activity

Deer Sightings & Notes

Date   **Observations**

Daily Weather Log

Date	Temp.	Moon	Rain	Snow	Wind	Sun	Other

206